Justice for
Helen

A mother's quest to find her
murdered daughter

Justice for

Helen

MARIE McCOURT
WITH FIONA DUFFY

JB

First published in the UK by John Blake Publishing
An imprint of Bonnier Books UK
80–81 Wimpole Street, London, W1G 9RE
Owned by Bonnier Books
Sveavägen 56, Stockholm, Sweden

www.facebook.com/johnblakebooks
twitter.com/jblakebooks

First published in paperback in 2021

Paperback ISBN: 978-1-78946-291-3
Ebook ISBN: 978-1-78946-292-0
Audiobook ISBN: 978-1-78946-325-5

British Library Cataloguing-in-Publication Data:
A catalogue record for this book is available from the British Library.

Design by www.envydesign.co.uk

Printed and bound in Great Britain by Clays Ltd, Elcograf S.p.A.

1 3 5 7 9 10 8 6 4 2

Text Copyright © by Marie McCourt and Fiona Duffy, 2021

The extract from *Flowers in God's Garden* by Bernard O'Mahoney (True Crime Publishing, 2012) is reproduced by permission of the author and the publisher. Copyright © Bernard O'Mahoney 2012; all rights reserved.

The right of Marie McCourt and Fiona Duffy to be identified as the authors of this work has been asserted by them in accordance with the Copyright, Designs and Patents Act 1988.

Every reasonable effort has been made to trace copyright-holders of material reproduced in this book, but if any have been inadvertently overlooked the publishers would be glad to hear from them.

John Blake Publishing is an imprint of Bonnier Books UK
www.bonnierbooks.co.uk

IN MEMORY OF HELEN

On the day you were born you were my ray of sunshine.
Since the day you were taken from us the world has turned grey.
No more laughter, no more smiles but you have left so many
lovely memories.

MUM

My big sister and best friend. Not a day goes by
that I don't miss you.
In my heart forever − love you Sis.

MICHAEL

LOVED EVERY MINUTE − MISSED EVERY DAY

Introduction

B ack in February 1988, I was your average, hard-working, devoted, mum. My dilemmas revolved around having pork or lamp chops for tea and whether I should risk those grey clouds by pegging the washing out. I watched the news. I read the papers. My heart went out to those who suffered tragedy, loss and heartache. But, for me, life was good. Money was always tight, but I had two wonderful, almost grown-up children, who were finding their way in the world. A daughter and a son, a pigeon pair. Faded family photos show us smiling. Laughing. Hugging. The sun was always shining back then.

As they left school and made their way in the world, I looked forward to engagements, weddings and the arrival of grandchildren.

Then the storm struck. Literally.

One wild, windswept night, in February 1988, my beautiful twenty-two-year-old daughter, Helen McCourt, left work, as usual, but never arrived home.

She came within a few hundred yards of the family home before disappearing.

1

The search for Helen became one of the biggest missing person's inquiries the country had ever seen. Overnight, I became that woman in the newspapers and on the news bulletins, wringing my hands and begging for help.

I've been that woman ever since.

Overwhelming, and groundbreaking, evidence – which has only ever been strengthened over time – proved beyond doubt that she had been murdered by the local pub landlord. The trial made legal history.

Had I been able to lay my daughter to rest, I daresay my life would be very different. I'd have grieved and learned, over time, to live with my loss. But despite the heroic efforts of so many people Helen has never been found.

This story tells of my quest to bring Helen home.

And to secure justice for her … and for all missing murder victims.

Chapter 1

A twinkle in
my eye

Looking back, it's a miracle I made it onto this earth at all – let alone brought new life into it. Before I was even a twinkle in my mother's eye, she came within a whisker of death during the Christmas Blitz of 1940.

Liverpool, my home town, was badly bombed during the Second World War as the Germans tried to wipe out its precious docks. As the air-raid sirens wailed through the ink-black, frosty night on 21 December, my mum Sarah Gallagher, twenty, had quickly pulled on her winter coat, tied her headscarf under her chin, and – along with hundreds of other local residents – scurried through the gloom to the nearest underground shelter in Blackstock Gardens, Vauxhall, Liverpool.

Fastening the buttons on her coat would have been a struggle. She was heavily pregnant with her first child – my older sister, Margaret. Like most women, she was coping alone. She'd married my dad, Michael, soon after war broke out; he was now serving overseas in the Navy. Heaven knew when she'd see him next.

That night, the shelter was bursting at the seams; two trams had made an emergency stop nearby so that passengers could disembark and seek safety underground. But even amid such chaos there was a sense of etiquette. The raids had been going on for months now; locals had their own regular seats, with visitors squeezing in as best they could.

Mum had settled down for the night in her usual spot when she heard her name being called excitedly. Her best friend, Mary, was down the other end of the shelter – along with her new baby! I like to imagine Mum craning her neck to spot her through the crowds. She and Mary had been thrilled to learn they were both in the family way.

Now Mary had given birth, Mum had to see her – and find out what it was like. She turned to a lady trying to get comfortable on the hard floor. 'Would you like my seat till I get back?' she said kindly. 'I'm just nipping down to see my friend – she's just had a baby!'

With a protective arm held across her swollen tummy, she'd carefully stepped her way through the sitting, sleeping, huddled crowds. She never got there. Seconds later, the shelter took a direct hit.

Because of wartime news blackouts, we'll never know the exact death toll from that night; estimates range from 74 to 200. But the end where Mum usually sat was decimated. No one in that section, including the poor, grateful, woman who took Mum's seat, survived. Entire families were wiped out in an instant.

I dread to think of the pandemonium that must have followed – the wailing, the crying, the suffering. Mum's family were out of their minds with worry, frantically visiting every hospital in the city to find her. It was hours before my grandad Paddy (her father-in-law) found her in Sheil Road Hospital, where she'd been stretchered, unconscious. She was covered in so much dust and cuts that he only recognised her coat. I don't even know the colour, but I imagine it to be distinctive. Bright red or crimson; a rare flash of hope in dark times.

The hospital itself was under attack that night. As my grandad arrived, staff were moving patients down to the safety of the basement. 'Come on, girl,' said Paddy, helping Mum to her feet, 'let's get you out of here.'

I never tired of hearing that story over the years. The enormity of realising that I owe my life, and my children's and grand-children's lives, to a newborn baby, has never faded.

As a result of the bombing, Mum suffered flare-ups of Trigeminal Neuralgia (we called it German neuralgia!) – known as the most extreme pain a person can suffer. She used to cry with agony and said it was like someone pushing red hot needles into her face. She was also terrified of the dark and even when the war was long over, would sleep with the bedroom light on if Dad worked nightshifts.

After that near-escape, Mum's family insisted Liverpool city centre was too risky for a woman in her condition. She went to stay with her sister, Mary Brown, who lived in the outlying countryside. Margaret was born less than a month later, on 23 January 1941, at Whiston Hospital, Merseyside.

Dad came home to visit every two years. We joke now that every time his ship pulled out of Liverpool, Mum was expecting.

As bombing intensified, Mum – who was now pregnant with me – and baby Margaret were evacuated to a small village on Anglesey. I was born on 9 July 1943 in Bangor Hospital. Although I was christened Mary, I've only ever been called Marie – pronounced Marry. My younger sister, Pat, followed on 17 May 1945.

When Dad finally came home for good, he got a job as a printer's assistant at the printers JC Moores (John and Cecil), who ran the Littlewoods Pools. The family continued to grow, with a run of boys arriving thick and fast.

Michael came first – followed by Tez, Peter, David and then Gerard – arriving at just seven months. I can remember the midwife coming to our house and wrapping him in newspaper to keep him warm. Sadly, as well as being very premature, I suspect there were underlying complications. He only lived for eight hours.

My brothers were all born at home, during the night, and I don't recall ever hearing a sound.

Aunty Mary would wake us up the following morning and whisper: 'Now, come on in, girls, and have a look at your new baby brother.'

We'd stumble in, wide-eyed and messy-haired, and there would be Mum sat up in bed, cuddling the new arrival. I must have been about fifteen before I learned that, to have a baby, you didn't just go to sleep and wake up with one in your arms.

One cot did us all – although if a toddler was still using it (there was always one in the oven and one in the pram), the new baby would go in a cupboard drawer lined with a blanket.

We lived in a small terraced house in Huyton – the girls in one bedroom, the boys in another. Downstairs consisted of a living room, a tiny kitchen and an outside toilet in what we called 'the entry' – or yard – just outside the back door. Bathrooms and indoor loos were a luxury few had.

My own near-brush with death came when I was four. But, in those days, there was no such thing as counselling or speaking openly about fears and worries. You coped by pretending nothing had happened.

Years later, a few days before my twenty-first birthday, Mum asked me to come into Liverpool for a meeting with her solicitor. Sitting side by side, on the bus, she said: 'Now, you won't remember this, but when you were four you were run over by a motorbike ...'

Interrupting her, I said: 'I remember that! They didn't stop, did they? I can remember being dragged along, then the sound of the motorbike revving off into the distance – and you crying. I was in someone's house and I could hear voices and you were saying, "She's dying, she's dying." I was put in the back of an ambulance and it was all dark when they shut the door. And I remember thinking, "Oh, I must have died."

'Then, we were at hospital and I was being wheeled into one of those old-fashioned lifts. I can remember the metal criss-cross gates clanging shut behind me, and sensed we were going up, and I remember thinking, "Oh, I must be going to heaven now." Then I can't remember anything after that ...'

As my voice trailed off, I realised Mum was looking at me, open-mouthed. 'You remember all of that?' she asked, clearly shocked.

I nodded. 'As if it happened yesterday.'

Mum had been taking the three youngest for a walk to my Aunty Mary's, three miles away. Michael was in the pram, with Pat – who was a toddler – while I walked alongside, one hand obediently holding onto the frame.

In Stockbridge Lane, in Knowsley, we needed to cross over. For some reason which I never understood – perhaps she was sorting out a grizzling baby or naughty toddler – Mum said to me: 'Marie, you run across and wait for me on the other side. I'll follow you over.'

But I never reached the other side. The motorbike came from nowhere, apparently. I was caught by its back wheel and dragged along the road for a few yards before it broke free and sped off with an ear-splitting roar.

I still have the scar on my right temple from the impact of banging my head on the road. I've no idea what happened after I was taken into hospital – whether I underwent surgery or had stitches, or how long I was kept in for. All I do know is that, after arriving home, no one ever talked about it. But I was obviously traumatised because, for the next eight years, I suffered horrendous night terrors. I'd be engulfed by the most bizarre, terrifying dreams, of hands trying to catch my feet so they could pull me down into hell. I'd wake up kicking and screaming hysterically.

Our GP prescribed a type of sedative, called phenobarbitone, to help me sleep. Although it kept the terrors at bay, it also affected my memory and concentration. Most of my childhood memories are, at best, patchy, and at worst, non-existent.

At the age of twelve, I can remember the doctor saying: 'We're going to have to wean Marie off these tablets, Mrs Gallagher. If she doesn't come off them soon, she'll be on them for life.'

That afternoon, on the bus going into town, Mum explained that the young motorcyclist had realised I was badly injured, sped straight to the police station to summon an ambulance and returned, with officers, in a terrible state.

'He thought he'd killed you,' she said. 'He always wrote and enquired how you were.' Then she lowered her voice. 'He went to court and had to pay £400 for you to receive when you were twenty-one. That's why we're going to the solicitor today – for you to receive it.'

I looked at her, astonished. 'Four hundred pounds?' I whispered. That was a huge amount of money back then. 'Why didn't you use that money, Mum? You needed that.'

She shook her head. 'That wasn't my money, Marie. It was yours. No one knows about it, only your dad and I.'

By then, I was engaged. Three months later, that money paid for our wedding and a week's honeymoon in Jersey.

But back to my childhood. Along with suffering from night terrors I was painfully shy and what you'd call a sickly child. If any lurgy was doing the rounds, I was guaranteed to pick it up. When I was eight years old, I was rushed to hospital in an ambulance with either scarlet fever or pneumonia. After recovering, I was sent to a convalescence home to build up my strength.

I have a distinct memory of getting off the bus in Huyton

with Mum and gazing around in wonder at how different everything looked. Flowers and trees must have been bursting into bloom while I was in hospital. It's a memory that's stayed with me, as clear as some of the memories I have of Helen … Pin-sharp and vivid.

Our primary school, St Columbus, was just across the road from where we lived in Bruton Road. There was a real community spirit – we're still in touch with old neighbours now, a lifetime on.

Once, when I was off school with yet another ailment, the teacher sent my two best friends, Kathleen and Elizabeth (who we all called Betty), to find out why. On my return, I was asked to stand at the front of the class and tell everyone why I'd been absent.

Mortified, I made my way to the front of the desks, turned to a sea of expectant faces and, blushing furiously, mumbled, 'Shingles.'

Suddenly, the entire class erupted into raucous laughter while I stood there, bewildered. Even the teacher's face crinkled as he urged everyone to calm down. It turns out that, after their visit to my house, Kathleen and Betty had returned and announced solemnly to the class that I'd had either jingles or dingles. They couldn't remember which one. No wonder there were peals of laughter – but I was still curling up with embarrassment.

Because of frequent illness and poor sleep, I missed a lot of schooling and ended up leaving at fifteen to work in the local biscuit factory. I'm the first to admit I'm a bit thick – especially compared to my brothers who were blessed with brilliant, analytical, minds and went on to have successful careers. However, I do know right from wrong and over the years, I've taken on, and stood my ground against, the most educated, intellectual, authoritative figures in my fight for justice.

Mum had worked part-time at the same Huntley & Palmers

biscuit factory and wasn't impressed when I announced I'd got a position there. Without her knowledge, we'd been taken on a school trip there and invited to apply for work if we were interested. By the time she was shouting 'You're not working there!' it was too late: I was starting the following Monday.

Mum had her reasons. She knew it was hard, physical work and worried it would be too much for me. Initially, it was great. We were really looked after with a free bus there and back, a hot lunch in the canteen for 4p (with a pudding costing an extra tuppence) and I took home three pounds and ten shillings a week (£3.50 in today's money) which was great money. Sadly, there were no cheap biscuits (or 'brokies' as they were called then) but I was more than content with my lot.

Margaret was only earning £3 a week at a jewellery shop and she had to pay for bus fares and lunches. And even Dad was only on £9 or £10 a week.

I remember feeling so proud going home with my first pay packet and handing it over to Mum, saying: 'Here you are.'

She was reluctant to take it and the envelope went back and forth a few times before I agreed to keep a small amount back. 'Just give me ten shillings, Mum,' I volunteered. 'That's plenty.' Eventually, we settled on twenty shillings – a pound in today's money.

All went well until the day I was moved onto a new machine that made the cardboard inserts that slotted inside the biscuit tins. It worked so quickly, firing cardboard at me at faster intervals, that I struggled to keep up and grew increasingly flustered and red in the face by the second. One of the bosses came over to help, but he struggled too. By now, panic was setting in. As someone else took pity and pulled the plug on the machine, I promptly fainted and came to, being carried to the site nurse.

When the factory car pulled up at home, with me lying

sheepishly in the back, Mum went mad. 'That's it,' she insisted. 'You are not going back there.'

I was so upset; I loved the job and the money was great, but Mum was adamant. Besides, it was easy to get work back then – you could literally leave one job on a Friday and start another on the Monday.

Mum asked Dad to put a word in for me at the Littlewoods Pools office and within days, I'd started there as a clerk – quickly joined by Margaret.

Despite being shy, I had a good circle of close friends and we loved going out to dances. When I was eighteen, my friend Sheila (who lived around the corner) and I arranged a coach trip to see the Blackpool lights. It was such a success that we started organising regular trips out to little pubs in the country. People would come up to us and ask: 'When's the next coach? Put me name down.'

The arrival of a new family, with a lad our age, two doors up from Sheila caused a stir of excitement among locals. Sheila said to me: 'Shall we ask this new lad if he wants to come on our next coach trip?' Mick Murphy said he would and could he bring his friend, Billy McCourt?

Our friend Barbara had her eye on Mick. He agreed to go on a date with her so long as we made it a double date with me and Billy. Initially, I refused – I had no interest in Billy. But my friends went mad. 'Oh come on, Marie – don't be mean,' they cajoled. 'What sort of a so-and-so mate are you?'

Eventually, I caved in. Barbara and Mick very quickly became an item and eventually got married. Sheila got married to her boyfriend, Ray. One by one, our friends settled down and started families as Billy and I ambled along together.

When he suggested getting married as well, I replied, 'OK, if you want to.' I suppose we just fell into it – it was what you did in those days.

We married in 1964 – using some of my unexpected windfall to pay for it. I wanted a baby so much and so I was over the moon to find I was expecting a few months later. At that point, Billy and I were living with his family in Bootle but I was desperate to have our own little place – I didn't want to wait for a council house.

When a little two-bedroomed bungalow came up in Ashton-in-Makerfield, near St Helens, I set my heart on it. Back then, they didn't take account of the woman's wages – even though I was earning a little more than Billy. Everything went on the man's earnings and every bank we approached for a mortgage (which we'd pay back in monthly sums of £11, 9 shillings and 11 pence) turned us down flat.

Across the road from the Littlewoods Pools offices was a convent. Even back then, I was a devout Catholic and would pop across to lunchtime mass every day. One day, as I was filing out, this little nun came up and asked: 'Are you all right, dear? You always have such a happy face, but recently, you look like you are carrying a burden.'

I tried to insist I was fine but eventually admitted that, yes, something was troubling me: 'We're trying to get a mortgage before the baby comes but they won't take my wages into account, sister,' I sighed.

'Hmm,' she said thoughtfully. Then she said, 'Wait here,' and scuttled off.

She returned, minutes later, with a prayer neatly copied onto a piece of paper. 'Say this novena to St Martha of Bethany every Tuesday and light a candle. You will have your mortgage before the ninth Tuesday,' she added confidently.

St Martha of Bethany – the patron saint of housewives – was the sister of Lazarus, who Jesus had raised from the dead.

I gasped incredulously. 'You can't pray for things like that!' I said, but she simply smiled and pressed the paper into my hand.

As directed, I lit a candle every Tuesday evening and recited the prayer. For the next few weeks, work was busy and I couldn't get to daily mass but on the Monday before the ninth Tuesday, I made a point of going. Afterwards, I hovered outside, waiting for the nun. 'Sister,' I said excitedly, 'I have got some really good news. My husband is going down to the bank to sign for the mortgage today.'

This little nun clapped her hands with delight. Then, tilting her head to one side, she glanced at my bump and said: 'Wouldn't it be lovely if your baby was a little girl and she was born on 29 July – St Martha's feast day. You could call her Martha.'

I immediately laughed: 'Sister, there isn't a cat in hell's chance of that,' I responded. 'I'm not due until the end of August or maybe even the beginning of September.' (We didn't have accurate arrival dates then.)

She just smiled serenely. 'St Martha has her ways …,' she said, patting my hand.

We moved into our little bungalow on 4 July – Independence Day, which was apt! We couldn't even afford a radio, let alone a TV. My sister Margaret gave me her old wireless and I'd have it on in the background as I cooked and cleaned, proud as punch to own our own home.

Even though we'd moved, I was still booked with my GP near to my in-laws in Bootle and had a routine check-up on 29 July. I was glad of the appointment – I'd been waking all night with terrible backache.

Despite being the height of summer, it was a cold, rainy day as I caught the train into Liverpool, then the bus to Bootle. The GP had a sheepskin coat on – that will tell you how cold it was.

'It's just standard backache, Mrs McCourt,' he said, scribbling out a prescription for painkillers. 'If it's no better next week, we'll have to book you into hospital for some bedrest.

My wife's in hospital with the very same thing,' he added, knowledgeably.

I walked wearily to my mother-in-law Cissy's house to wait for Billy to pick me up after work. 'You look tired, girl,' she said. 'Why don't you go and have a lie down upstairs?'

I lay down on our old bed but couldn't settle. The pains were worsening and coming and going quite regularly. Frightened, I called down to Cissy.

'Let me get Mrs Morrison from next door,' she called back. She'd had eleven children – delivering quite a few, unassisted, apparently.

This small, elderly, woman took one look at me and said: 'Cissy, get her to the nursing home before she has this baby on your doorstep.'

My mother-in-law bundled me into my coat, tied a scarf around my head and knotted it under my chin to keep out the cold, then linked my arm in hers as we walked slowly to the bus stop. As it was the summer holidays the bus, when it finally came, was packed with kids all heading to the swimming baths.

With Cissy's help, I heaved myself onto the rear open platform of the bus and made my way gratefully to the seats that two children had just been unceremoniously turfed out of. The pains gripped me again, twice, on the journey and I closed my eyes and took deep breaths to get me through.

Walking from the bus stop to the Balliol Lodge Nursing Home in Bootle took an age as I kept having to stop, taking slow, deep breaths. As Cissy rang the doorbell, I was clinging to the gatepost, doubled up in agony. Suddenly, a matron appeared beside me. 'Mrs McCourt, you can't just turn up here like this,' she said, crisply. 'You're not due for another month. You need to go back home and see your doctor.'

'I've just been!' I whimpered. Then the tears came. 'Please don't make me get on the bus again,' I begged.

14

At that, she relented and led me indoors, where she asked me to 'hop up' onto the bed – a feat in itself. 'Leave your coat on, love,' she instructed. 'We just want to take a quick look.'

For a few seconds, all was quiet. Then she suddenly exclaimed, 'Oh God!' A loud bell clanged and the room was full of nurses. 'Take her coat and scarf off,' someone ordered. Another barked at Cissy to dash home and get my overnight bag.

There was a flurry of clothes being unbuttoned and removed, a sheet being draped over me. As the pains came thick and fast, my head span as instructions to push and pant filled the air.

Seconds later, at 2.50pm, 29 July 1965, a baby's cry rang out. 'It's a girl,' I heard someone say. 'Congratulations!'

Nowadays, newborns are placed straight into the mother's arms, but back then, babies were whisked away to be checked and weighed first.

I lay there, alone, stunned and in pain, waiting for the doctor to come and administer stitches. Mum and Margaret were on holiday in North Wales with Aunty Mary. Cissy had gone to get my bag; Billy was at work. And my baby had surprised everyone by arriving a month early – on St Martha's feast day, just as the nun had predicted.

Finally, I was sitting up in bed with my baby being placed in my outstretched arms. She was 6lb 13oz – a little scrap of a thing but not a bad size, considering she was early. She had a perfect little face and a shock of jet black, thick, glossy hair.

'Would you look at that,' one of the nurses said. 'We've got our very own Bootle Beatles baby!' (Beatlemania was at its height in the mid-sixties).

As I smiled proudly down at her little button nose and perfect rosebud mouth, her eyes flickered open and she stared, solemnly, back at me. In that moment, melting deeply into those beautiful blue pools, I felt a stirring, then a surging of love from my very soul. It was so tender, but so strong, so primitive and raw, it took my breath away. As she blinked once, then twice, I buried my face in her hair, then planted a kiss softly on her cheek.

Even in those first few moments of motherhood, I knew, without a flicker of hesitation, I would lay down and die to protect my child. More than fifty years on, that instinct has only ever grown stronger.

Chapter 2

A dream daughter

Every mum is biased but Helen really was a dream daughter, beautiful both inside and out. From the moment she entered the world, she was sweet-natured, content and loving.

We stayed in the maternity home for two weeks. It sounds so strange compared to these days when sore, shell-shocked new mums are turfed out of hospital just a few hours after giving birth.

Back in the sixties, becoming a mum was a big deal and new mothers were revered, supported and cosseted. Between feeds, cuddles and nappy changes, babies were looked after in a nursery while new mums rested and recuperated and visitors were confined to the evening.

Helen and I were discharged on a Thursday – and she was baptised the following Sunday. You didn't hang about in those days; babies were christened before even being registered to ensure a smooth path to heaven if, God forbid, anything happened to them.

I had already decided on the name Helen after my maternal grandma (it was years before I discovered she was actually Ellen, not Helen!) As a second name, I'd chosen Sarah after Mum. But following Helen's early arrival on St Martha's day, I thought we should honour the Saint's day by calling her Helen Martha.

Certain family members had other ideas about both names. 'I can't believe you're not calling her Mary,' complained one of Billy's devout elderly aunties. 'You're having her christened on our Blessed Lady's birthday and there's no greater saint in heaven. Her mother's Mary, her godmother's Mary, she should be called Mary.'

Back then, relatives were very free and easy with their opinions – and there was no let up. In the end, I abandoned second names completely. As holy water was poured through her glossy black hair, our baby was simply christened Helen McCourt but I vowed that when it came to her making the Catholic sacrament of confirmation, I'd tell her the story behind her birth in the hope she'd take Martha as her confirmation name.

As I've said, Helen was a model baby and once she mastered smiling, she never stopped. Trouble only ever flared when I wasn't quick enough with her feeds.

We were visiting Aunty Mary, one day, when Helen woke crying. Mary watched me try in vain to pacify her before declaring knowledgeably: 'That child's hungry.'

'But I've just fed her before coming out,' I argued.

Mary scooped Helen into her arms and nuzzled her gaping mouth with a crooked little finger. In a split second, Helen had clamped onto the digit – and was sucking for dear life. Mary gasped. 'If she'd have had teeth, she'd have had that off!' she cried. 'And look at her thumb, girl – it's all red and dry. She's been sucking her thumb in your belly, waiting for proper food.'

Handing Helen back to me, she started rattling pans. 'This will help,' she said, expertly mixing evaporated milk with cool boiled water before tipping it into a bottle. Helen guzzled it greedily then went out like a light. As I said, things were done very differently in those days!

After weaning, Helen became even more impatient. She could scream so loudly, I genuinely worried about her vocal cords.

We were still at the local shops, one lunchtime, when she stirred from a deep sleep. *Uh oh*, I thought, glancing at my watch. I'd never get home on time. For a few seconds, all was quiet as the hunger messages travelled to her brain. And registered. Taking a deep breath, she scrunched up her face and erupted. It was like a volcano.

Screeching to a halt outside the chemist, I slammed on the pram brakes, sprinted inside – almost taking the door off the hinges – snatched a jar of Virol (a malt extract preparation that Helen loved) from the shelf, then hurried outside, unscrewing the lid as I went.

'OK, Helen. Just coming,' I soothed, trying to make myself heard above the racket.

Grabbing her dummy, I scooped it into the dark brown, gloopy contents, quickly jammed it into Helen's wide-open mouth, then watched, relieved, as she sucked furiously. Apologies to the stunned shop assistant who had to abandon her post to chase me outside and get me to open my purse but any mum would have done the same!

Our next-door neighbour, an elderly lady called Amy, was a godsend. She'd sit outside, her hands a blur with wool and knitting needles, watching Helen in her pram – meaning I could get on with my jobs.

Just doing the laundry took the best part of a day. I had to feed water into our old-fashioned top-loading washing machine – donated by a cousin – wait for it to heat up, then use wooden tongs to dunk clothes and sheets into the scalding steam.

While mopping my brow, I'd call, 'Amy? All OK?' through the kitchen door so often that Helen's first word was 'Ai-ee!' She'd sit up and peer around the pram hood until she spotted Amy, then, mischievously, call her name over and over like a little parrot.

Helen grew into a very 'busy' toddler – chattering ten to the dozen while playing with her dolls or flicking through picture books. Her favourite doll was Emma Kate – a knitted doll made by Billy's younger sister, Geraldine's, mother-in-law. It was a real work of art – pale pink face, knitted pale green dress and curly blonde hair. Helen adored that doll, even after she'd lost her left arm from being dragged around everywhere.

Long after Helen had outgrown her dolls, Emma Kate took pride of place on her pillow. She's still there to this day. It's strange to think that this little doll with her sad, grey, eyes and determined pink mouth outlived her owner by so many years.

* * *

Aged two, Helen was delighted to learn that she was going to be a big sister: 'A baby? In your tummy?' she repeated, eyes wide with wonder.

She didn't mind if it was a boy or a girl, she just wanted a baby. On the train to my mum's one day a group of teenage boys clambered on and sat nearby. Helen eyed them for a few seconds, then loudly announced: 'My mummy's got a baby in her tummy.' After a dramatic pause, she repeated, louder this time: 'My mummy's got a baby in her tummy – because she swallowed a jelly baby.'

I flushed with mortification. It was the first thing that had come into my head when she'd asked how babies got into tummies. The boys exchanged grins before looking away, while I tried to interest Helen in the cows in the fields we were speeding past.

Two Saturdays before Christmas 1967, a neighbour appeared, breathless, on my front doorstep: 'Your dad's been taken to hospital.' Phones were few and far between then, so it was usual for relatives to reach out to neighbours in an emergency.

Billy drove like fury to get us to Liverpool, but we were too late. Dad had died of a heart attack – aged just forty-eight. He'd taken on extra overtime at work to make Christmas special. It was a bitterly cold morning and he'd struggled to get the car – one of those ones where you cranked a handle at the front to get it going – started. Flustered and late, he realised he'd already missed the bus so sprinted to the next stop and made it by the skin of his teeth. His relief must have quickly changed to confusion – then fear – as pain gripped his chest. Back then, men worked hard but never exercised. He was rushed to hospital but couldn't be saved.

Poor Mum, still in her forties, was left a widow of seven children with three still at school. Even worse, she hadn't been speaking to Dad that morning as he'd chosen extra shifts over Christmas shopping. His last words had been: 'Look, Sarah, we'll do it next week when we've got a bit more money to get things. I'll see you later.'

We all rallied to comfort her. Losing Dad at such a young age shook us all, but strengthened the already close bond we had with Mum and prepared us for more heartache ahead.

In April the following year, my son Michael arrived safely and calmly in a planned home birth. From the moment she was led into our bedroom, eyes as wide as dinner plates, to meet her baby brother, Helen was besotted.

Baby Michael was her baby, not mine, she'd say. One afternoon, when Michael woke, crying, Helen looked up from her dolls: 'I'll give him his bottle, Mummy,' she offered.

'You sit there and don't move. If you're a good girl, I'll let you hold him,' I told her.

I was in the kitchen, cooling the bottle, when I realised how quiet it was in the living room. Too quiet … Peeping in, I found Helen jiggling her baby brother on one shoulder, just as she'd seen me do. I froze in horror as she swung him across to the other shoulder – just missing his head on the wooden arm of the settee.

'Helen!' I screeched, rushing forward and scooping a startled baby out of her arms. 'That's naughty!' I cried, soothing a by-now hollering Michael. 'I asked you to sit still. Well, you can't feed him now.'

I'd never seen her cry so hard. Finally, I calmed her down by sitting her on my lap and we fed Michael together – once she'd promised never, ever, to pick him up again.

I can picture us, sitting there in contented silence. My toddler and my new baby in my arms. Occasionally, Helen gave a little involuntary shudder as a leftover sob escaped her. She turned to give me a sheepish, watery, smile then planted a kiss on her baby brother's forehead. She was a born mother, even at that age.

Over time, their bond only ever intensified. Occasionally, they got up to no good – like the time we had building work done and I caught them sticking their chubby fingers in the fresh window putty. But, on the whole, they were as good as gold.

Our estate was filled with young families. Most, like Helen and Michael, attended Our Lady Immaculate Catholic primary school, nearby in Bryn. After school and all through the weekends, the estate would ring with the happy sound of children playing outside.

If Michael hurt himself, I never got a look in! For his fifth birthday he'd got a gleaming bike and couldn't wait to try it out with his friends. Minutes later, I heard a commotion outside and found his friends carrying him dramatically up the garden path: after braking too hard, he'd been catapulted over the handlebars. My hands flew to my face at the sight of the blood trickling down his chin and knees.

As I dabbed gingerly at the gravelly wounds with cotton wool, Michael switched from weeping silently and bravely to screaming hysterically. Suddenly, Helen appeared at my side. 'Mum, you're making it worse,' she said firmly. 'He can tell you're upset and it's scaring him. Let me do it.'

I watched in amazement as she ushered me to one side. There

wasn't a peep out of Michael as she expertly cleaned the wound, dabbed antiseptic cream on and finished with a plaster. She'd long decided she wanted to be a nurse when she was older. 'There,' she said with a flourish, planting a kiss on his forehead, 'all done.' And off Michael trotted, to show off his war wounds.

The kids yearned for a television like their friends but it was a luxury we couldn't afford. I'd always lived by Mum's motto: 'Make sure you have coal for the fire, money for rent, and a little bit left over for food. Never, ever, get into debt.' It's stood me in good stead.

When the lady over the road announced she was upgrading her TV and asked if I'd like her old one, I was touched … until she added, 'For £25 …'

It was a lot of money, but an eavesdropping Helen and Michael had already started jumping up and down with joy. Billy and I scrimped and scraped to get the money together and, after taking delivery, we all stood back to admire it. It was beautiful – a piece of furniture in its own mahogany case.

Helen and Michael loved finally catching up on shows like *Blue Peter*, *How*, *Magpie and Crackerjack!* – and spent many happy hours curled up together, transfixed by this whole new world.

Money was tight but we'd have lovely family days out. Margaret had three children, while our younger sister Pat, like me, had two. We'd all meet up for a picnic on the beach at Formby. As a toddler, Michael was terrified of the sand and Helen would laugh as she patiently coaxed him off the picnic blanket.

I wish I could remember more of those times. Many evenings spent listening to my siblings reminiscing has made me realise that whole chunks of memory have either never registered or been erased by my brain – possibly, due to the motorbike accident or the sedatives I was on for years.

I've cried really angry tears railing at God: 'Why didn't you give me a good memory – or at least let me remember more of those happy times?' But, remarkably, from the moment Helen disappeared, my memory is pin-sharp. There is nothing I don't remember about that night – Tuesday, 9 February 1988.

Maybe my early memories had to go in order to make room for the heartbreaking ones. The ones that would ensure her killer was caught. Whatever the reason, I treasure the few happy memories – and photos – I do have. (Even developing a film was pricey then so you rationed photo-taking!).

While the children were still young, I went back to work, at Littlewoods Pools, part-time. We needed the money – for bills, but also for the children's activities. Helen loved her dance classes and both children learned to swim and attended Cubs, Brownies and Girl Guides – earning badges galore.

Helen got on with everybody – I don't recall a single occasion when she fell out with a friend or a mum came to my door to complain about something she'd done or said. She could be stubborn and mule-ish, though. At eleven, she moved to senior school – St Edmund Arrowsmith school in Ashton-in-Makerfield.

The day we shopped for school shoes is etched in my memory. We headed to the local shoe shop, where Helen dismissed every single plain black shoe as too tight, too big, pinchy or feeling funny.

'What about these?' she suggested, pointing to a pair with a forbidden two-inch heel.

'No, Helen,' I said, firmly. 'The school specifically says "flat shoes".' Her face fell. Around us lay a sea of abandoned shoes, discarded boxes and tissue paper. The assistant coughed – 'I'll just go in the back and see if we have any other styles.'

Meanwhile, I marched my mutinous-looking daughter outside. 'Helen, I am not having this,' I said firmly.

Her bottom lip trembled. 'But, Mum, all my friends have shoes with heels, I'll be the only one.'

'Well, all your friends with heels will be sent marching back home to change,' I continued.

As Helen stared forlornly down at her feet, I did some quick mental arithmetic with my housekeeping money for that week. 'OK, let's sort this between us,' I said. 'Why don't we get flat shoes for school and heel shoes you can wear playing out?' Watching her face light up was like the sun coming out from behind a cloud. She flung her arms around me.

'Oh Mum, that's brilliant!'

I can still see her striding out of the shop, proudly clutching a shiny carrier bag with not one, but two, pairs of new shoes. It was the most extravagant thing I'd ever done but it was worth it.

At thirteen, she came home full of news. 'I'm making my confirmation – and we get to choose a new name!' she enthused. Wiping my hands on a tea towel, I asked her to sit down while I told her the story of how she came to be born on St Martha's day.

Helen listened, rapt, only for her face to fall when I suggested Martha for her confirmation name. 'Oh Mum, that's lovely,' she said, 'but we've chosen our names. I've picked Ann.'

Suddenly, a thought occurred to me: 'Why don't you ask your teacher if you can have two names – Martha Ann?'

Helen thought about it, then nodded: 'That's nice – and different!' she agreed. We were thrilled when her teacher agreed. At last St Martha was going to get some recognition – and Helen loved having such a personal story to tell.

Her choice of sponsor – the person who would stand by her side when she made her confirmation – took us all by surprise.

'Aunty Pat?' I repeated incredulously. Mum used to joke that when she went into hospital to have my younger sister she came home with the wrong baby! 'But your Aunty Pat doesn't even go to mass,' I began.

'Mum, I love me Aunty Pat,' Helen said firmly. 'She's funny and she makes me laugh with her jokes.' One of my favourite photos shows a teenage Helen leaning across the back of the settee to hug a seated Pat. I don't know what had just been said but they were both creased up laughing.

On the day, we all gathered at our local church in Ashton-in-Makerfield and one by one, the children – and sponsors – snaked their way to the front of the church to make their sacrament.

I craned my neck to see Helen, in a smart new dress, kneel down in front of the Archbishop, Pat with her left hand placed on her niece's shoulder. Helen uttered her confirmation name and listened attentively to his quietly-spoken words: 'Helen Martha Ann, be sealed with the Gift of the Holy Spirit,' while making the sign of the cross on her forehead with holy oil. I beamed with pride. Sacraments like first Holy Communion and confirmation are huge rites of passage for Catholic families. *One day, please God, she'll stand at this altar and make her wedding vows*, I thought. *Bring new life into the world, make me a proud Grandma.*

As Helen and Pat made their way back down the aisle, I nudged Margaret. 'What's wrong with our Pat?' I whispered. 'She looks like she's been hit over the head!'

Margaret followed my gaze. Pat was literally floating back down the aisle, a serene, rapt, dreamy expression on her face. Afterwards, I pulled her to one side: 'Are you OK?' I asked.

Pat's face lit up all over again. 'Oh Marie,' she said. 'You wouldn't believe it. When Helen told the Archbishop her confirmation name he closed his eyes, smiled and repeated: "Martha Ann, how beautiful! That was my mother's name."'

We were all astounded. What on earth were the chances of that? It still wasn't enough to make Pat go to mass, though!

* * *

As time passed, we outgrew the bungalow. We'd built a small extension to make a third bedroom but there was no privacy if the children wanted their friends around.

I fell in love with a brand-new estate being built in the nearby village of Billinge, four miles away, and in 1979 we were the first family to move in. The kids loved the novelty of finally having stairs and a spare bedroom. Shortly afterwards, Helen proudly announced she'd got a babysitting job after answering an advert in the post office window.

'You can't babysit,' I told her, 'you're too young.'

Helen's face fell. 'But, Mum, she chose me out of all the girls who applied.'

After meeting the mum, who told me how impressed she was with Helen – and how her kids had loved her – I relented on the condition that me or her dad would walk her home afterwards. Helen earned £2 a shift and loved treating herself to hair clips from the chemist or a little cake from the bakery.

In time, Helen became the most popular babysitter on our estate. Children always asked for her when their parents were planning nights out. She adored playing silly games and reading bedtime stories.

Helen also became an Avon representative, knocking on doors all over the estate to take orders. With her commission, she'd buy herself pretty little soaps to keep in her drawer – I've still got some of them.

Had she lived, Helen would have made a brilliant business-woman. For her thirteenth birthday, I'd bought her a desk for her bedroom and a typewriter in one of those little cases that opened up. She loved typing out letters and filing her Avon orders. She might not have been the tidiest of people but her paperwork and clothes were always immaculate.

By now the cracks that had always run through my marriage to Billy became chasms. As a devout Catholic, divorce wasn't something I'd ever contemplated and it wasn't something I entered into lightly, but it was clear that our staying married was never going to work. Early in 1984, we finally divorced. The children were heartbroken, of course. But they also knew we hadn't been happy for years and, very quickly, accepted it as the right decision for us both.

As a single mum, I watched every penny and worked my socks off. After leaving Littlewoods Pools I worked as a catalogue rep for Empire Stores before moving to a sales job for Dolphin Showers. I also worked for a kitchen company near Manchester, took on a window craft job and also ran a little business with my sister-in-law doing house parties with 'seconds' clothing from Marks & Spencer. Sometimes, I'd have a good month with bonuses, other times, there'd be hardly anything. Helen and Michael knew how hard I worked and really appreciated everything I did for them.

Of course, they had the usual teenage rows but they never lasted for long. Those two were as thick as thieves and squabbles quickly blew over.

I prided myself on being a good mum. I'd prepare dinner late at night when they were in bed, peeling vegetables while watching *Coronation Street*.

Helen loved cooking (but not so much the cleaning up afterwards) and would experiment with pasta and lasagne in comparison to my meat and two veg, sausage and mash repertoire. I did my best, but looking back, I sometimes grow tearful, thinking, was it enough? Did I give them enough attention? Had I known then that I'd only have Helen for another few years I'd have happily lived as a pauper if it meant more precious time with her, but hindsight is a wonderful thing.

* * *

After her O-levels, Helen went to college, hoping to enrol on a nursing course at eighteen. In the meantime, her friend Janet got her a job in the dole office in Wigan. Helen was a clerical assistant there for just over five months before redundancy struck. 'She's got such a nice way with people,' Janet told me. 'A lot aren't happy when they come in, but Helen calms them down and is really friendly with them.'

Helen loved office work so much that nursing lost its appeal. Jobs were scarce in the Northwest – but her cousin, Gaynor was working at Tooting Bec Hospital in South London and helped her get a job as an office assistant there. 'I'm going to London!' Helen cried excitedly.

Initially, the novelty was great. 'Our Helen's only got everyone going out to the pub on Friday after work,' Gaynor told me proudly. Apparently those Friday nights were a roaring success. But Helen was such a home bird. Our Friday evening phone chats always ended with her crying, 'I just want to come home, Mum.'

Three times I drove straight down to dry her tears and spend the weekend with her, but after a couple of months I said, 'Helen, if you're not settling down here, come home.'

So that's what she did.

Her old colleagues kept their Friday night drinks tradition. She'd only worked with them for a short time but they were all distraught at her murder three years later …

It was lovely having her home. We'd shop in Liverpool at weekends and puff and pant our way through a weekly aerobics class.

With no sign of regular work, Helen took up her Avon position again and even started bar shifts at the local pub – the George and Dragon – on busy nights. She also fundraised for Guide Dogs for the Blind and would rattle her tin in there enthusiastically.

The pub was just around the corner, on Billinge Main Street. For years, it had been an old-fashioned pub, but then a new manager, Frank Keralius, refurbished it. The traditional snug bars and ale made way for a modern lounge with discos and quiz nights. It became popular with a lot of the youngsters in the village, including Helen. That's where she met her boyfriend, David, who she dated for two years.

I was surprised when she handed in her notice and switched to bar shifts at the Conservative Club. Finally, she confessed that it was because of the new bar uniform: a mini skirt and low-cut top. 'I hate letting them down, but I can't wear that,' she said. 'It's just to get more blokes to the bar so that if we're bending over, they can see up our skirts and down our tops.'

I was so proud of her principles. Helen had a lovely figure but she was quite self-conscious. Even on family holidays, she only wore a swimsuit – never a bikini. Naturally pretty, she wore the tiniest amount of make-up: a slick of mascara and lip gloss.

My cousin's husband, a docker, was a keen amateur photographer and had entered a work's 'portrait' competition. 'I can't get over how beautiful your Helen is,' he told me. 'Do you think she'd pose for me?'

I managed to talk her into it. He set up a little studio, with special lighting, then photographed Helen in front of a window – looking back to the camera.

We saw all the 'takes' and they were lovely so I was really surprised when I saw his entry.

'Where's our Helen's lovely smile?' I asked, disappointed. 'She looks really serious.'

Don't get me wrong, it was a stunning shot of her gazing solemnly into the lens. Her curly hair cascaded around her and her blue eyes were piercing. But when Helen smiled, her whole face lit up – her eyes danced and twinkled. You couldn't help but smile along with her.

He explained that the shot was enigmatic and atmospheric. When he admitted he hadn't won, I couldn't help myself: 'I'm not surprised!' I retorted. 'If you'd entered a smiling shot you might have.'

He presented us with a framed photograph and I have to admit, the more I looked at it on the coffee table, the fonder I became of it.

When Helen failed to arrive home that awful night in February 1988, that was the photo the police took to use in media appeals and searches. Over the years, it's become such an iconic, instantly recognisable image of my daughter – and it's the picture that graces the cover of this book.

I can see now that a carefree, laughing shot wouldn't have had the same impact. The image needed to be pensive and thoughtful. It needed to highlight the grave injustice of a killer not only taking the life of a young woman so cruelly but perpetuating our grief in denying us her funeral. She was just eighteen, with her whole life ahead of her. That image has resonated with people all over the world. It's pulled at their hearts and stirred them into supporting me. 'Such a beautiful girl'… 'my heart goes out to you'… 'I have a daughter the same age and can't imagine your loss' were typical of the many heartbreaking comments I received from other mums.

* * *

We were all chuffed when Helen got a job as a computer operator with Liverpool Royal Insurance in 1986, aged twenty. It was a bit of a trek for her to get there – a bus to St Helens, a train to Liverpool Lime Street and then another local train to Moorfields Station, opposite the offices (she became an avid reader on her commute!), but it was a great position.

Helen was responsible for buying parts and replacements for staff computers – and there wasn't a single worker there she didn't know.

Life was looking up – for all of us. Eighteen months after my divorce I'd met John Sandwell through friends. I wasn't interested in a relationship and was quite standoffish whenever he spoke to me, but, thank heavens, he persevered.

Gradually, he became my rock, my best friend, my harbour for life – and there isn't a day goes by when I don't thank God for sending him into my life. It was a while before I introduced him to the children but they were thrilled to see me happy.

Before then, we had another big celebration – Helen's twenty-first in July 1986. She'd been on holiday with a group of friends, including her boyfriend, David, and was lovely and brown.

'Here you are, love,' I said, handing over her present – a beautiful gold necklace. 'And I couldn't resist this as well – for your party,' I added. She tried to smile at the yellow dress I'd bought from the Freemans catalogue. It was a strapless, ballerina-style design and absolutely stunning. At her Aunty Pat's insistence, she slipped the dress on and we all oo-ed and aah-ed. 'Helen, you look like a film star,' Pat insisted. But Helen shook her head. 'It's not me,' she said. 'I don't like bare shoulders.'

Our Pat was nearly tearing her hair out. 'If I was your age and had your figure, and our mum bought me a dress like that, I'd wear it for twelve months!' she ranted.

But Helen was adamant. Reluctantly, the dress was packaged up and returned. Instead, she bought a demure coat dress with a high neck and three-quarter length sleeves. 'Oh Helen, we can barely see your necklace,' I sighed. But Helen was thrilled with it. And with her hair pinned up, elegantly, she looked a million dollars.

Another year flew by. She and David were love's young dream. He'd recently returned from a trip to Canada and she was thrilled to have him home. 'Do you like the mitts he brought me, Mum?' she asked, waving her hands in the air.

'Good God, Helen,' I laughed, 'you won't get knocked down wearing those! They'll see you coming a mile off!'

They were the brightest, most vivid shade of green I'd ever seen. 'Well, I love them,' she declared, stretching her hands out to admire them. 'They're proper Canadian – I'll never feel the cold in these.'

Helen had recently passed her driving test. Michael had left school too and was now working and it felt like John had always been with us. When he proposed, in the summer of 1987, I remember asking Helen what she thought.

'If you don't want me to, I won't,' I assured her.

She hugged me. 'Mum, why wouldn't you marry him? He adores you and makes you happy. Go for it! And,' she added mischievously, 'I can be your bridesmaid … again!'

The story of how she had embarrassed me on a bus when she was a little girl had gone down in family history. She'd insisted on us sitting upstairs so that she could see everything going on at ground level. Across the aisle from us were two, head-scarved women, smoking. As we passed a church, a wedding was clearly going on. A beaming new bride, a vision in white, was smiling up at her husband, while the wedding party threw confetti. 'Oh Mum, look!' Helen breathed, steaming up the window. 'Isn't she beautiful? And look at the bridesmaids!'

She gazed at the scene for a moment, smiling dreamily, then turned to me and loudly said: 'Remember when I was your bridesmaid, Mum?'

Immediately, I reddened. Back in the sixties there was a real stigma about having children before you were married. 'Shush, Helen,' I said. 'Don't be silly, you weren't born when I got married.'

But my daughter was adamant I'd got it wrong. 'Yes, I was,' she said, her voice rising. 'I was your bridesmaid. I wore a lovely dress and a hat. I'm on the photos.'

'No, no,' I argued. 'You were a bridesmaid for your Auntie Geraldine, not for me.' But she was having none of it.

Glancing across, I caught the eye of one of the two women, who was trying not to laugh.

'Eee, don't they make a show of yer, girl?' she said in a thick smoker's voice.

Helen loved hearing that story when she was older. 'Go on, Mum,' she'd grin. 'Tell the bridesmaid story!'

We set the date for April 1988 and decided on a small register office service. Michael and John's sons, Stephen and James, would also be involved. We were an ordinary, happy family, looking forward to the rest of our lives. We had all the time in the world to sort outfits.

That summer passed with only the odd hitch. In June, I was signed off work after a car ran into the back of John's car on the motorway, leaving me with painful whiplash. And, late one night, I heard sobs coming from Helen's room: David had broken up with her. 'Oh love,' I soothed, climbing into bed to console her, 'he's not worth your tears. No man is. You'll come through this, I promise.' I held her close as she cried herself to sleep.

To ease her broken heart, I encouraged her to start socialising with her single friends again. Her friend Lynn – who was working away as a nurse – came to stay for the weekend, in October, and they went to Blackpool to see the lights. Others encouraged her to join them at the George and Dragon, which had been turned into a 'fun pub' by a new landlord called Ian Simms. They were there every weekend night. As Helen started arriving home later and later, I realised she was staying for lock-ins long after the discos and themed entertainment had finished. She was a grown woman, but she was still my little girl and I couldn't help but worry. 'Helen, I don't like these stay-behinds,' I said. I'd heard rumours in the village that drugs were being dealt at the premises and the police were planning a raid. 'If you're caught at a stay-behind, you could end up in prison.'

But that wasn't my biggest fear. I was terrified about her walking home, alone, in the early hours. The street lighting wasn't great and I worried about the thick row of conifers in next door's front garden.

'You don't know who could be lurking ready to jump out,' I continued. My next words were strangely prophetic: 'I could get up one morning and find you dead on the doorstep!' It was as if, deep down, I had a sixth sense that something awful, connected to that pub, would happen to Helen. Over the years, I'd actually yearn to have been confronted with that horror. As awful as it would have been, at least we'd have been able to have a funeral and grieve properly.

Occasionally, and much to Helen's mortification, I'd ring the pub, asking her to come home. 'Oh Mum, I wish you wouldn't do that,' she'd say.

'And I wish I didn't have to,' I'd retort.

One night, it was well after midnight when I rang and asked her to come home. I started reading a book but must have drifted off. Next thing I heard her key in the lock. Glancing at the clock, I gasped. As I marched downstairs, wrapping my dressing gown around me, Helen at least had the grace to look sheepish as she tiptoed up the stairs.

'What time do you call this?' I cried.

I knew exactly what time it was – 6am.

'Mum, Mum,' she said, 'there was a bit of a party. It wasn't just me. And I was waiting for it to get light so I could walk home.'

In desperation, I asked my youngest brother, David, to have a word while she was babysitting his three young boys one weekend. There were only eight years between her and David. 'She'll listen to you more than me,' I said.

Thankfully, it worked. By November, she was no longer staying for lock-ins. We had a lovely, happy family Christmas and New Year. And despite Helen's vows to stay boyfriend-free until she was thirty, she began courting a lovely boy called Frank, who lived in a nearby village. Apparently, he'd liked her for ages. Each time he went to the pub, he'd think, 'When she stops talking for long enough, I'm going to ask her out.'

By February, they'd gone on a few dates and things were going well. I was so happy for her.

On Sunday, 7 February 1988, a friend who was home for the weekend called around and persuaded Helen to go to the pub for a quick drink.

'Oh Helen, please don't be late,' I urged. 'You've got work in the morning.'

She was back earlier than usual and popped her head round the living room door before saying she was going straight to bed as she was tired. When I checked on her, she was fast asleep. The following afternoon, however, her friend called to make sure she was OK 'after last night'.

'Did Helen not tell you?' she asked. 'There was a bit of a to-do in the pub. A girl threw her drink over Helen and there was a row in the toilets. The landlord barred Helen ... she's really upset. She was crying.'

I gasped. 'Barred her?'

When Helen arrived home that evening, I asked what had happened in the pub the night before. She immediately looked stricken but assured me it was a misunderstanding. 'Oh Mum, the girl was drunk,' she insisted. 'She was unsteady on her feet and spilt her drink accidentally. It was nothing.'

I could tell she was upset, though. 'Oh Helen, I think it's best if you keep out of that pub,' I sighed.

This time, she nodded determinedly. 'Don't worry, Mum,' she said. 'I have no intention of putting my foot through the door ever again.'

Her mouth was set; I knew she meant it.

That night, I looked in on her as usual, before going to bed. I parted the curtains to check her window was locked. The weather men were warning of gale force winds sweeping across the UK from tomorrow lunchtime – I didn't want her windowsill getting drenched if they came early with downpours.

A full moon streamed in through the pane, illuminating her face on the pillow. She looked so young and peaceful. I felt a protective pang and stirring of anger at the thought of someone upsetting her last night, even accidentally. Every mum knows that yearning to wrap their child up in cotton wool – no matter how old they are – and keep them safe from hurt and harm.

After pulling her blue curtains together, I stooped and gently kissed her cheek as I'd done every night, since she was born. She might have been twenty-two – the age I was when I had her – but she was still my baby and always would be.

More than thirty-two years on, if I close my eyes time melts away and I can still feel the warmth of her breath, the yield of her soft, full cheek under my lips, the pure love that passed from me to her in that moment, our final kiss. 'Night, night, Helen,' I whispered before tiptoeing to the door and closing it softly behind me.

Had I had the slightest inkling of the evil about to be unleashed upon us all, I'd have climbed into bed beside her once more, held her in my arms and never, ever, let her go.

Chapter 3

Where is she?

As the pips for the 6pm news sounded, I retraced my steps to the living room window, pulled apart two slats on the Venetian blinds and peered out anxiously into our wild, windswept, road.

Helen should have been home forty minutes ago. She'd rang me often enough today from work to remind me that she was leaving early and could I have her tea ready. But, now, an uneasy prickle of anxiety crept up my spine. You could set your clock by our Helen. When she said she'd be home at a certain time, hell or high water wouldn't stand in her way. Back in 1988, mobile phones were still light years away, but if she missed a train or bus, she would always, without fail, fish in her purse for a 10p and phone me from a public phone box.

'Hiya Mum,' she'd say brightly over the connective pips. 'I've missed me train, I'll be fifteen minutes late.' And if anything happened to *that* train, she'd ring me again. It might sound strange – a twenty-two-year-old woman ringing home to warn her mum she'd be a few minutes late – but that's just the way we were. Maybe it's because of what happened to her grandad: setting off for work on a bus and never coming home. Maybe it's because she loved my dinners and knew how cross I'd be to see prepared food left to shrivel in the oven. Helen still loved her food as much as she did when she was a baby. But she also knew how much I worried about her and her younger brother, Michael, who was nineteen at the time. Ask any parent. You don't stop fretting about your children just because they're in long trousers. If anything, you worry about them even more – especially on wild nights like this.

The predicted storm had hit with a vengeance at lunchtime with gale force winds of more than 85mph sweeping in from the Irish Sea, battering Merseyside and the whole Northwest. Trees and telegraph poles had been uprooted, roofs torn from buildings and power supplies disrupted. As I stood, anxiously, at the window, I could hear howling winds whipping around the house – toppling over plant pots and the bird table in the garden.

The weather had already scuppered the nice girls' day out we'd planned for today – Tuesday, 9 February. When Helen had learned I was taking Mum for a late morning appointment at St Paul's Eye Unit, next door to the Royal Insurance offices in Old Hall Street, where she worked, she'd immediately started making plans.

'Let me take you and me nan for lunch – my treat,' she'd said excitedly. 'Afterwards, you can spend the afternoon shopping, then I'll meet you from work and drive us home.' We both loved it when Helen drove; I was still nervous eight months after my accident.

All morning, we'd hoped the weathermen had got it wrong. But by midday, fierce gusts were coming thick and fast.

Even now, I often think back to that 'sliding doors' lunchtime moment when I rang Helen from a phone box and called off our lunch.

'Your nan was almost blown over crossing the road,' I told her. 'It's too dangerous for her to be out.'

I could hear the disappointment in her voice but she understood. 'You get Nan home,' she said. 'We'll do lunch another time.'

It's funny to think how protective we were of my mum back then. She was only sixty-eight – nine years younger than I am now – but we thought of her as elderly, especially as we worried about her failing eyesight.

Had the weather not been so atrocious, that Tuesday would have been another lovely memory (that I'd hopefully be able to recall!) chalked up with my daughter and mum – three generations of one family enjoying time together. Instead, that date will forever be remembered for another reason: the anniversary of her murder.

It would be etched on her gravestone.

If we had one.

Following the main road out of Liverpool to St Helens, then turning off for the twisty, climbing road to Billinge, I'd gripped the steering wheel as the wind buffeted the car.

Billinge village has the honour of being situated on the highest point of Merseyside. From the upstairs back of the house you can see the Welsh hills in the distance and from the top of Billinge beacon on a clear day you can see all the surrounding counties.

It's always 'fresh' – even on a calm day – and great for getting a line of washing dry. But, today, it was wild. I heaved a sigh of relief pulling onto the drive. 'Tell you what, Mum,' I said. 'I'll rustle us up some soup, then we can catch a film I recorded for you – see what you think. The wind might have eased off by the time I drop you home?'

I can still picture us now, side by side on the sofa, glued to the screen as we watched, ironically, a film about a young couple who went missing in the Australian outback. One scene – where the woman's father coldly watches from a hilltop as the entire town searches for the pair – has stayed with me even after all these years.

Of course, he turned out to be the killer – murdering them in an inheritance row. It was weeks before the bodies were discovered hidden in a river.

'Wicked, wicked man,' I found myself murmuring.

I had to pause the film when the phone rang. I smiled. 'That'll be our Helen,' I said to Mum. 'Again.' She'd already rung once to let me know she was leaving work early that day as she was going out on a date with Frank.

The hotline from her desk to the McCourt home lit up at least ten times a day with vitally important questions like 'What's for tea?' and 'How's me cardigan coming on, Mum?' I was in the middle of knitting a lovely cardigan for Helen and she couldn't wait to wear it, but it was quite intricate – featuring rows of black cats with blue collars – and taking longer than usual. Occasionally, she'd ring and suggest a quick cheesy beans on toast for her and Michael's tea so that I could spend more time knitting and purling.

'Hiya Mum,' she said now. 'Just to remind you, can I have tea a bit earlier tonight, please? I want to give myself plenty of time to shower and do my hair. I'll be home at twenty past five. No later.'

I can remember holding the remote and staring at the frozen TV screen, listening to her voice. 'Yes, love, you've already told me,' I reminded her. 'I'll have tea ready for then.'

'Oh, and Mum,' she added quickly, before launching into the real reason for her call. 'Please can I borrow your car on Friday? We're having a girls' night out in Liverpool. I can drive myself and leave it at Gaynor's mum's overnight.

'Where they live, it's really nice,' she continued, rattling off words at ten to the dozen. 'And they have a gate in front of their house so it'll be locked up safe behind it. And I can just drive home the following day. Please, Mum?'

I hesitated. 'Let's discuss it when you've tidied your bedroom. And you're not going out tonight until it's done,' I added.

'Ah, Mum,' she wheedled. 'I won't have time tonight. Janette's coming over to show me her wedding plans while I get ready. But I'm staying in tomorrow night – I'll do it then, I promise. Please, Mum?'

Grinning to myself, I refused to be swayed. 'We'll talk about it when you get home,' I repeated. Of course, I'd let her borrow the car but I didn't want her thinking I was a complete pushover.

'OK, Mum – bye!' she called, and she was gone.

I often replay that conversation, longing to hear her voice again. How many times, since then, have I yearned to be back in that moment in my eighties living room. For Mum to be beside me on the couch, for life to be well, and for my biggest worry to be my daughter's messy room. I'd give anything, *anything*, to walk into her room and find her clothes strewn on the unmade bed, make-up and hair clips scattered on the dressing table – and know she was coming home to me that night.

After finishing the film, I dropped Mum home to Skelmersdale, twenty minutes away. On the way back, I stopped off at the butcher in Billinge to get pork chops – Helen's favourite – for tea.

By now, the wind had really picked up. As I opened the car door a fraction, a sudden sharp gust almost whipped it clean out of my hand. Clambering out, there was an unseemly struggle as I tried to hold onto the door with one hand and stop my skirt from blowing up with the other. *Blimey*, I thought, *I'll be giving the butcher an eyeful if I'm not careful!*

Back at home, I prepared dinner, popped it in the oven on a low heat, then laid the dining room table, ready for when Helen, then Michael, arrived home – starving. I loved sitting across from each of them as they tucked in hungrily and filled me in on their busy days.

When the hands on the kitchen clock inched towards 5.30pm, then 5.45pm, I tried not to worry. The severe weather warnings and news bulletins were coming thick and fast on the local radio and TV, urging commuters to take care. My ears pricked up at an update – a tree had come down on the line between Liverpool and Wigan, meaning all trains were delayed. She's probably stuck on a train somewhere, between stations, I reassured myself.

I jumped as the phone rang. *That'll be her*, I thought. But it was Janette, explaining she'd only just got home because of delays. She was surprised to hear Helen hadn't arrived. 'I was supposed to pop round but it's a bit late now. We'll do it another time,' she said.

Poor Janette was always so upset that she never got to see Helen that evening, as planned.

At 7.15pm, a key turned in the lock. *Here she is now*, I thought, jumping up. But it was Michael, home from a late shift at the factory in St Helens where he worked. 'Isn't Helen with you?' I asked, peering behind him hopefully. Michael frowned. 'Why would Helen be with me, Mum?' he asked, frowning as he took off his motorbike helmet.

I'd been so sure that she would have got a message to him at work to pick her up from a nearby station if she was stranded. He'd been her knight in shining armour a number of times when there were problems on her commute. 'Trees are down on the line,' I said. 'I thought she'd have rung you.'

Michael could see I was worried. He dug out the telephone directory (remember, this was in the days before the internet) and I began calling the local train information lines but they were constantly engaged. 'The world and his wife must be calling,' I muttered.

It was 7.45pm by the time I got through. 'Can you tell me where the tree has fallen onto the railway line between Liverpool and Wigan?' I asked. 'My daughter should have been home hours ago and I'm a bit worried.'

'Where does your daughter get off?' the person asked. When I explained she caught the train as far as St Helens, they immediately tried to put my mind a rest. 'Ah, her journey's not affected,' they said. 'The tree has come down after her stop – between St Helens and Wigan. The trains from Liverpool are going as far as St Helens, then turning back.'

Perhaps the buses aren't running, I thought, dialling the local bus depot. But they assured me that the 362 bus from St Helens to Chorley, via Billinge, was also running normally. 'So, where on earth is she?' I asked Michael, as a knot of anxiety tightened in my stomach. 'She's two and a half hours late.'

A knock at the door sent my spirits soaring – then plummeting when I found Frank on our doorstep, all dressed up ready to take Helen out. 'She's not here, love,' I told him. 'She hasn't arrived home from work yet.'

Concern flashed across his face, as he stepped inside. This was only their fourth date but he thought the world of Helen. Suddenly a terrible thought occurred to me. 'What if she's been hit by flying masonry?' I asked him. 'What if she's lying unconscious in a ditch somewhere – or has lost her memory?'

Frantically flicking through the pages of the phone book once more, I rang the Royal Liverpool University Hospital, then St Helens and Whiston hospitals to see if anyone matching Helen's description had been admitted.

'Five foot four, shoulder-length curly hair, pretty face,' I said, hopefully.

'OK, thank you,' I replied, replacing the receiver in the cradle each time with a click. By now, John had arrived home and helped look up numbers for me.

Next, I tried a few of her workmates – who'd all arrived home safe and sound. They assured me Helen had left the office early, as planned. 'She should have been home hours ago,' one said. I even tried the Royal Insurance bar in Liverpool city centre where her colleagues would sometimes gather for a drink before heading home.

'Everyone's gone, love,' the manager said.

Finally, John dialled the George and Dragon. 'There's no way she'd be there,' I insisted, remembering our conversation from last night. And the thought of Helen popping into her local on her own and leaving me fretting, her dinner getting ruined and her boyfriend high and dry was unthinkable. But, by now, we were desperate. Grasping at straws. The barmaid put a message out over the tannoy before returning: 'Nope, Helen hasn't been in tonight,' she said.

Replacing the receiver, I grabbed my coat, bag and a photograph taken on New Year's Eve of Helen and me from the mantlepiece. 'We need to look for her,' I decided.

John drove, with me in the passenger seat and Frank in the back. We travelled in silence – all three of us scouring the deserted streets and pavements for any sign of her. Michael stayed at home to man the phone and let her in if she'd lost her keys.

After checking St Helens station, we tried Moorfields (the station near Helen's workplace), but, by now, it was locked up with heavy gates firmly closed. Twice we stopped at phone boxes to ring home. Each time, Michael snatched the phone up on the first ring. I could hear his heart sink when he heard my anxious voice instead of his sister's.

'No word, Mum,' he sighed.

Finally, we headed for Lime Street station in the centre of Liverpool. My heart felt leaden as we parked up and hurried inside to the information office. 'I need to speak to the station master urgently,' I said. He confirmed the trains to St Helens had been running only a few minutes behind schedule and, yes, it was further along the line that a tree was blocking the track.

Pulling the photo of Helen out of my bag, I thrust it under his nose. 'This is my daughter,' I said. 'She gets the train here every night. Have you seen her?'

He looked at the image closely. 'She looks familiar,' he finally said. 'But I can't say as I've seen her tonight as we've been so busy. Sorry, love,' he added seeing the desperation in my face.

Tears of terror and despair welled. *Something has happened to my daughter. I just knew it.* There was nowhere, and no one else, to try. 'Can you tell me where the nearest police station is?' I asked in a shaky voice. It was 9.30pm when I hurried up the steps and into the tiny lobby of Copperas Hill police station, which has long since closed.

'I'd like to report my daughter missing,' I told the desk sergeant. 'Her name's Helen McCourt.' Our visit coincided with a shift changeover and there were lots of officers coming and going behind him. He wrote her name down but when I gave her age, his pen paused. I could almost see the urgency evaporate. *Twenty-two? She's a grown woman.* He looked up. 'Perhaps she's with friends?' he suggested.

I shook my head. 'I've checked them all – they haven't seen her.'

'Maybe she's met up with someone and gone for a drink without realising the time?' I could see it written all over his face: Over-protective mother.

Again, I was adamant. 'You don't know my daughter. She wouldn't do that without letting me know.'

Whatever suggestion he made, I gave the same response: 'She'd have rung me. She'd have found a phone box and rung me. I've tried the train stations, the hospitals, and there's no sign of her.' My voice was rising with every word.

Seeing that I wasn't going to let this go, he picked up his pen again. 'OK, let's get some details, shall we?'

I handed over the photo of Helen and reeled off facts: 'Dark hair, slight build, five foot four ...'

Meanwhile, John had slipped outside to use the phone box to ring home. As he came back in, I looked up hopefully. He shook his head.

I started to cry. 'Please,' I begged the sergeant. 'She should have been home five hours ago. Something's happened to her, I know it has. What if she's lying somewhere injured and doesn't know who she is or where she is? She won't even be able to phone.'

The officer tried to reassure me. 'Look, I'll ask the night shift to keep a lookout for her, but why don't you get yourself off home? In fact, she's probably there now – waiting for you.'

I gulped back a wave of annoyance and gripped the counter. 'She's not,' I said through gritted teeth. 'We've just phoned home and she's not there.'

Behind him, an officer was calling for his attention. Another was waving sheets of paper.

'Leave it with us,' he said, hurriedly. 'But I'm sure there's nothing to worry about.'

He turned to speak to his officers but I didn't leave. One coughed.

She's still there, Sarg.

He turned back to see me still standing there. 'What can I do now?' I asked, helplessly.

He took a deep breath. 'Get yourself home,' he repeated. 'I've got your details. If we hear anything, we'll let you know.'

I nodded sadly. Then a thought occurred: 'Can I ring you?' I asked. I could sense his patience wearing thin.

'Erm, if you want to,' he replied, scribbling down the desk number.

I took the slip of paper. 'How often can I ring?' I persisted. I didn't want to be a nuisance but I didn't want him to forget me. It was like I was five years old again – back at school and raising my hand to speak to the teacher.

'You can ring every hour if you want,' he said.

I could tell he thought I was mad – planning to stay up ringing all through the night, enquiring after my grown-up daughter who hadn't arrived home from work.

I understand that, back then in the late eighties, police only sprang into action if a juvenile under seventeen was reported missing. Otherwise, although an unofficial risk assessment was carried out, they tended to wait for twenty-four to forty-eight hours before acting. Because of my persistence they acted straightaway. I thank God they did. Because had they followed protocol and waited until forty-eight hours had passed, my daughter would now be a long-term missing person. And her killer would have, quite literally, got away with murder.

Things are very different now, of course, with police acting promptly on all missing person's reports. My heart breaks for all those other unfortunates who have never arrived home – and who will never be found, either. What sort of torture is that for their loved ones? Always hoping, always praying, for a phone call, a birthday card, a text, a message on social media … Anything to end the misery of simply not knowing.

Later, I learned that the duty sergeant was upset when he realised that my concerns were founded. He felt he hadn't been able to give me his full attention as the station was so busy. However, I will always be grateful to him for setting the search in motion. Because he did issue alerts to the night squad. He distributed Helen's photo and a description of what she was wearing – a grey-brown coat (I couldn't remember the name of the shade), brown trousers, suede brown boots, maroon scarf and her favourite green mitts.

'She's not arrived home from work and her mother's panicking,' he told them. 'Keep an eye out for her.'

He also rang the hospitals, only to be told: 'We've already had a call off the mother. There's no one of that description here.'

The half-hour drive home took much longer due to the terrible weather. Over and over, I prayed Helen would be there when we arrived – mortified at having caused us so much worry. I imagined myself calling the police station and telling them, with relief: 'Don't worry, officer. She's turned up.' Maybe even given a rueful laugh as I agreed: 'Yes, she's in a lot of trouble.'

As we pulled onto the drive, the front door opened sharply. My heart leapt – then sank. It was Michael. Alone. 'Have you found her?' he called, as John switched the engine off. The look of complete and utter anguish that washed over his young face as he watched just three of us – John, Frank and me – emerge from the car, will stay with me forever.

'Let's go in, Michael,' I said, placing my hand gently on his shoulder.

Frank headed off home – assuring us he'd ring the moment he heard anything, and vice versa.

As it was late now, I sent both John and Michael to bed. 'You two have got work in the morning, you need your sleep,' I said. 'I'll wait up.'

I sat bolt upright in the chair by the red brick fireplace, facing the window, with the lamp on. The blinds were closed but through the little holes where the threads went, I could see into the street outside. The little gold carriage clock on the mantlepiece ticked away the seconds.

The central heating had long gone off and there was a chill in the air. I pulled my cardigan around me, tighter. At midnight, I made the first of my hourly phone calls to the police station. 'It's Mrs McCourt,' I began. I'd close my eyes, silently begging for positive news. *Please, please, please* ... Each time, I replaced the handset, slightly more dejected than before.

I thought back to her last words that morning: 'I'm going now, Mum. I'll see you at lunchtime,' she'd called up the stairs cheerily. It seemed a lifetime ago, now.

At 4.20am, my ears pricked up at the sound of a car approaching. We lived at the far end of a cul-de-sac so didn't get passing traffic. The car drew closer, then stopped outside our house. For a moment, the room flooded with red light as the brake lights lit up, then died.

With my heart in my mouth, I leapt to my feet and yanked open the front door to find two men on the doorstep. I craned my neck to see behind them. Was she injured on the back seat? 'Have you found her?' I cried.

One of the men held out his police identification badge. 'Detective Sergeant John Ross,' he told me, and introduced his colleague. 'We'd just like to get a few more details about your daughter, Mrs McCourt,' he said.

I swallowed back frustration as I led them into the living room. *More questions?* He picked up the framed photo of Helen that took pride of place on the coffee table and gazed at it before putting it back down. Later, DS Ross wrote to me, explaining that he'd recognised Helen straight away. They'd often caught the same train from St Helens to Liverpool Lime Street. In fact, he'd once mentioned her to his wife: 'There's a pleasant young lady who gets my train. She always dresses really well, has a lovely smile and says good morning to everyone. If our daughter grows up to be like her, we can give ourselves a pat on the back.'

I'd smiled, reading those words. He must have only ever seen Helen on a good day – when she'd caught her train on time! But deep down, I swelled with pride. Because, yes, Helen really was a dream daughter and I couldn't have been prouder of her.

DS Ross had instinctively known that my fears weren't unfounded. 'I know this girl,' he'd said when going through calls from the shift and seeing the New Year's Eve photo I'd left. 'She's from a nice area. If her mum's worried, I believe her. There's something not right here.' He'd picked up his car keys, recruited a colleague and paid me a visit. Again, it was thanks to him that things moved so quickly.

At this point, I was still convinced Helen was lying somewhere injured, or in a hospital bed. These days, mobile phone and CCTV mean it's impossible for someone to go missing just like that. Three decades ago the world was a very different, old-fashioned, place.

'So, Mrs McCourt, what time were you expecting your daughter home?' DS Ross asked.

My heart sank.

I've been through all this at the station.

With hindsight, they were obviously checking I wasn't telling lies or had mental health issues – reporting a phantom daughter missing. I fought the urge to scream: 'Why aren't you out there looking for her?' and patiently went through all the information again – what time she left work, what she was wearing. I even went upstairs and checked her wardrobe to make doubly sure the description was accurate. 'She was wearing new trousers and a smart blouse under her long grey-brown coat, with brown suede knee-length boots. She'd only bought the trousers and blouse the day before,' I recalled.

Helen had arrived home from work on the Monday, clutching a shopping bag. 'Hiya Mum,' she'd called as she dumped her handbag and kicked off her boots in the hall. 'I've bought some new trousers and a ...'

Her voice trailed off as she'd seen the look on my face. I'd just learned, remember, that there had been an incident in the pub the night before, and Helen had been barred.

After reassuring me there was nothing to worry about and that she'd never be going there again, I'd felt happier.

'Come on, then. Let's see these new clothes,' I'd said brightly.

Helen didn't need asking twice. She'd pulled off her coat, maroon scarf and green mittens and tossed them over the back of the two-seater settee. There was a perfectly good closet in the hallway with a hanger for coats and space for boots and bags, but she never used it. Then she'd taken the stairs two at a time, clutching her shopping bag, to try on her new clothes for me. As I heard her on the landing, I'd called out to her to wait: 'Don't come down, love. I'm doing chips and the smell will get on your new clothes. Stay there.'

I'd closed the kitchen door behind me, went to the bottom of the stairs and peered up at Helen on the landing – wearing her new outfit, dark trousers and a cream satiny blouse.

'Ta da!' she'd called, doing a little twirl.

I'd beamed. 'Smashing, love – you look really smart. And it means I get my blouse back!'

Helen had taken to borrowing my best blouse for work. Cream and satiny, double-breasted, with long sleeves and a fitted cuff, it was quite 'cocktaily' with pleats down the front and a little gathering at the back.

'It's far too good for your office,' I'd sighed, each time she swiped it.

Now she'd bought one quite similar my blouse would be safe. I've never worn it to this day …

Next morning, she'd headed off – earlier than usual so she could leave early that afternoon – with a spring in her step. It's funny the difference a new outfit and an upcoming date can make …

'Is there a possibility she might have stayed with a friend?' the second detective asked, breaking into my thoughts.

I shook my head. 'She'd have rung to let me know,' I repeated.

There was silence apart from the detective's pen scratching in his notebook.

'What happens now?' I asked, as he snapped the book closed.

The DS looked up. 'We'd like to borrow this photo,' he said, gesturing to the portrait. '… and put an appeal out on the news. We'll also be going to Helen's office and checking what she was wearing, and what time she left.' I tried to hide my exasperation. *I've already told you all that.* But I can see now they have to check every single piece of information – they couldn't take anything at face value.

John had to remind me afterwards that they also searched the house, garden and garage during that visit. I honestly don't remember. But he'd heard them coming upstairs and shown them to Helen's room where they looked inside her desk and under her mattress. With hindsight, they were searching for any clues that she was unhappy or planning to run away.

It was still dark as their car pulled off the drive. I continued to ring the station on the hour, every hour. They were used to me now: 'Not yet, Mrs McCourt. We'll be sure to let you know, Mrs McCourt.'

Upstairs, I heard Michael stirring. Stiff and cold from a night upright in the armchair, I walked to the kitchen to flick the kettle on. My haunted reflection stared back at me.

This is bad. This is very bad.

At 7.45am, I dialled Helen's work number. It sounds ridiculous now but a tiny part of me was still praying for a miracle, that I'd hear her pick up in her usual 'Good morning, Liverpool Royal Insurance,' sing-song voice. That she'd taken leave of her senses, been locked in the toilets overnight – anything but this complete absence.

Instead, it was a voice I didn't recognise: 'Helen McCourt's phone?'

It was her boss.

'Oh hello, Mrs McCourt,' he began cheerily. 'She's not here yet. I've been up half the night as the garden gate was banging in the wind, keeping me awake. Eventually, I decided to get up early and beat Helen into the office. She always takes great delight in getting in before me and then greeting me with a "What time do you call this, hmm?" tapping her watch,' he laughed.

That sounded like our Helen.

There was a stunned silence when I explained that she hadn't arrived home from work the evening before. That she'd been missing for more than fourteen hours; that the police were involved. 'But she left early to get her train,' he insisted. 'I saw her.' Again, he went through all the possible scenarios: Could she have gone for a drink? Stayed with a friend?

Colleagues arriving at work were stunned to find the police there – searching Helen's desk and establishing her movements the day before. They were devastated. The woman who came in every Wednesday to restock the vending machine was so upset, on hearing the news, that she had to be sent home. Helen had chatted and laughed with everyone in the building, from the highest boss to the cleaners.

Back in my kitchen, pips signalled the 10am news. The lead item was a person killed in the winds the evening before. 'And police are searching for a twenty-two-year-old office clerk who vanished on her way home from work yesterday evening. Helen McCourt, of—' I rushed out of the kitchen with my hands over my ears. If I didn't hear it, it wasn't real. Then I thought of Mum – I couldn't have her waking up to this.

'John?' I called. 'You'd best get to Skelmersdale and pick up me mum.'

No matter how old you are, when things go wrong, when you're scared, you revert to being a child again: you just need your mum. I needed Mum beside me.

For more than thirty years I have lived with the awful realisation that, in her final moments, when Helen needed me, I wasn't there. Occasionally, and out of the blue, it still hits me like a sledgehammer to the chest. Did she call out for me? Did she cry? It causes a physical pain, a heartache, that takes my breath away.

One by one, my family began to arrive. Mum came first; worry was etched into her face and her skin was ashen as she hurried towards me, arms outstretched.

Next was Margaret, then Pat.

'Marie, what's going on?' Pat cried. 'The police are stopping all the cars coming into the village and searching boots.'

Helen's dad was away working down south. The police contacted him and brought him home. My brothers, working all over the country, received word to come home urgently. One by one, they arrived, their faces pale with worry. 'Is it true,' they asked, stunned, 'our Helen's missing?'

More police officers turned up. A family liaison officer (FLO) introduced herself. 'I'm here to support you,' she said gently.

At one point, someone switched on the TV and I did a double take as my daughter's beautiful face filled the screen. It was the lead item on the lunchtime news.

This can't be real. This can't be happening.

I closed my eyes and rocked forward and back in my chair. 'Mother of God and all the saints in heaven,' I whispered, 'please, please, please, bring Helen home.'

More than three decades on, my prayers, my intercessions, my pleas, have never changed.

Chapter 4

Please come home, Helen

The kettle boiled continuously that day as family and friends of Helen's arrived, wide-eyed with disbelief and desperate to help. Everyone racked their brains to think of something, anything, we might have overlooked. Each time we drew a blank.

Helen would have let us know.

An incident room was set up in the village hall. Police officers came and went in a blur, searching every inch of the house. Michael and John were taken into different rooms and questioned about their whereabouts the evening before. Frank and David, Helen's previous boyfriend, were also questioned, but quickly eliminated from inquiries.

A search of Helen's room revealed her diary and her passport, both filed neatly in her desk. (Helen's room might have been untidy but she was meticulous about order when it came to paperwork.)

'So, she hasn't gone abroad,' one officer said.

'I know that!' I wanted to scream. 'Please find her.'

Having confirmed with her colleagues that Helen had

switched off her computer, called her goodbyes and left her office, as planned, at 4pm that day – Tuesday, 9 February – the police painstakingly retraced her movements. By interviewing commuters and station staff, showing Helen's photograph, they quickly established that she had caught the train from Moorfields to Lime Street station in Liverpool, before catching the 4.16pm connecting train for St Helens. Passengers remembered her sitting in the front carriage, engrossed in a book.

So, she'd reached St Helens – we knew that – two-thirds of the way of her journey home. Police then focused their attention on the last leg – her journey on the 362 bus from St Helens to Billinge.

More than three decades on, I'm impressed at how thorough the police were. At 5pm, they waited until all the passengers had boarded outside the Theatre Royal in St Helens – Helen's usual bus stop – before asking for their co-operation in an investigation into a 'missing person who was believed to have been on this bus twenty-four hours earlier'.

'Anyone who did not take this exact bus last night should disembark and board the bus behind,' one officer announced. 'All those passengers who did take this bus last night, please move to the same seat you took then.'

Within minutes, they'd established exactly where Helen had sat – chatting to another passenger – all the way to Billinge.

'Helen was a real chatter-box,' one passenger had commented.

At 5.15pm she'd got off at her usual stop – at the junction of Main Street and Rainford Street, just outside Billinge Clinic. From there, she had just a 700-yard walk home. One female passenger remembered looking out of the window and seeing Helen struggling to walk into the wind as the bus went past – 'She was clutching her coat and bags and her hair was blowing everywhere,' she recalled.

Shielding her face from the driving wind, Helen had last been seen walking along the pavement, following the road as it veered left into Main Street. From there, she headed towards the few shops on the left and the pub and restaurant on the right – that stood between her and home.

And then – on this wild, windy, night – Helen had vanished into thin air.

* * *

The *Liverpool Echo* featured Helen on their early front page that evening – under the headline 'Riddle of Office Girl Who Didn't Arrive Home'. The story reported how extra police had been drafted in to scour woodland around the village. Police divers were on standby to start searching local lakes and rivers.

Later, two new police officers from Merseyside Police arrived at my home. They introduced themselves as Paul Acres, Senior Investigating Officer, and his boss, Detective Chief Superintendent Eddie Alldred – head of Merseyside CID. It was clear they were now taking this very seriously.

The questions continued. Did Helen have any money worries or relationship issues? Had she been planning any holidays? I shook my head. She and her friend, Hilary, had been planning a trip to Majorca and were looking at brochures, but that was as far as they'd got. There was no way she'd have gone on the spur of the moment. Besides, her passport was in her room!

DCS Alldred then shifted in his seat. 'Mrs McCourt, did your daughter have any enemies?' he asked. 'Can you think of anyone who might have wanted to hurt her?'

I shook my head vigorously. 'Absolutely not,' I said. 'Helen has never upset anyone. She's popular with lots of friends.' It never occurred to me to mention the incident in the pub on the Sunday night. Helen had been so dismissive of it – it had been just an accident, a misunderstanding.

He nodded. 'Was anyone pestering her?'

I frowned. 'Not that I know of,' I said. I racked my brains. Then a thought occurred. I felt awful saying it, but …

'Mrs McCourt?' he prompted.

I hesitated. 'The manager, Ken Booth, had started sending drinks over to Helen,' I said. 'It made her feel a bit uncomfortable.'

Helen had come home one night feeling a bit awkward about some banter that had gone on at the bar. Apparently, Ken had put his arm around her and joked about running away with her. He'd said to his wife, 'You'd better be careful. This is my girlfriend and one day, we're going to ride off into the sunset together.' His wife had burst out laughing and said, 'Will you do me a favour, Helen? Let me know when it's happening and I'll have everything packed – even his toothbrush!'

'I didn't like it, Mum,' Helen had told me. 'His wife's lovely' – everybody was lovely according to our Helen – 'and I get on well with her. He's started sending drinks over to me, too. I don't want them, but I don't want to be rude.'

Soon afterwards, John and I had gone to a charity quiz at the pub. Halfway through the night, Helen and her friend, Brenda, had pulled up chairs and joined us.

When Ken came over with ordered drinks for John and I, he also placed a drink in front of Helen: 'Here you go, love,' he'd said. 'On the house.'

I placed my hand on his arm and lowered my voice. 'Excuse me, Ken,' I said. 'Will you do me a favour and take that drink away? Helen doesn't need it. And if she does want a drink, we're here to buy it for her.'

Without a word, Ken picked up the drink and slipped away. Helen glanced across at me: 'Thanks for that, Mum,' she mouthed. As far as I know, the drinks and banter stopped.

'But Ken's harmless,' I stressed now. 'There's no way he'd have hurt Helen.'

The officers listened and nodded. 'Thank you, Mrs McCourt.'

Three decades on, I thank God that I mentioned that incident, because it was only by going to speak so quickly with the manager that police made such a major breakthrough in the investigation. Another few hours and my daughter's killer would have successfully covered his tracks.

* * *

Helen's disappearance had been leading the news bulletins all day. Reporters regularly knocked at the door, asking for comments and interviews. As the numbers congregating outside on the road swelled, John closed our blinds so they couldn't see in.

Then my family liaison officer said BBC News had requested an interview with me the following morning.

I stared at her in horror. The BBC? The very thought of it terrified me. Then I paused. There must be a reason why families made appeals on television. 'If I do it, will it help?' I asked.

She nodded. 'Definitely,' she said.

I spent a few moments considering it. The prospect of appearing on camera had me running for the hills, but if it helped Helen …

'OK, I'll do it,' I said.

After another sleepless night, I sat ramrod straight on our settee as cameras and microphones were erected around the room. My hands were clasped rigidly in my lap to stop them shaking and I could feel my knees trembling – I had never, ever done anything like this before.

Billy, my ex, had been asked to take part, too, and took a seat beside me. Just before the cameras started rolling, he reached across and took my hand. I pulled it away.

'Don't,' I said through clenched teeth.

From the moment Helen had gone missing I hadn't allowed anyone to touch me – not even my son, my mum, my beloved sisters or John. If they reached towards me, I stepped back.

If there was no room behind me, I moved briskly to the side, out of range.

It was as if I was in a bubble and no one else could join me. I needed to keep my wits and sanity about me – stay in the moment, remember every minute detail to help the police with whatever it was they needed to know. Years later, people would ask incredulously: 'How on earth did you know what your Helen was wearing?' But I did – right down to her jewellery.

My memory had never been great, but right now it needed to be – and remain – pin-sharp. Terrified of the impact falling apart might have, I had to stay strong. I sat stiffly, clenching my jaw to stop the tears from spilling over. My eyes were so dry, they stung.

I had to behave like this just to survive, but looking back, it breaks my heart to think of the impact this had on my loved ones. I was an empty vessel. A husk. All I wanted, all I needed was to hear the words: 'We've found Helen.' Nothing else mattered.

'Please,' I begged beseechingly into the camera lens, 'if anyone knows what has happened to my daughter, let the police know. If she's being held against her will, please let her go. We need her home.'

No sooner had the cameras packed up than another crew turned up. 'Sorry,' said my family liaison officer (FLO). 'It's Granada TV.'

I sat back down and nodded. 'If it will help, I'll do it.'

Outside, there was a growing throng of reporters. 'Do you think you could come out and briefly talk to them?' my FLO asked. 'If you just answer a few questions then they'll go away.'

Taking a deep breath, I went outside. They all thronged towards me. Some had notebooks and pens, others held up dictaphones. As camera bulbs popped, I felt like a rabbit trapped in headlights and had to fight back the urge to run back inside and slam the door. I had to do this for Helen. The questions came thick and fast. How was I coping? Did I think Helen was being held against her will? What would I say to her?

TV dramas often show journalists in a bad light – hounding families and ruthlessly chasing exclusives. However, I've found the vast majority are fair and trustworthy and simply trying to do their job well – as all of us are. Even then, in those early days, I knew it was important to work with them if I wanted to find Helen. Once I'd stammered a few words, they – and their editors – were happy. They went away and highlighted my plight.

Over the years, I have made a point of always trying to answer every phone call, grant each and every requested interview. Without the press continually writing stories I wouldn't have been able to keep Helen's story alive for three decades and have such success with my campaign to change the law in her name. Some have become lifelong friends.

I always urge families: 'Work with journalists, they can help you. Yes, they don't always get things right, but if that happens, contact them and let them know.'

Taking a deep breath, I now spoke to them. 'If anyone has information, no matter how small, please call the police,' I stammered, before breaking down. 'We think Helen is being held – though heaven knows why. All we want is for her to be home, safe and well. I haven't slept. The worry is agonising ...'

* * *

'Mystery of Girl Who Vanished into Thin Air' ... 'Puzzle of Missing Girl's Journey', the headlines screamed on the front pages of the evening newspapers. In just forty-eight hours Helen was topping the list of Britain's most baffling missing person's cases. Diana Lamplugh, mother of estate agent Suzy Lamplugh, twenty-five, who had vanished two years earlier, offered support through the *Liverpool Echo*. 'Helen McCourt's mum has my every sympathy,' she said. 'There is nothing worse than not knowing. It is absolutely dreadful.'

The Suzy Lamplugh case was still so fresh and raw. My heart had gone out to her poor mother. I shook my head in sheer disbelief that I was now in exactly the same situation. *But Helen would be found, surely? There was no way this could happen to me.* The thought of another three decades going by without either young woman being found was unthinkable.

That same day, Thursday, 11 February, the police started door-to-door inquiries – at every building Helen would have passed on her way home, searching gardens, sheds and outhouses.

It was only during the trial, a year later, that I learned how quickly they made a breakthrough that day due to the quick observations and reactions of their officers. At one point, I became aware that three people were being questioned at St Helens police station, but, as it was still so early in the investigation, the police couldn't give me any further details.

That evening, Father Ashton, the priest at our local church, St Mary's in Billinge, was saying a mass for Helen's safe return.

'I'd like to go,' I decided.

A convoy of family and friends wrapped up and headed down there for 7pm mass. Someone volunteered to stay behind and answer the phone and front door but I can't for the life of me remember who it was.

Clutching my rosary beads and gazing up at the crucifix beseechingly, I whispered fervent prayers: 'Please God,' I begged. 'Please, please, please ...'

Behind, more people filed in – colleagues, neighbours. As Father Ashton uttered my daughter's name, offering the mass and prayers for her safe return, I felt an aching in my heart. This was like something from a film.

Afterwards, as we filed out, Father Ashton took my hands in

his. 'God bless you, Mrs McCourt,' he said. 'I pray your daughter comes home safely.'

More people congregated around me.

Stay strong, Marie. We're thinking of you. She'll be found.

I nodded gratefully. 'Thank you,' I whispered.

Mum and my sisters supported me on the walk back home, hands gently cupping my elbows. I was staring down at my feet.

Just put one foot in front of the other, I kept telling myself.

As the George and Dragon came into view, I heard Lynn, a neighbour, exclaim, 'That's strange, the pub's shut.'

Glancing up blankly, I vaguely remember thinking, *So it is*. The George and Dragon, normally ablaze with light, music and chatter, was dark, empty and silent. But I barely gave it a second thought. Maybe the landlord's famed lock-ins had finally caught up with him? Whatever the reason, I didn't care: finding Helen was all that mattered.

A tiny flicker of hope sparked as we turned into our road. Maybe God had heard my prayers, seen the pitiful state of me and how much I was suffering, and shown mercy. Maybe, even while we were praying, Helen had managed to escape from whoever had been holding her prisoner, or regained her lost memory.

As the front door opened, I craned my neck, hoping to catch a glimpse of her sitting on the bottom step of the stairs – a foil blanket around her, paramedics tending to her cuts and bruises. She'd look up, see me and burst into tears of relief. 'Oh Mum,' she'd sob, 'you'll never believe what happened.' I'd kneel beside her, smooth her hair, kiss her face, dry her tears as she told me all about how she'd fallen down an uncovered manhole, been pulled into the back of a van, or abducted by aliens. 'Oh Helen – you had me so worried,' I'd weep, weak with relief. 'But it's OK, love. You're home now, you're safe.'

The image evaporated. The stairs were empty, Helen wasn't

home. As I was helped inside, an overwhelming, suffocating sense of sadness engulfed me.

There was a flurry of activity in the kitchen as the kettle was boiled, teapots warmed and crockery clattered onto the counter. A cup and saucer were pressed into my hand. I watched the steam unfurl, but couldn't drink it. My throat felt constricted.

I'm not sure how long I sat there, watching blankly as life bustled on around me. Tea was poured and passed out, teaspoons clinked against china, biscuits tipped onto plates.

'Mrs McCourt, can we have a word, please?'

I looked up. It was Eddie Alldred and Detective Sergeant Tom Purcell.

My heart leapt. Did they have news? Struggling to my feet, I ushered them into the dining room and closed the door. Their faces remained blank.

DCS Alldred reached into an envelope and pulled out a transparent cylinder. It looked a bit like a test tube – a plastic test tube with a lid. Tentatively, he held it out to me.

'Does this mean anything to you?' he asked.

My eyes focused on the tube. It took a few seconds for my brain to whirr, then click into gear ... to register the small jewel nestling at the bottom. Recognition flickered and I gave a small, involuntary jolt.

The familiar white opal, surrounded by tiny sapphires, twinkled under my dining-room light. Small and intricately designed, it looked lost as it rolled sadly around in the container.

I swallowed. 'It's identical to earrings Helen was wearing,' I said finally. 'She'd chosen them herself with twenty-first birthday money ... eighteen months ago.'

Even then my brain was protecting me.

It's not Helen's. It can't be. Helen's fine, she'll be home soon. As soon as they find her ...

My response must have been pitiful. The earring was obviously

Helen's. I'd already described in minute detail everything she was wearing when she'd left home on Tuesday morning – right down to her jewellery. By going through her wardrobe and jewellery box I'd known exactly what she was wearing. Don't forget, she and I pored over the same catalogues, planned shopping trips together and wore the same-sized clothes. But I was holding onto a tiny nugget of hope and saying the words, 'It's Helen's' would see it evaporate.

Eddie and Tom exchanged the slightest of glances. Then Eddie slid the tube back into a folder. 'Thank you,' he said. I waited for them to say something else. Seconds crawled by. This was tortuous.

Low murmurs and the gentle clink of teacups in the next room sounded far away. Deep inside me a swell of frustration and despair rose like a wave, threatening to drown me.

'So, have you found her?' I finally asked. 'Is she OK?'

Eddie shook his head. 'Not yet, Mrs McCourt. But our investigations are continuing. We're doing everything we can.'

My voice cracked at my next question: '*When* will you find her?' I asked desperately, wringing my hands together.

The detective chief superintendent's eyes finally met mine.

'I don't know, Mrs McCourt,' he replied.

He paused, then quietly and sadly murmured five words which to this day chill me to the bone: 'We may never find her.'

Eddie, like all the officers who worked on Helen's case, became a good friend. Years later, I'd asked why he'd used those words.

'I don't know,' he said, looking a bit uncomfortable at the memory. 'It was just a gut feeling I had.'

But, back then, in that moment, had I any inkling that he had just prophesised the hellish path I was about to embark on I'd have slumped to the floor of my chilly dining room, closed my eyes and refused to go on.

Deep down, in the pit of my stomach, I knew something bad

had happened. I knew that my beautiful, vivacious, life-loving daughter would never walk through my front door again. But I honestly and truly thought, hoped and prayed that she would be found. The alternative – a lifetime of searching and unresolved grief – didn't bear thinking about.

Chapter 5

Never coming home

On the morning of Friday, 12 February 1988, Senior Investigating Officer Paul Acres informed me that two of the three people being questioned by police had been released, but a third was still 'helping police with their inquiries'. It had always seemed such a polite, civilised phrase. Now it had such sinister connotations. At that very moment, someone was sitting in an interview room being asked questions about my daughter. Where was she? What had happened? Were they being open and honest, or stubbornly and cruelly, sat arms crossed and refusing to answer?

I thought of notorious kidnapping cases – like Black Panther victim Lesley Whittle who was found dead in a draining shaft in 1975. What if Helen was tied up in a cave that was gradually filling with water? Had a ransom note got lost on its way to us? Was she dehydrated? Weak? Injured? Even conscious? Was she calling out to be rescued? Horrendous thoughts whirled around my brain. I felt so helpless sitting at home, waiting for news.

At one point, my neighbour Lynn popped in with groceries and said there were rumours in the village that Ian Simms, landlord of the George and Dragon, had been arrested. It would explain why the pub was shut the previous night, but I just presumed he'd finally been caught by the police having lock-ins. I never, for a minute, dreamed he had anything to do with Helen going missing. Alone, inside my bubble, I was still hopeful that Helen would be found safe and well. I was completely oblivious to the news reports stating that police were now fearing the worst – that the RAF had been called in to fly over the countryside using heat-seeking equipment – the same used in the search for the poor Moors murder victims some twenty years earlier. In an interview years later, Michael recalled heading to our newsagent to buy a paper, seeing that headline, and walking straight out again, stunned. He went to his room and never told a soul.

Newspapers also reported that police believed Helen's body might have been hidden in an area of 'thick clay and surrounded by thorny undergrowth'. More stories told of how upset I was after police warned me to expect the worst, but I honestly don't remember that conversation. Perhaps my brain decided to block it out or refused to register it. All I know is that, at that point, while everyone else was looking for a body, I was hanging onto hope that my daughter was alive.

My spirits soared when the police announced a massive search around the village for Helen the following morning at 10.30am and appealed for volunteers to join them.

Thank God, I thought. *They'll definitely find her.*

The response to their cry for help left police reeling. Coach after coach, packed with people from all over the North and even the Midlands, arrived, clad in wellington boots and warm coats – leaving the village gridlocked.

It was the biggest search for a missing person the Northwest had ever seen.

Billinge Main Street was completely overwhelmed. I'm still

shocked to see black and white newspaper photos of crowds 2,000 deep, thronging along Main Street, which was packed with police vehicles.

I was touched that so many people – mostly strangers – had seen the appeal on the news and wanted to help. Billinge, previously a mining community, was still very close-knit. My brothers, sisters, an ashen-faced Michael and Frank, Helen's friends and colleagues, all joined the search that day. Both John and I had pulled on our wellies and coats only to be told to stay at home: 'If we find anything, we'll need to speak to you quickly,' the police advised. 'But Billy can take part.' Disappointment and frustration surged through me. I needed to be doing something ... anything. But I had to trust the police. They knew what they were doing.

After having to turn some volunteers away, police divided the remainder into squads, led by search experts, to scour farmland, fields, undergrowth and open spaces around Billinge. Top-ranking detectives and uniformed officers worked side by side. Farmers checked outbuildings and barns, mounted police covered huge tracts of open land. Sniffer dogs strained at the leash as they pulled their handlers along, eagerly snuffling at the ground. Eyes were peeled for disturbed ground, footprints, discarded belongings, anything that would give a clue to where Helen might have gone or been taken.

John and I sat at home, waiting for news.

None came.

At one point police appealed for anyone who had seen a Volkswagen car parked in remote areas to come forward. There were also reports of clothing, possibly blood-stained, being abandoned on a remote path.

Frogmen and police divers dragged a section of the Manchester Ship Canal while officers scoured the nearby rubbish tip. They worked relentlessly.

As Saturday turned to Sunday – Valentine's Day – all across the country hearts were swelling with love.

Mine was breaking.

Police continued to bring regular updates. They had been granted a further detention order from St Helens Magistrates Court to continue questioning the man in custody and had until 10pm that night to charge or release him.

On Monday morning, Senior Investigating Officer Paul Acres visited and asked me to sit down: 'Late last night, we charged a man with Helen's murder,' he began.

My stomach lurched so violently I clapped my hand instinctively to my mouth. Through the rushing in my ears I could barely hear his next sentence… that the perpetrator would be appearing at St Helens Magistrates Court that morning.

Just one word was resonating around my head. Murder.

Murder?

I can remember Paul's ashen face but nothing else from those moments. As the enormity of that awful word 'murder' dawned upon me everything went black.

By now, police had revealed the man's identity: he was Ian Simms, thirty-one, landlord of the George and Dragon. TV news bulletins and daily newspapers showed him being led, in handcuffs, into St Helens Magistrates Court.

I was stunned. We barely knew the man. He'd only taken over the pub eleven months earlier, in March 1987, and wasn't even behind the bar that often – letting his staff do all the work apart from when he threw his regular stay-behinds.

Why on earth would he want to hurt Helen?

It also meant that if Helen had reached the pub, she'd come unbearably close to home – just 483 yards – before vanishing.

Deep down, I prayed there was some mistake. That Helen was still being held somewhere against her will, that she was still alive. That she would come home to me. 'You can lose an earring, easily, can't you?' I'd say, clutching at straws. 'Those butterfly backs can be useless …'

My brothers had exchanged glances on hearing that Ian Simms had been charged with Helen's murder. As I would discover at the trial a year later, they weren't surprised at all. All I'd known about Simms was that Helen didn't like him: 'Someone new has taken over the pub,' I remembered her telling me. Then she'd grimaced. 'He's a horrible man, Mum. He's got a lovely wife and children but he's carrying on with other girls.'

It became an open secret in the village that, while his wife and children lived with his mother in the nearby family home, Simms told his wife he had to stay on the premises to prevent break-ins. Then he'd brazenly moved his young girlfriend into the pub's living quarters. Apparently, he'd even waited until his wife, kids and mum had gone on holiday for a week, then flown to Tenerife with his girlfriend. 'He sounds lovely,' I remembered commenting, sarcastically. To top it all, there had even been rumours about drug dealings and money lending going on at the pub since he took over. But dubious morals and extra-marital flings were his own affair. What did he have to do with Helen disappearing?

* * *

Tuesday, 16 February dawned with an awful sense of finality and foreboding. Helen had been gone a whole week, an entire seven days and seven nights.

Where is she? Where is she? The question was on a continual loop, echoing around my head.

Police announced they would be staging a reconstruction of my daughter's five-mile bus journey home from St Helens to Billinge that evening in the hope of jogging memories. A young dark-haired model, dressed in a knee-length coat, played the part of Helen. They urged anyone watching to come forward with information, no matter how small. 'A passing motorist may hold the vital clue to what happened to Helen,' DS Tom Davies said. 'Our search will continue until we find Helen and we are confident that we will.'

I felt so helpless watching the news reports on the early teatime news. And then, from the depths of my brain, a thought flashed: *St Martha's novena.*

Scrabbling in my dressing table drawer, I found the little prayer that the nun had written out for me all those years ago when I was pregnant with Helen and desperate for a mortgage. My heart surged with hope. It had worked then. If I prayed hard enough now, it might work again.

John drove me to St Oswald and St Edmund Arrowsmith Church in Ashton-in-Makerfield – our old church where the children had made their holy communions and confirmations. I thought there would be less attention there than St Mary's, the Catholic church in Billinge. It's also a particularly beautiful church – the inside seems more like a cathedral, with dramatic, sweeping, Norman-style domes.

After the 7.30pm mass, with the smell of incense still thick in the air, I made my way to the candle stand tucked away in the side chapel, dropped a donation in the box and picked out a tealight candle. As I held the wick into the flame of an already-lit candle, I watched, mesmerised, as it glowed, then burst into life. Placing the candle carefully into the stand, I knelt down and prayed like I'd never, ever prayed before – beseeching St Martha for her help.

'O St Martha,' I whispered, reading from the faded piece of paper, *'I resort to thy protection*
And, as proof of my affection and faith, I offer thee the light which I will burn every Tuesday.

> *Comfort me in my difficulties and, through the great favour*
> *thou didst enjoy when our*
> *Saviour lodged in thy house, intercede for my family that*
> *we may be provided for in all our wants.*
> *I beseech thee to have pity on me with regards to the favour*
> *I ask of thee ...'* I took a deep breath and closed my eyes
> tightly. *'...To please, please bring Helen home safely.'*

I finished with one Our Father and three Hail Marys.

Back at home, I lit another candle, placed it in front of Helen's framed portrait and repeated the prayer. My faith, as always, comforted me.

'Helen will be found before the ninth Tuesday,' I told Paul Acres confidently. 'My prayer will be answered. You'll find her, you'll see.' He never said a word. Just looked at me sadly. Later, intrigued, he would gently ask me about my faith in novenas. I never tired of explaining.

It was years before I learned that prayers, no matter how fervently they are said, aren't always granted in the way you want them to be. But, my God, St Martha has come through for me so many times in other ways. Every Tuesday, coming home from that mass, I'd have a tiny bit of good news or something essential would pop into my head: an answer to a question from the police or the location of a crucial piece of paperwork needed for their investigation.

On that first Tuesday night, I learned that the reconstruction had led to more bus passengers coming forward, including the man who had sat next to her. The police had also been desperate to establish exactly what Helen had been wearing when she disappeared – down to the last tiny detail. I'd been really struggling to pinpoint the colour of her coat. It wasn't brown, or beige or fawn, all colours suggested to me.

The second week, driving home from my church novena, I

suddenly said to John: 'When we're home will you have a look in Helen's desk and see if you can find any receipts?'

Later, he appeared with a file. 'Here they are,' he said, astounded. 'All carefully filed in date order.'

There was a receipt for her coat from Etam. I'd been with her when she'd bought it in Manchester, eighteen months earlier. 'Taupe!' I cried, reading the receipt. 'That was the colour.' There were also receipts from 8 February for her new blouse and trousers – all clothes she'd been wearing when she went missing.

Another Tuesday, I remembered how Helen had been so upset when she lost one of her opal and sapphire earrings at a New Year's Eve family party. 'Get yourself another pair and that way, you'll always have one spare,' I advised. Lo and behold, in another file we found receipts for both pairs of earrings from the same jeweller – essential evidence when it came to Simms' trial.

Helen might have been messy when it came to her bedroom and tidying up after cooking, but when it came to paperwork and filing, she was meticulous: her desk was pristine.

* * *

By now, police and frogmen were searching the warren of old mineshafts – some flooded – that snaked around the area. The Coal Board provided intricate maps of known pits but some shafts were so old, they weren't even marked.

The headline on one story – 'Needle in a Haystack' – chilled the blood in my veins. Journalists used words like 'daunting task' and 'vast area' in their coverage. I swung constantly between hope and despair.

With every day that passed, you could sense the growing frustration among the police too. 'It's disturbing, from the point of view of the family that we have not yet found the body,' DS Davies said in one newspaper interview. 'We still have high hopes of finding her … We would like to hear from anyone who has any idea of likely places where she could be located. Someone might have a brainwave. If so, please let us know.'

The thought of coping with this for weeks, let alone months, years or decades, was impossible to imagine.

'Why don't you have a lie-down?' my family liaison officer would ask. I'd shake my head, blankly. How could I sleep when my daughter was missing? I'd sit up at night, watching the window, willing her to return. In the mornings, I'd imagine I heard her pitter-pattering to the bathroom. At 5.50pm, her usual time for arriving home from work, I'd strain to hear Helen's footsteps approaching the house, her key turning in the lock, her cheery call of: 'Hiya Mum, it's me.'

Closing my eyes, I could almost see her kicking off her boots and dumping her bag in the hallway before draping her coat across the back of the settee (I'd wince, remembering the times I'd told her off for not using the cloakroom). Then she'd stretch out on her stomach across the oriental rug I'd won at a local auction house. Helen had been so delighted when it was delivered and dramatically unfurled. 'It's huge!' she'd exclaimed as it filled the entire length of our living room. 'Oh Mum, it's lovely.' She would ignore the armchairs and settle down on the rug to watch the news or flick through the local paper that she'd picked up on the way home, humming to herself.

'I love this rug, and I love this house,' she'd sigh dramatically, glad to be home. I'd relish the image and smile, but now I dreaded opening my eyes to find the rug, empty.

Doctors prescribed sleeping pills and tranquillisers in the hope of getting me to rest but I couldn't even swallow water, let alone tablets. Someone suggested strawberry jam as it's more slippery that way. With a conscious effort, grimacing and holding my eyes tightly shut, I'd drag my top lip over the spoon and the tablet would finally be forced down.

But it didn't work. Nothing did. How could I sleep while

my daughter was out there, lost and alone? I'd lie there, limbs twitching, brain whirling, until I thought I'd go stark raving mad if I stayed there. A fog of exhaustion, of weariness, of misery, settled around me like a cloak. My bones felt as heavy as lead as I walked downstairs slowly. It was like wading through thick treacle.

Looking back on those awful days, my heart goes out to Michael. At the age of nineteen, he'd lost his best friend, the sister he adored and his mum had become a zombie, a husk of her former self. I refused to cry in front of him – I didn't want him to see me upset. Years later, he confessed that he'd adopted the same coping mentality. He'd spend hour after hour in his room, playing music – he'd turn it up so no one could hear him cry.

Years later, his Victim Impact Statement revealed how much he'd been hurting:

> Helen was everything to me. We were extremely close
> and did everything together. She was the perfect big
> sister, always there … an integral part of my life …
> often waking me up so that she could sit on my bed
> and tell me everything she had done that day. We were
> both starting out in life, and I thought she would be
> there forever.
>
> In the weeks and months following her death I
> closed myself off from everyone – spending most of my
> time alone and not wanting any other company. I could
> not share my pain or grief with anyone as the only
> person I could open up to was Helen and she was no
> longer there.

But for him the hardest moments came years later, on his wedding day, and, later still, when he became the proud dad to two beautiful children. Gazing down at his daughter, and the son who followed two years later, he'd wept for the loving, proud, funny aunt they would never know and for the nieces and nephews he should have had. He envied his wife's close relationship with her sisters and the close, tight network of cousins at family gatherings. All of this had been snatched from him on that wild, wind-lashed night.

At times, my family liaison officer would urge me to let go of all that pent-up pain, to shed a cathartic tear: 'Why won't you have a good cry, Marie?' she'd ask. 'You'll feel better.'

But I shook my head. If I cried, I'd weaken. I needed to stay strong and alert – Helen needed me. 'I'll cry when Helen is found,' I said blankly. If I started crying, I was terrified I'd never stop. The questions were coming thick and fast and I needed to be able to answer them.

What shampoo did Helen use? How long were her fingernails?

The days and nights blurred into one. On Friday, 26 February, two and a half weeks after Helen had gone missing, I asked Father Ashton to say a mass in the house. 'I'd like all of Helen's friends and colleagues to come,' I decided.

Thankfully, we'd moved all the furniture from the living room into the garage. As word spread, the house was bursting at the seams. Throngs of vibrant young people who had all loved Helen spilled out onto the hallway and stairs.

Eyes would have been wiped as Father Ashton dedicated the mass to my daughter: 'We are gathered here together to pray for the safe return of Helen McCourt.' We were all united in prayer. I imagined hundreds of prayers floating up to heaven.

God would listen, wouldn't he?

Afterwards, I helped Father Ashton pack away his chalice and Holy Communion plate carefully, then walked with him to the front door. He gently reassured me that God was listening. That I should keep praying. As I waved him off, Paul Acres arrived, with another officer. 'Mrs McCourt,' he began. 'Is it possible for me to have a word with you …?' Then his eyes took in the crowded house, the sea of young people sitting on every step of the stairs, chatting and sipping tea: '… in private.' The living room and dining room was busy, too.

'Come upstairs,' I said, weaving my way through knees and feet. Passing a queue of people for the bathroom, I opened the door to my bedroom and gestured inside to where a mountain of coats was piled on the bed. Then, taking leave of my senses, I uttered a line that mortifies me to this day: 'There aren't many men who get an invite into my bedroom, Paul.'

Even as the words were coming out of my mouth, I wanted to curl up with embarrassment. I suppose it's an example of the impact trauma and shock can have, making you say things you'd never ever say in normal circumstances. A therapist would no doubt say I was trying to lighten the mood in a desperate attempt to shield myself from what I knew was coming. To his credit, Paul allowed a tiny smile before speaking.

'Mrs McCourt, Manchester Police have found a handbag and some items.' He paused, then said: 'We believe them to be Helen's.'

The words swirled in the air, then floated away. 'We have officers guarding the site and will be embarking on a thorough search of the area tomorrow with police divers,' he continued. 'At some point, we would like you to identify whether they are your daughter's or not. Until that point, we would ask you not to share this information with anyone.'

Breathing shakily, I lowered myself onto the coat-covered bed. I opened my mouth but nothing came out. Finally, I nodded to show I'd understood.

'We'll be in touch tomorrow about you identifying the items,' he said gently.

I nodded again.

They slipped away as quietly as they had arrived. John and

Michael didn't even know they'd been. Having given Paul my word, I told no one. Taking a deep breath, I went back downstairs and bustled around the kitchen.

The house gradually emptied and Michael went to bed, until it was just Mum, my sisters and a couple of neighbours in the living room. The thought of them going, leaving me alone with these terrible, terrible thoughts, sent my adrenaline soaring. The bag the police had found might not be Helen's, but Paul Acres seemed pretty confident.

Had her purse and work identification card been inside?

And if Helen's bag had been found somewhere, after weeks of looking, something was definitely wrong. There was no way she'd have tossed it aside herself.

I went from jittery to manic, chattering non-stop, pointedly ignoring tired yawns and discreet glances at watches. At around 11pm, John started dropping heavy hints: 'Marie, it's time to let these people go to their beds,' he said gently.

'They're fine – you go to bed if you want to, John,' I snapped. 'Now, who's for another cuppa? Or would you like a glass of wine?'

No one had the heart to leave me sitting there all alone. As midnight struck, I was still talking ten to the dozen. John, who had gone to bed, came back downstairs and popped his head around the door. 'Marie, you need to let these good people go home—' he began.

I don't remember much about what happened next, but apparently, wild-eyed and hysterical, I'd leapt to my feet. 'I want them to stay!' I shrieked. Turning to them, I'd insisted, 'You're fine, aren't you?' Then I turned back to John: 'See? They're happy to stay.'

They watched with growing horror as, in front of their eyes, I fell apart at the seams. My voice rose higher and higher until it was a persistent screech. As John stepped forward in a bid to calm me down, I'd lashed out wildly, growing hysterical. I could hear someone screaming continually. It took a few moments for me to realise it was me, but by then, I couldn't stop.

Everything is a blur from then on. I vaguely recall seeing my GP, Dr Bhaduri, in the room, reaching into his black medicine bag. Firm hands steered me onto the couch and there was a sharp pain in my thigh as I was injected with a sedative. Sinking into the cushions, a blissful darkness lapped around the edges of my vision, then washed over me ...

Suddenly, I was standing in a blindingly white room, gazing up into a corner where the walls met the ceiling to form a triangle. A sense of happiness I thought I'd never experience again flooded through my veins. Rapturous delight washed over me in waves. For there, smiling down at me, was Helen. She was dressed all in white and had never looked more radiant or beautiful. My brain whirred trying to make sense of it all.

Helen! It's Helen! She's here! She's safe! The nightmare's over – it's over.

I smiled, laughed, beamed up at her. 'Helen!' I cried. 'Thank God! Where have you been?'

As she continued to smile down at me my relief quickly gave way to other emotions that every parent of a lost and found child will recognise: frustration, anger – even fury – at being put through such fear and heartache. 'Why haven't you called?' I cried. 'The police have been looking everywhere for you, Helen. A man's been locked up.'

She looked beseechingly at me. 'Mum, I'm sorry. It was in the window and the plane was taking off and I had to be on it.'

Her voice was so clear and calm. It sounded so rational. She and her friend, Hilary, *had* been planning a summer holiday in Spain. Helen had been flicking through brochures and scanning window displays (this would explain 'it was in the window') for suitable apartments.

'Well, why didn't you ring me when you got there?' I demanded.

She gave a slight shake of her head and her hair danced. 'I couldn't, Mum,' she said, apologetically. 'There are no telephones here.' Then an expression of pure happiness washed over her face. 'Oh Mum,' she smiled. 'It's so beautiful here, I want to stay.'

I felt a prickle of panic. 'You'd better get home right now, Helen,' I ordered. 'Do you hear me? This minute!'

Once again, she shook her head. 'Mum, I can't.' Then she smiled dreamily. 'It's so beautiful here, Mum,' she repeated. 'You should see the flowers. The colours are amazing.'

My throat constricted. With a growing sense of horror and panic I realised that her face was beginning to shimmer and fade as she floated upwards. 'No, no!' I whimpered. 'Helen! Helen!' I stood on tiptoes, plaintively reaching up to her disappearing image. If I could reach her, I could hold on. I had to stop her. But as she slipped further away, my cry became a scream: 'Helen! You can't leave, come back!'

I was desperate now. 'What about me and Michael?' My voice became a screech as she floated away. 'What about me and Michael? We need you to come home!'

I was gazing up into an empty space. She'd gone. Shuddering sobs racked my body. Opening my eyes, I realised I was back on our silvery-grey settee, flailing and screaming. Mum, Margaret and Pat were hovering helplessly nearby. Margaret had buried her face in her hands and Pat was consoling her. Tears ran down Mum's face as she dropped to her knees beside me. I will never, ever forget her stricken face as she gathered me in her arms: 'Oh Marie, Marie,' she soothed.

I crumpled into her as she rocked me back and forth. 'I saw her, Mum,' I gasped. 'I saw our Helen. And she's gone. She's gone!'

It was as if a dam had been opened. As the last fragments of hope I'd been clinging to drifted away, out of reach, the tears I'd been holding back for weeks finally flowed. In that instant, I knew that my daughter would never be coming home alive.

Chapter 6

The 'no' year

My drug-induced dream had left me drained and exhausted. One thing was for sure: no matter how upset or distraught I was to become, I was never sedated again.

Years later, I'd described this particular dream to one of the many mediums I met over the years. The search for Helen led to many people, mediums and otherwise, contacting the police with messages and suggestions as to where Helen's body might be; there were so many, Merseyside Police actually set up a separate desk to deal with the phone calls and letters. Despite my strong Catholic beliefs, I became open to anything that might help me find my daughter.

This particular medium told me I'd had a very spiritual encounter; the white room and Helen being dressed all in white represented purity, while the 'tri-shaped' corner of the room she appeared in symbolised the Holy Trinity – Father, Son and Holy Spirit. 'She was letting you know she was all right,' she explained gently. I nodded, gaining comfort from her words.

The police had spent Saturday, 27 February 1988, the day after our house mass, scouring the area where the handbag had been found – on the banks of the River Irwell, in Irlam – and found clothes.

A woman's clothes.

On Sunday, Paul Acres asked if I would be able to visit St Helens police station, with my family liaison officer, to identify the items.

'Would you like me to come with you, girl?' Mum asked softly.

I looked up. 'Will you be OK to?' I replied.

She nodded. 'I'd rather be with you than here waiting.'

* * *

Paul Acres greeted us at the door to the station and led us into a side room. There, labelled and spread out in polythene evidence bags, were damp, crumpled items of clothing.

'We've tried to dry them out as best we can,' someone murmured.

Taking a deep breath, I focused on the items within the plastic. Despite being streaked in mud and dirt, they were instantly recognisable. My legs felt weak and I clutched the table for support. There was Helen's smart, taupe coat, her navy-blue handbag, work identification card and purse, maroon scarf, those distinctive green mitts she'd loved – and one brown suede boot. I winced at the final item: her underwear.

My daughter had always taken such pride in her appearance, kept her outfits so pristine. It was heartbreaking to see her lovingly chosen and cared-for clothes in this state.

I looked up and met Paul's quizzical expression. 'They're all Helen's,' I whispered. He nodded. 'Apart from the trousers,' I added. 'Helen was wearing brown trousers. These are navy, they're not hers.'

It was a year later, at Simms' trial, that I learned the trousers were Helen's after all. Although she'd originally set off that Monday lunchtime to buy brown trousers, the shop only had navy in stock. After trying them on for size, she liked them so much that she decided to buy them and order the brown. When she'd put them on for me that evening, and twirled at the top of the stairs, I'd just presumed they were the brown ones ...

We never did find out if those brown trousers had arrived for her. I presume they were sent back to the warehouse once it was clear they were never going to be collected and worn. We travelled home in miserable silence. I realised that after everything that had happened, I'd still been holding out for a miracle. For the impossible ... for Helen to, somehow, still be alive and well.

Anyone can lose an earring. But you don't just lose your boot, your mitts, your coat ... This was it. It was over, she was dead.

An image of Helen's underwear flashed into my mind and I instantly batted it away. Those thoughts, those questions, were too disturbing, too upsetting, too horrible to think about, yet. I needed to brace myself.

These days, homicide cases move quickly through the legal system. Suspects are charged and committed to crown court quickly, with trials usually underway within six months. It's all so much better for the families of the victims. Back then, however, things moved at a snail's pace. Simms was repeatedly brought back before magistrates before finally being committed to Liverpool Crown Court in August 1988 – a full six months after Helen went missing. Although he'd been arrested very quickly after she disappeared it would be another six months before the murder trial began – the longest twelve months of my life.

John, Michael and my brothers and sisters made a point of attending every hearing at St Helens Magistrates Court, sitting on pull-down seats in the public gallery. Each time the magistrate said: 'You are remanded in custody, take him down,' my family would immediately stand up as one. The noise of the pull-down seats snapping back into place was like a gunshot going off.

The first time it happened, Simms looked around, startled (as did the magistrate, clerks and prison officers) and met the cold, staring faces of Helen's loved ones. 'We were telling him "We're here. We are a family and we're not going anywhere,"' John told me afterwards. But there was no mouthing, no gesticulation, no issue of threats. Through my work with victims' families over the years, John and I have always urged them to show the court that you are respectful. I've always tried to show dignity and respect in any official setting relating to my murdered daughter and my quest for justice – whether that be a crown court or the Houses of Parliament.

Throughout all this time, my weekly novena kept me going. Being in church, gazing up at the stained-glass windows, watching the flickering candles brought me some comfort and gave me strength.

Five weeks after Helen went missing, John, Mum and I slipped into a pew towards the back of the church just as mass was about to start – I didn't want sympathetic glances or looks of pity. As the familiar words washed over me, I immersed myself in prayer. I'd accepted Helen had been taken from me. All I wanted was for her body to be found so she could be laid to rest.

Please, please, merciful God in heaven, bring Helen home to me. Mother of God, pray for me. St Martha, pray for me. End this torment, I beg you.

As the priest came to the consecration of the bread he lifted the paten (small plate) and asked God to bless its contents. As I've always done, I looked up, struck my breast and whispered, 'My Lord and My God.' It's a ritual left over from the days when Catholic masses were said in Latin. The little altar bell rang out to symbolise the miracle taking place then died away. I bowed my head.

Next, the priest lifted the chalice, looked to the skies and asked

God to bless the wine it contained. Once more, I looked up, struck my breast, opened my mouth to whisper … then froze.

The shock that jolted through me couldn't have been stronger if I'd stuck my wet finger in an electrical socket. One hand flew to my mouth, the other gripped the bench in front of me so tightly, my knuckles turned white. My heart literally froze in my chest.

I sensed John and Mum, either side of me, turn their faces towards me, bewildered. But I continued to stare straight ahead, without blinking.

There, just above the altar railings, where the congregation knelt to take Holy Communion, Helen had appeared.

I could just make out the top half of her, floating serenely. She was wearing a red silky vest top. Even from this far away, I could see her make-up was natural – just a gentle arc of lilac eyeshadow and a sheen of lipstick – and she was wearing her heated hair rollers. In her right hand, she clutched a half-full glass of red wine. She was gazing right back at me with sparkling eyes and smiling that beautiful smile.

Instinctively, one of my hands floated up from the pew. I reached out to her. Then, as before, the image shimmered, then evaporated. As the altar bell died away, so too did my daughter.

A long, juddering whimper escaped me. I sensed people turning their heads. Burying my face in my hands, I wept. Again, she'd been so real. And, again, she'd slipped away.

The rest of the mass passed in a blur. Religious stories from the Bible I remembered from my childhood raced through my mind. Jesus had brought his best friend, Lazarus, back to life, after seeing how distraught his sisters, Mary and Martha, were. Could he … they … not see the impact this was having on me? Jesus himself had been resurrected from the dead on Easter Sunday. Why not Helen, my daughter?

I want her back …

I was aware of John and Mum helping me up to the altar to take Holy Communion. Tears streamed down my face and my hands trembled as I took the offered host, whispered amen, placed it on my tongue and made the sign of the cross.

As the priest gave his final blessing, I turned to John: 'I need to go. Please get me out,' I begged. He put one strong arm around me and literally carried me out of the church and into the car.

I was shaking like a leaf and my body heaved as dry sobs continued to rack through me. 'What is it, love?' Mum kept asking. But I shook my head.

How could I tell her? How could I tell anyone that my dead daughter had just appeared to me in the middle of mass?

I don't remember getting home or being put to bed. It was Thursday morning, a full thirty-six hours later, that my eyes flickered open. I'd heard a familiar creak on the stairs followed by my door opening. Seconds later, Mum tiptoed into my room.

'Are you OK, love?' she asked softly.

'Yeah,' I whispered blankly. 'I'm OK.'

'Do you want some tea and toast?' she offered.

I sighed. 'Who's in the house?' I didn't want to face anyone.

She smiled. 'Only me and you, love,' she said. 'Margaret and Pat will be down later. Why don't you come downstairs? The kettle's on.'

Wrapping a dressing gown around me, I stepped weakly down the stairs, holding onto the rail. As I entered the kitchen, Mum looked up from pouring tea and I could have wept. She tried to smile encouragingly but the lines on her face were so etched and there were dark shadows under her eyes.

'Are you all right, girl?' she asked gently.

This is killing her.

Pain was emanating from every pore, I couldn't keep her in the dark.

'Shall I tell you what happened in church, Mum?' I asked.

She nodded.

Tears slid down her face as I described how I'd seen Helen on the altar – the rollers in her hair, the red vest top.

'She was there, Mum. I swear. As clear as you are to me now. She was so serene, it was so beautiful.' I shook my head. 'And I couldn't deal with it.'

She nodded and reached out a hand to briefly squeeze mine. We sat there for ages, drinking tea in silence, listening to the clock ticking in the background and nursing our hurt.

'That must mean something,' Mum murmured at one point.

I nodded. 'Maybe,' I agreed.

That evening, the phone rang. It was Lynn – Helen's friend, who had taken her to Blackpool in October of the previous year. 'Hello, Mrs McCourt,' she said. 'I'm coming to Cheshire tomorrow to visit my sister who's just had a baby, the first grandchild in the family. It's not that far from you. I'd love to call by and see you … if that's OK?'

I often think what courage that phone call and visit would have taken. She was celebrating a great family occasion, but took time out to visit the mother of her missing, murdered, friend.

I smiled. 'That would be lovely, Lynn,' I said. 'Do come over. Please.'

When she pulled up the following morning, I suddenly remembered we'd found some photos of her in Helen's drawer and wearily headed upstairs to get them. Coming back downstairs, I found Mum, my sisters and Lynn all stood in the doorway of the living room.

'Sorry about that, Lynn,' I said. 'I just wanted to grab some photos for you …' But my voice trailed away. Pat, Margaret and Lynn were all looking, concerned, at Mum. The colour had drained from her face and she was trembling as she gazed at the photo in her hand. An age seemed to go by, then she held it out to me.

'Marie?' she began. 'Lynn's got something she wants to give you.'

Taking the offered photograph, I looked at it and gasped: it was a picture of Helen I'd never seen before. It was as if I was back in that church pew, gazing at the altar again.

There was Helen in her bedroom, wearing that red, silky top. Her hair was in curlers – apart from one curl which had worked its way loose. She was beautifully made up, with lilac eye shadow and pink lipstick. And she had the prettiest, widest smile on her face. Only one thing was missing – the glass of wine.

Beside me, I sensed Mum crying. I looked up, stunned, at Lynn.

'Wh— where did this come from?' I asked.

Lynn swallowed, unsure of what was going on. 'I took it that weekend when I was down visiting. We were getting ready for our night out in Blackpool. It's such a lovely picture ... I thought you might like it.'

I ran my finger over the image. 'Lynn, were you and Helen drinking red wine in her room before going out?' I asked.

Lynn coloured. She would have known I disapproved of Helen drinking in her room while getting ready. Drinking was something you did with friends, not on your own. But you could see her brain working.

How on earth did you know that?

'Erm, yes, we were, Mrs McCourt,' she confessed. 'But, don't tell me mum – she'd kill me.'

I smiled. 'It's OK, love,' I reassured her. 'It's just that I saw Helen, just like this – in church, two days ago,' I explained. 'Me mum knows. She was on the altar, holding a glass of wine. This is exactly how she looked.'

I can't thank Lynn enough for bringing that photo to me that day. It has brought me such comfort over the years. After the initial shock of seeing my daughter in church, I realised I'd been blessed in being allowed to see her one more time.

Some divine intervention, perhaps St Martha, had allowed me a glimpse of her, smiling and happy. They couldn't bring her back to me but they could let me see her just one more time. And thanks to the photo, that image has stayed fresh in my mind.

* * *

I was so touched by gestures of kindness, both from loved ones and complete strangers. Flowers, cards and little gifts would arrive from well-wishers and local congregations at churches. They'd tell me they were thinking of me and praying for me. Some were simply signed 'from a mum' or 'a parent whose heart goes out to you'.

Meanwhile I continued to say the novena, so sure that Helen would be found by the ninth Tuesday. I spent all day, right up to midnight, willing the phone or doorbell to ring, imagining my relief at hearing those three words: 'We've found her.' But the house remained silent.

I've stuck to my novena religiously. Tuesday evening mass has long since stopped, but wherever I am in the world, whatever I'm doing, on Tuesday evening I light a candle to Helen's confirmation saint. Then I kneel, bow my head and fervently say my novena. I lose myself in the words and finally emerge, blinking. Afterwards I feel exhausted and spent, but a little more at peace.

I was so touched when a dear friend, who has since died, bought me a statue of St Martha to use for my novenas. For thirty years she has stood on our mantlepiece watching over us all, one hand on her heart, the other holding her staff. On Tuesday evenings, I place Helen's framed portrait beside her, then add softly flickering candles.

Those novenas kept me going during the darkest, darkest times that descended upon me. With no date even set for the trial, I found myself in an horrendous no man's land. I entered a long period of 'No' days, as my mum called them. She'd moved in to support me, sleeping in Helen's bedroom, and would make tentative knocks on my door throughout the day. The curtains remained closed but sleep still eluded me – I just lay there, hour after hour, staring up at the ceiling.

'Would you like a cup of tea, Marie?' she'd ask.

'No.'

'Shall I run you a bath?'

'No.'

'Are you going to get dressed today?'

'No.'

On and on it went. No matter what was asked, my answer was always the same. Even if the police visited with an update, I'd go down in my dressing gown (much to Mum's horror) to listen to them. Why should I care what people thought? Over time, I've come to realise that they're used to dealing with grieving, distressed families. The sight of someone in their dressing gown isn't going to phase them in the slightest.

I tormented myself, reliving that evening over and over. I knew the weather was going to be horrendous so what was I thinking, sitting in the house? Why didn't I go and pick her up? Why did I let her make that journey in those appalling conditions? Why? Why? Why? What sort of a mother was I to let her down in the worst way possible? I know now, through my work with the families affected by homicide, that those 'what ifs?' and 'why didn'ts?' are incredibly common. We berate ourselves over and over.

Over time I came to accept that what happened couldn't be changed and in my work with other families, have helped them to do the same. For a long time, however, that pain, that anger towards myself, was there. But no matter how low and miserable I felt, I would drag myself to church every Tuesday evening and Sunday morning. To this day, my faith has kept me going.

Looking back, my heart goes out to so many of my loved

ones who were also struggling, but particularly John. After the initial media interviews following Helen's disappearance, I had no further contact with Billy, my ex-husband, and the situation remains to this day. No doubt he has his own grief to deal with, and his own story, but it's not mine to share.

Poor John must have wondered what he'd taken on. He'd fallen in love with a happy-go-lucky woman who was blessed with two lovely children. We were a great, little unit – the happiest of families – looking forward to spending the rest of our lives together.

As it would be the second wedding for both John and me we only wanted a small do with family and close friends. We'd booked St Helens register office but we hadn't even got around to sorting outfits or booking a venue for a meal afterwards. In a way, it was just as well: there was only one phone call to make to cancel the service.

John was the strong glue that held our family together through those dark times. I'd been an old-fashioned mum who had prided herself on providing for her children. There was a meal on the table every night but from the night Helen went missing, I stopped cooking.

Her dinner had been ready that night. And she had never come home for it. I was simply never able to cook again.

It was the same with clothes shopping. Helen and I used to spend all our Saturdays together, choosing outfits. To this day, I dread shopping for clothes.

John stepped in, doing all the shopping and cooking. Our house which once rang with laughter and music was now stifled with misery and grief. There were times it was so engulfing I found it difficult to breathe – it descended from the ceiling, rose up from the floor and leached off the walls, no matter how many windows I opened. Anyone who came into our house couldn't fail to feel it settle across their chest and shoulders and sink into their clothes. I imagined it as a dank, damp fog, wrapping itself around visitors.

I urged John to leave. To get out. 'Go and find yourself a nice, ordinary woman – someone who can make you happy,' I'd say, blankly.

He would shake his head and smile a sad smile. 'I'm going nowhere, love,' he'd reassure me. 'I love you and I'm staying.'

* * *

Along with every member of my family, John threw himself into the physical search for Helen. To start with, he, Michael, my brothers, sisters, brothers-in-law and cousins would join the police on their searches.

They were focusing on two areas: the first was near to where a man's clothes had been found dumped the morning after Helen disappeared, on wasteland, at a place called Hollins Green, near Warrington – near the Manchester Ship Canal. A car (the Volkswagen police had appealed for information on in the early days after Helen disappeared) had also been spotted backed up to the canal, its boot open. Police had spent an entire week just dragging the murky waters.

The second area was where Helen's clothing had been recovered three miles from this spot – on the banks of the River Irwell.

'Give us something to do, we want to help,' my brother Tez and John would say to the police. Usually they were given a spot off the beaten track, but they'd watch the police carefully and look and learn from their methods. They learned how to plan a search, how to ensure no area was missed, how to record results and tick off an area completely once they were sure it had been covered.

After months of relentless work, I was heartbroken when the police searches were wound down. They had done all they could, they explained. The search would always remain open, but from now on, it would be a matter of 'acting on positive information' that came in.

I understood, but the disappointment was unbearable.

I turned to my brothers. 'Please, please, can you carry on?' I implored, tearfully.

'We'll do everything we can,' they promised. And they did. The police, God love them, continued to support the family – assigning officers to direct the team and analyse soil samples.

The family went out every weekend without fail, searching from morning till night. I couldn't go with them to begin with. First, I didn't have the strength, emotionally or physically. But there was another reason: *What if someone rings?*

There were no mobile phones, emails or social media in those days. The house phone was the only way police could reach me and I was going to be there to answer.

Sitting there, willing the phone to ring became an obsession. The thought of not being here to respond straight away, to spring into action, to get the wheels in motion for bringing my daughter home was unbearable. I didn't want her out there, God knows where, for a minute longer than she had to be.

The house became a prison. Sometimes I felt it closing in on me but I couldn't leave. 'They may ring,' I'd say simply.

One day, John came home with a box under his arm. 'Here you go,' he said, getting to work with a machine and a tangle of wires. 'It's a phone with an answer machine. Now, you can go out.'

Even now, thirty years on, the first thing I do when I return to the house is listen to messages. It could be a journalist, someone with information, an old schoolfriend of Helen's ringing to catch up. Or it might be the police with those three longed-for words: 'We've found Helen.'

One Saturday night, I dug out my wellies and waterproof coat: 'I'm going with you, tomorrow,' I told John.

It was time, I was ready.

Setting off in the car with flasks and sandwiches, we must have looked like any other family heading for a day out. Except we weren't going to picture-postcard spots or breath-taking areas of natural beauty. We were seeking out God-forsaken hell-holes: old mines, rat-infested sewers, stagnant ponds, litter-strewn ditches, lonely woods. Places off the beaten track ... Places suitable for hiding a body.

Those searches were to become a focal point of my life, a purpose for getting up each morning, a reason to keep going.

Helen was gone, I knew that. No miracle was ever going to bring her back. But I had to find her, I had to bring her home.

Chapter 7

The trial

As with all events relating to Helen, the trial of her killer, at Liverpool Crown Court, started – and finished – on a Tuesday.

The first anniversary of her disappearance had been just over a fortnight earlier. I'd organised a remembrance mass at St Mary's, Billinge, and was touched and comforted when 400 people attended. Gazing up at the familiar stained-glass windows, I prayed this nightmare would soon be over. After conviction, there would be no point in the killer staying silent.

Surely to God, he'll do the decent thing and let us know where she is.

For years, I'd imagined the joy of watching Helen walk up this aisle on her wedding day. Now, all I wanted was the relief of seeing her coffin being carried slowly to the front of the church on the shoulders of those who loved her.

We'd have a requiem mass and her coffin would be blessed and sprinkled with holy water before being laid gently into consecrated grounds.

For now, though, I had nothing.

People often commented on the resemblance between Helen and myself, particularly our similar thick brown hair. I'd always kept mine short and neat, but after Helen went missing, I stopped caring. Over twelve miserable months my hair had grown long and unkempt.

As the trial approached, I decided not to get it cut.

I want him to look at me and see Helen.

The trial had been due to start on the Monday but for some reason it was held over to Tuesday, 21 February 1989, which I took as a good sign.

I used rollers to style my hair in thick, full waves, like Helen's, then pulled on one of her smartest work suits. I wanted to make her proud – to do her justice and get her justice.

Walking towards Liverpool Crown Court, I focused on the ground as press cameras flashed and whirred. Seeing cuttings now, I'm shocked at how gaunt and drawn I looked. Misery emanates from every pore.

My heckles rose as our bags were searched and we were patted down by security guards: 'We're not the criminals,' I hissed indignantly to my sisters and Mum.

As a key witness, one of the last people to speak to Helen and the person who reported her missing, I wasn't allowed into the court itself until I was called to give evidence. But I was determined to be present from the outset – and I wasn't the only one.

The placed was rammed.

Not only were murder trials without a body still incredibly rare but the prosecution would be presenting a brand-new scientific discovery as a vital part of its case.

Nowadays, we're all familiar with DNA profiling and genetic fingerprinting, but back then, these were breakthroughs. A conviction, using DNA evidence in the absence of a body, would make legal history. No wonder people were interested.

Helen's dad (who also attended the trial each day) and I had provided samples of blood for analysis. I had also handed over Helen's baby teeth from her keepsake box and her Velcro rollers to which the odd strand of hair still clung. How it would all fit together we had no idea.

I missed the jury selection, Crown Prosecutor Mr Brian Leveson (now Sir Leveson) setting out the case for the prosecution – and the first glimpse of him, Simms. The man accused of my daughter's murder standing in the dock, listening to the charge, entering his Not Guilty plea.

I'd hoped for a blow-by-blow account when my family finally streamed out, but they were exhausted and drained. My mum, flanked by Pat and Margaret, had dark shadows under her eyes as she tried to give me a cheery smile. My heart twisted. This had only just begun. The trial was expected to last for three weeks, calling more than 100 witnesses.

That evening, John and I went to mass as usual. *Give us strength to get through this, St Martha*, I implored silently. *Help me get justice for Helen.*

On day two of the trial, the judge arranged a visit to the George and Dragon so the jury could see the complex layout of the pub. Family members were among a small crowd that watched silently as the judge, jury and defendant himself arrived. The evening papers were filled with dramatic images of Simms being led back into 'the pub where time has stood still' flanked by prison guards.

After lunch, the court resumed. 'Mary McCourt,' called an usher, using my official name. This was it. My shoes clicked along the polished floor as my trembling legs carried me to the witness box. Placing my right hand on the Bible and vowing to tell the truth before bewigged barristers, solemn solicitors and officious clerks felt surreal – like being on a film set.

Before answering questions, there was something I needed to

do. Taking a deep breath, I turned towards the dock until he came into view: Simms. The accused. I was shocked at how different he looked from his committal, just six months earlier.

His once-full head of hair was visibly receding and his thick, bullish neck – sinewy from years of weight training and martial arts – had become skinny and scrawny. He looked so much older than his thirty-two years and lost in a dark suit that was clearly too big for him. But he still had the same distinctive moustache – he looked like a little Hitler.

I stared, unblinking, silently urging him to look at me. But he didn't. Not once throughout the entire trial. He fixed his gaze straight ahead to where his counsel was sitting. Occasionally, he'd glance across at the jury – doubtless weighing them up, wondering what they were thinking. One attractive blonde woman seemed of particular interest. Or he'd look down, scrutinising his hands or feet.

Over three weeks my eyes must have burned a hole in the side of his head. *Look at me. Look at me,* I willed silently. I wanted him to see Helen. I wanted him to break down and admit what he'd done, say where he'd hidden her and put a stop to this torture once and for all. But his eyes never once met mine.

'Mrs McCourt …' Mr Brian Leveson began.

We'd started.

In a trembling voice, I answered his questions. How every mum is biased but Helen really was an extra-special girl – caring and considerate and never giving us a moment's worry … Until the night she went missing. Step by step, I relived that awful evening – how we'd searched frantically before reporting her missing.

I recoiled slightly as a taupe garment, inside clear plastic wrapping, appeared.

'Do you recognise this, Mrs McCourt?' Mr Leveson asked gently.

Our trip to the Trafford Centre to buy it … Helen's new

winter coat in 1986 seemed like yesterday. I nodded. 'That's Helen's winter coat,' I whispered. 'It was her favourite. She ... she loved it.'

Seeing it now, so dirty and dishevelled, after lying in a river for three weeks was soul-destroying. Mr Leveson mentioned a missing button, a tear in the lining under one arm. Deep in my brain, a disturbing memory stirred, then slotted into place.

In the committal hearing I'd attended the previous August, a barrister had briefly summarised what the Crown believed had happened that night – that Simms had lured my daughter into the pub, dragged her upstairs into his living quarters and murdered her before hiding her body. Just hearing those words was horrible. But now, seeing the damaged coat, it was all too real.

Without warning, my stomach lurched violently.

The coat was damaged – while she was being dragged.

Terrible images and thoughts flooded my mind. Was she aware of what was happening, or, worse, what was about to happen? Did she, oh dear God, did she call out for me?

Helen was five foot four, not even eight and a half stone and a gentle soul, a slip of a thing. Simms was a powerfully-built kickboxer and bodybuilder – five foot ten and over thirteen stone. We also learned afterwards of his violent temper, his Jekyll and Hyde personality and how he revelled in the nickname 'Psycho Simms'.

Helen never stood a chance.

My breath juddered. I bowed my head and watched fat tears splash onto my skirt. A tissue and a glass of water were placed in front of me.

'Would you like to adjourn, Mrs McCourt?' someone asked.

But I shook my head firmly. Gripping the damp tissue, I shakily sipped water through parched lips. I had to get through this.

For Helen.

I identified that sad little opal and sapphire earring again and Helen's favourite green mitts, a red comb, a pearl coloured hair slide ...

Mr Leveson also asked me about the incident in the pub two nights before Helen had gone missing.

'Helen wasn't the type of girl to get into arguments,' I insisted. 'She said it was all a misunderstanding, but she was adamant she wouldn't be going there again. There's no way she'd have gone into that pub on the Tuesday of her own accord,' I added, fixing my stare at Simms. 'She was never late.'

Finally, I was allowed to step down. The prospect of being cross-examined the following morning by Simms' counsel filled me with dread.

More than thirty-two years on it's all a blur, but I remember at one point, John Kay QC pondering whether Helen's coat was already damaged before that night.

'My daughter took pride in her appearance,' I said coldly. 'She would never have gone out in a torn coat. And the buttons were always fastened. I'd have noticed if one was missing.'

He asked me about the earring that I'd been asked to identify. I explained how they were Helen's twenty-first birthday earrings; she'd bought a replacement pair after losing one. Since then, there had been three in her jewellery box – she wore two and always had a spare.

I confirmed Helen had been distraught after breaking up with her boyfriend, David, in September 1987 and started frequenting the George and Dragon, drinking more than usual. Yes, she'd occasionally stayed behind for lock-ins, returning home in the early hours. No, I wasn't particularly happy about it, but it was just a phase. By November, things were back to normal.

At last it was over. 'No more questions,' he said.

Drained, I stepped down from the stand and gratefully joined John and my family in the gallery. Opening my handbag, I rooted inside until my fingers clasped around what I called my 'holy cards'. One was my well-worn novena to St Martha, the other was a gift passed on by my Aunt Bibby – who was a Carmelite nun: 'One of our sisters made this for you, Marie,' she'd said.

It was a delicate pencil drawing of Our Lady reaching her arms comfortingly towards a kneeling child. Tears of compassion were streaming down her face. Underneath, in beautiful calligraphy, were the words, 'Mother Mary, Pray for Me'.

'Keep this with you,' Bibby said, gently. 'Look at it every time you feel low.' Helen had adored Bibby – and had been so looking forward to seeing her 'take the veil' in July 1988 (five months after her murder).

Those 'cards' gave me the strength to attend day in, day out, and listen to every harrowing detail.

Afterwards, in my support work with other families, I would lend that precious Mother Mary card out for court hearings. 'Hold this, it will give you strength,' I'd say gently. Unfortunately, after one such loan, it never came back. I was sad, but took comfort in the fact that its new owner needed it more.

* * *

The evidence against Simms was, as the prosecution had stated on the first day, overwhelming. Very occasionally, in my long quest for justice, I have encountered the odd person who ventures that, perhaps, Simms doesn't know where Helen is because he didn't do it. Maybe the jury got it wrong. Maybe his conviction was a tragic miscarriage of justice and the real killer is still out there. I would urge anyone with the slightest doubt of Simms' guilt to read the next two chapters and see if you still feel the same.

Rather than recount the trial, day by agonising day, witness by endless witness, I'll try to take you through the prosecution evidence in chronological order. There was so much forensic information that jury members were issued with files of evidence – with overlays of plastic sheets, maps, diagrams and studies – to help them follow.

Firstly, there was the incident in the pub on the Sunday night, which I found out more about as the trial progressed. It turns out Helen had photos in her bag from the pub's New Year celebrations and was showing them to a lad she knew from the village. One picture showed her good friend, Karen, with whom she'd been on holiday to Majorca the previous year – along with a group of girls. But unbeknown to Helen, this lad had actually gone out with Karen while they were at school. Staring across the pub at them now, with a face like thunder, was his current girlfriend … who had been drinking all day. (Simms had even lent her a tenner when she ran out of money).

When the girlfriend, who we'll call Susan, weaved across the pub towards them, Helen's friend hissed at her to put the photos away. But it was too late. The girl saw them, got upset and accused Helen of 'stirring' things. While trying to grab the pictures, she spilt her wine over Helen.

(I have to stress here that Helen was anything but a trouble-maker. Don't forget, she hadn't gone to the local school with any of the villagers so had no idea who'd gone out with who back then).

When Helen slipped away to the ladies' toilets to sponge down her skirt, this girl stormed in after her. Helen's alarmed friend immediately ran to the bar for help saying: 'Susan's going to kill her – Helen's not a fighter'. Ian Simms hurried in and found Helen, crying, holding a furious Susan's wrists to stop her lashing out.

Grabbing Susan by the shoulders, Simms had ordered Helen out of the toilets and told her she was barred. My daughter left the pub crying. Simms shouted at her and humiliated her in front of everyone like that and she'd done absolutely nothing wrong. Even now, all these years on, my heart twists at the thought of her sobbing as she walked home – then drying her eyes before coming inside and pretending everything was OK. On the Monday evening, she'd vowed never to step foot in that pub again – and I believed her.

And so we come to 9 February 1988 – the last hours of Helen's life.

If you remember, she had left work half an hour early that day, at 4pm – keen to have her tea, then have plenty of time to get ready for a date with Frank, her new boyfriend, at 8pm.

She'd read some of a Mills & Boon book (they were small and fitted into her handbag) and eaten a bag of crisps on the 4.16pm train from Lime Street to St Helens. Then, en route to the bus stop, she'd popped into Superdrug to buy a few bits before catching the 362 bus to Billinge.

At 5.15pm, she'd got off at her usual stop and was seen by two witnesses walking, head-down, into the gale-force winds, clutching her shopping in one carrier bag and her work shoes in another. The sun had set six minutes earlier so the village was dark.

She was never seen again.

Her short route home would have taken her directly past the George and Dragon pub – just 483 yards from our home.

Ian Simms admitted from the outset that he was alone inside from 4.20pm to 6pm. (Back then, pubs closed at 3pm and reopened in the evening.) Upstairs in the pool room, which was open to customers, Simms had fitted blackout windows and thick drapes so that he could hold secret lock-ins. They also gave him the advantage of being able to look out, unseen. One bar worker testified that, while getting the upstairs bar ready one afternoon, he'd been startled to see the curtain suddenly move. Pulling it back, he found Simms standing there ... silently watching schoolgirls getting off the bus.

That evening, he would have had a clear view of Helen struggling up a deserted Main Street, towards the pub, crossing at the pelican lights.

The George and Dragon was an unusual building; part of the ground floor had been converted to an independent restaurant called The Stone Barn (which Simms had run before taking over the pub). It also had the first-floor pool room with a bar, and on one side of the building was a bowling green.

A tall wooden side gate provided access both to the bowling green and a rarely used private door, which led to a staircase (referred to as 'Staircase A' in the trial) and the pub's living quarters upstairs. In seconds, Simms could have slipped down those stairs, opened the gate onto Main Street and called my daughter over.

As I testified, and told police, Helen would not have voluntarily called at the pub. But if he'd called her name, urgently gestured her over, she might well have gone out of politeness. The gate could have clicked shut behind her as he encouraged her up to the side door out of the howling wind and gritty air.

Just come up here for a second. I need to ask you something …

What could he have wanted? To discuss the incident in the pub two nights earlier? Or was there another, more sinister, reason?

The police investigation established that Simms was a lothario who boasted about his sexual prowess. While his wife and two young children lived just 500 yards away in the family home with his mother, Simms claimed he needed to sleep on the premises to prevent break-ins. He didn't sleep alone, however. Since the summer of 1987, his young mistress Tracey Hornby, who was twenty at the time of the trial, had virtually moved into the flat with him. Even that didn't stop his womanising. One of the advantages of being a pub landlord, he'd boasted, was being able to 'have' any woman who came through his door. His many conquests among young female customers, even while Tracey was sleeping in the main bedroom, were the 'perks of being a licensee'.

Simms admitted in the witness box that as recently as the week before Helen disappeared, he and Tracey had rowed in a club when she'd caught him 'all over' a girl.

As witnesses gave evidence, I learned that Helen had confided in a number of friends that Simms had made advances, was 'trying to get her into bed' and told her he'd 'fantasised' about her, but she had 'knocked him back' and wasn't interested. The police had no doubt there was a 'sexual attraction' to Helen on Simms' part.

After the incident in the toilets, Simms was heard by three separate witnesses saying he hated Helen. Was it because she'd rebuffed him? A few months earlier, he'd accused her of gossiping about his lock-ins and extra-marital affair and temporarily barred her. She'd assured him she'd done no such thing and it was all smoothed over – but was it?

We already knew that Simms had a temper … and he admitted he was 'steaming' that day with his manager who hadn't notified him when a rep from Labatt beer had called at the pub. Was he quietly fuming upstairs? Did he see Helen out of the window and decide to tackle her about the incident in the pub two nights earlier?

At 5.25pm, a villager returning home from work got off his bus in Billinge and walked up what we call 'the steps' or 'the cobbles'– a steep footpath on Main Street, about 100 yards away from the George and Dragon pub. This path leads to a high point which overlooks the village – and pub.

Just as he reached the top, Mr Leveson said, the villager had 'heard a sharp, fairly high-pitched, screaming call which stopped dead. He looked where he believed the noise had come from – down Main Street towards the George and Dragon public house – but saw nothing.'

Assuming it was children playing, he'd carried on home. But, on hearing his evidence, a chill went down my spine. That man had heard Helen's last scream as she was pulled into the pub. I knew she wouldn't have gone in willingly.

Between 5.45pm and 6pm, the manageress of The Stone Barn restaurant was in the bar serving area when she heard loud 'dragging' noises coming from upstairs. Directly above her was the back bedroom of the pub.

The ceiling was low – with a height of just 7ft 1½in – and the gap between the ceiling and the floorboards above was just 5½in. As Mr Leveson pointed out, 'every sound made in the back bedroom can be heard in the servery'.

The jury would have discovered that for themselves when they visited the premises early in the trial.

The sounds were similar to those made when the previous owner had been packing up furniture to move out, 'as though something was being moved around,' she said.

At 5.45pm, Simms was seen moving his VW Passat dark blue car from its usual position in front of the restaurant and reversing to the tall gate which led to the pub's private door. After stopping, he opened the boot.

It was no accident the car was moved to this position, Mr Leveson told the court '… for in that way the body of Helen McCourt could be removed from the flat essentially out of sight and away from observant passers-by.'

Back to Simms' affair. Every evening at 7pm, Tracey would arrive at the pub to spend the night with him. However, her grandmother became upset at overhearing gossip about a young woman having an affair with 'that rat at the pub'.

To keep the peace, Tracey agreed to no longer sleep at the pub but return home each night after seeing Simms. She wept as she told the court, 'I love him and still do.' She was going to start returning home on Tuesday, 9 February … the day that Helen went missing.

That very evening, Simms phoned her at 6.10pm, asking her not to come to the pub until 8.30pm – an hour and a half later than her usual arrival time. When asked why, he'd whispered 'Nadine.' His wife's name. She presumed Nadine was in the background.

At 5.55pm, a dark blue car pulled out from the pub car park without warning, causing a driver to perform an emergency stop and exclaim 'Silly idiot!' The blue car continued through the traffic lights towards St Helens.

Simms visited the family home between 6.30 and 6.45pm, said his wife, but he only stayed briefly before returning to the pub – again, reversing his car to the gate – at 7pm. He must then have spent the next hour upstairs – on his own – before coming downstairs at 8pm and telling staff he was 'nipping out for half an hour'. He was gone for two hours.

Between 8pm and 8.15pm, John rang the pub and asked if Helen was there. An announcement was made over the tannoy. 'Sorry, she's not here,' a new barmaid said. At 8.45pm, Tracey arrived at the pub and, as usual, headed upstairs to the flat via the main set of stairs (called 'Staircase B' in court). These stairs led to both the pool room on the first floor – and the locked front door to Simms' living quarters.

Tracey slid her key in the lock but it wouldn't turn. Downstairs, she fumed for a while before remembering there was a key to the other set of stairs, via the side gate, in the cleaning cupboard. She let herself in that way, but found the flat empty. There was no sign of Simms. Puzzled as to why she hadn't been able to unlock the front door, she'd checked it and discovered the 'snip' was on.

Someone had deliberately locked the door from the inside – preventing anyone from coming in.

It also meant, said the prosecution, that Simms could not have left the flat through that door because the snip could only be applied from the inside.

This had never happened before, Tracey agreed. Upset that Simms wasn't there, and suspecting he'd taken Nadine out for her birthday, which was later that week, she'd sat in the main bedroom watching TV, waiting for him to come home.

Finally, at 10pm, Simms returned to the flat. Popping his head around the bedroom door (keeping his body out of sight), he told a still-miffed Tracey that Nadine had 'gone berserk' after finding out about the affair. 'Look what she's done,' he said, pointing to two long scratches on his Adam's apple.

He then asked her to go downstairs and see if the new barmaid needed a hand while he had a bath. Tracey was surprised – she'd never been asked to help before and was only gone a few minutes as the barmaid was fine. Back upstairs, she watched TV until Simms emerged from the bathroom with a towel around his waist and wet hair.

After dressing, he'd popped briefly to the bar, where a customer alerted him to the pub sign swinging precariously in the gale force wind. Simms had looked out of the window and said he'd deal with it.

Simms returned to the flat 'subdued and not his normal self'. But not so subdued that it interfered with his sex life. I still vividly remember recoiling as Tracey told the court how they'd got into bed and made love. The word 'wonderful' was used.

Afterwards, she'd set her alarm for 1am and gone home, leaving him in bed. Alone in the pub …

Just after 5am, an air stewardess driving to work for an early shift spotted a car matching the description of Simms' Passat being driven at speed near Warrington, thirteen miles away.

At 5.30am, a local delivery driver to Billinge noticed lights blazing in the usually dark pub. There was no sign of Simms' car. It was still absent at 8.30am.

Fifteen miles away, Gordon Bannister, a local butcher, was taking his Alsatian dog for a 7.30am walk on Hollins Green waste land between the Manchester Ship Canal and the A57. He noticed a dark blue VW hatchback backed right up to the canal's edge. One big gust of wind and they'll be in the water, he remembered thinking. But his attention was taken by his dog running excitedly off along a dirt track. About 200 yards along the path, he found it sniffing at a blood-stained towel. As a butcher, he recognised human blood when he saw it.

Two feet away from the towel were a pair of muddy men's boots plus a pair of men's jeans, 'concertina-ed on the ground as though someone had just stepped out of them'. Nearby was a blue sweatshirt, inside out and crumpled up, 'as though it had been thrown off', a pair of underpants and one solitary sock – all heavily mud-stained. There was also another towel and a dishcloth.

Intrigued, Bannister put his hand over the crotch of the jeans. Despite the extensive mud on the legs, the clothes were 'bone dry'.

They'd only just been taken off.

Mr Bannister told the court he was so alarmed at the bloodstains, he'd looked around for a body before turning back. The car was now gone. After confiding in his wife, he rang Cheshire Police and led them to the site at 10am.

There isn't a day goes by when I don't thank Gordon Bannister for acting so diligently. His evidence would prove crucial to the case.

Back in Billinge, Simms was seen at a local garage at 8am, putting air into his car's rear offside tyre.

At 8.45am, the pub cleaner, Mrs Mary Smith, and her husband arrived at the pub for her morning shift. They were stunned when Simms answered the door immediately. Usually, it took five to ten minutes to rouse him from bed.

Although Simms was wearing clean clothes, his hands and face were dirty 'as if he had been working in the garden and then wiped his face with grubby hands'.

Yet, he'd only had a bath at 10pm the night before.

Inside, the pub seemed unusually clean. Brand new black bin bags, which had not been ordered by Mrs Smith, were strewn in the cleaning cupboard. And the usual roll of bin bags looked noticeably slimmer. While cleaning the toilets, she heard 'vigorous brushing' and was astonished to find Simms scrubbing the wooden floor at the bottom of the private staircase with bleach and a stiff brush. He said he was cleaning up dog dirt – a job he never normally did. The dog often messed there but Simms usually left the cleaning up to them.

At about 9.45am Simms announced he was going to Makro – a wholesalers at Kirkby – even though he'd only visited the day before to buy cleaning equipment. He had never gone twice in one week before. He told the police, in interviews, that he wanted paint and floor tiles to 'improve' his home. (But was he planning to decorate the pub to hide evidence?) Paint was actually delivered on the Thursday while police were speaking to him in the pub. I was told later that one officer actually commented, 'Someone's going to be busy.' (although this was not said in court). The police report also said that Simms brought in a vacuum cleaner from home as the pub one was being repaired and used it on the carpets. Again, this was out of the ordinary.

Leaving via the side door which led to the bowling green gate, carrying two black bin bags, Simms had locked the staff inside until the pub manager Ken Booth arrived later that morning. This was definitely out of character. Simms didn't trust anyone. He would remove the handle of the back bedroom, where he stored bottles of spirits, so no one could gain access.

At 12.30pm, Simms returned to the pub to meet Tracey for lunch. When she commented on a mark on his lip, he said he'd cut himself shaving.

Helen's disappearance was now all over the news. By that evening, police had established that she had reached Billinge before vanishing. DCS Eddie Alldred announced police would be searching every building Helen would have had to pass on her way home from the bus stop.

At that point, my loyal brothers had already embarked on some detective work of their own. While everyone had gathered at my house, frantic with worry, three of them had slipped out and visited the George and Dragon to mingle in the hope of overhearing something about Helen's disappearance.

Once inside, Tez had asked the pub manager, Ken Booth, if the landlord was in and if they could speak to him.

'What's it about?' the manager asked.

Our Tez wasn't in the mood for a chat. 'It's a private conversation,' he'd replied, coolly.

Five, then ten minutes went by, with no sign of Simms. After another prompt to the manager, Simms finally appeared – swaggering across to where they were waiting.

'What's up?' he'd asked over-casually.

All three had stared at him. Simms looked as though he'd just got out of a long soak in a red-hot bath. He was wearing a thick cream Aran sweater but his face and hands were red and literally gleaming. He made a point of trying, and failing, to look at ease – stretching out his arms dramatically, slowly scratching his neck and yawning, while he considered, then answered, their questions.

Tez had chosen his words carefully: 'When's the last time you saw Helen McCourt?' he asked.

Simms' demeanour instantly changed. His swagger evaporated. For the briefest of moments, a look of panic appeared in his eyes and his voice became hesitant and higher-pitched.

'She comes in here, sometimes,' he stammered. Then he quickly added, 'But I haven't seen her.'

Tez eyed him levelly. 'What do you mean, "you haven't seen her"?' he asked. 'I didn't ask that.'

Then David spoke: 'So how often did she come in?'

Simms' eyes darted about. 'Er, rarely,' he stammered.

'Did Helen ever stay behind for lock-ins?' David continued.

Simms shook his head quickly. 'No, never,' he said.

David stared at him. He knew for a fact Simms was lying – he'd asked Helen himself to stop having stay-behinds as it was upsetting me.

'Right, I'd better be off,' said Simms. 'Have a drink before you go – on the house,' he added, before sauntering off.

The brothers headed outside to the front of the pub and spoke quietly.

'He's lying,' said Tez.

David nodded. 'I know for a fact he's lying because Helen did have stay-behinds.'

Tez frowned. 'And what sort of landlord offers free drinks to strangers? There's something not right.'

Together, they'd gone to the police incident room to report their concerns before slipping back to my house – I hadn't even noticed they'd left.

The prosecution asked for just one sibling to testify. Senior Investigating Officer Paul Acres put Tez forward: 'I think you'll agree he's the strongest witness,' he said.

'No!' I said firmly. 'It has to be our David.'

Paul blinked – he probably wasn't used to having his brilliant mind questioned. 'He was the only one who knew about Helen having stay-behinds and he was the one who asked Simms about it,' I continued. 'The barristers will accept it from him. But if it comes from our Tez, it's just hearsay.'

I've no idea where that word 'hearsay' came from. I'd never even heard it before. Yet, suddenly, I was spouting legal jargon with the best of them – I'm sure it was down to St Martha.

And so it was my youngest brother, David, who took the witness stand. Sitting beside Mum, I shook with nerves. David had developed epilepsy as a teenager and, although it was controlled with medication, I was terrified that the stress would bring on a seizure. Thankfully, he remained calm and in control as he testified.

'When Tez told Simms we were Helen's uncles, he asked: "Helen who?"' David told the court.

Helen had been a regular in the pub for years – she'd worked there, for heaven's sake. Everyone knew her.

'Helen who?' indeed.

Next morning at 11am, perhaps before this information had even filtered through, police arrived at the George and Dragon.

DCS Eddie Alldred explained in later documentaries how they knew something had happened between the bus stop and Helen's home so decided to search every building she would have passed. Simms wasn't there but Ken, the manager who had been sending drinks to Helen, allowed them to start a cursory search of the premises. The judge reminded the jury that, at that point, the George was just one of the places they were visiting – the searches weren't in detail.

At 12.30pm, Simms arrived. Initially, he was helpful – offering to make tea and fetching a ladder so they could search the attic, outhouses and bowling green area. He told them he lived alone at the premises but was forced to confess to an extra-marital affair when police found Tracey's belongings in the main bedroom.

As the pub grew busier with lunchtime customers, police decided to take Ken's statement at St Helens police station. Aware that it would leave the pub short-staffed, Detective Inspector George Durno, flanked by Superintendent Tom Davies, asked Simms if there was anyone else who could help him behind the bar.

And there it was. The reaction that changed everything. Because within a fraction of a second, Simms' demeanour instantly, and dramatically, changed.

Even though he was wearing a thick Aran sweater, his chest began to visibly palpitate. And from speaking calmly and easily, he suddenly had difficulty enunciating his words. 'I-I-I'll g-g-g get Tr-r-racey,' he stammered.

Silence descended. Every single police officer stopped what they were doing and turned to look at this remarkable response from the pub landlord. Superintendent Davies, who had a degree in psychology, exchanged glances with his colleague.

He's panicking.

'Right,' Superintendent Davies decided. 'We'll have you down at the station, too.'

It was the one and only time that Simms' mask ever slipped.

Simms, Ken and Tracey were all questioned separately. Ken and Tracey's stories matched; Simms' didn't. It quickly became obvious that he was lying through his teeth about his whereabouts on Tuesday evening.

First, he told police he'd been upstairs with Tracey all evening. When Tracey's account differed, he made a second statement admitting he hadn't been truthful. This time he said that he'd left the pub, filled up with petrol at a garage in Main Street and called at the family home to confess to the affair but couldn't bring himself to do so. Upset, he had driven to Southport, parked on the prom overlooking the sea and cried about his marital difficulties. He said he hadn't wanted to tell the police this before in case they laughed at him. But neither of the two garages in Main Street recalled serving Simms. No one could vouch for his presence in Southport. And despite the strong gales, not a single grain of sand was found on or inside his car.

When police asked about the scratches on his neck, he said they'd been caused the previous Sunday by Susan when he'd pulled her off Helen in the ladies' toilets. But he had put make-up on them to hide them from Tracey, who disliked Susan.

Simms admitted that he was on his own in the pub – with his Rottweiler guard dog – from 4.20pm, when his manager, Ken, had left following the lunchtime shift, until 5.55pm, when Ken returned to open up for the evening. He said he was doing his books in the first-floor office and 'got his head down' for a bit.

Meanwhile, Simms' Volkswagen had been impounded and taken to the station. An examination revealed heavy mud staining, inside and out. On opening the boot, forensics found 'smears and spots of blood on the boot sill and its rubber seal … spots and splashes of blood on the inside of the boot lid and blood stains on the boot carpet'. And there, in the centre of the boot carpet, lay a solitary opal and sapphire earring with minute traces of blood on it.

I'd already described to police everything Helen was wearing when she left the house that day – right down to her favourite earrings, an opal surrounded by sapphires.

With heavy hearts, DCS Eddie Alldred and DS Tom Purcell made that fateful visit to my home and asked if I recognised it.

Back at the station, just after midnight, Simms was asked what he could tell police about the jewellery found in his car. When he replied 'nothing', he was arrested on suspicion of the abduction and murder of Helen. He insisted someone must have placed the earring there.

A detailed medical examination of Simms by a police doctor revealed scratches consistent with fingernails and vegetation on his hands, arms, legs and torso. Simms insisted the scratches were caused by brambles while walking his dog on the Monday – and the scuffle with Susan on the Sunday night. However, a police doctor examined Susan's fragile, weak fingernails and insisted they could not have caused those scratches. Helen, however, as Mr Leveson told the court, had strong, long fingernails. A bracelet and two rings that Simms had been wearing (one was so tight that it had to be removed with lubricant) revealed traces of pale, encrusted mud that matched sediment found on the car.

Meanwhile, back at the pub, which had been closed by police, forensic scientists were getting to work. Grit and sand were found at the bottom of the bath. Blood stains and splashes were found on the interior door, which led to the private staircase and at the bottom of the staircase itself – the area Simms had been scrubbing with bleach.

More stains were found on the wallpaper and banister rail at the top of the stairs. A further drop of blood was found on the fifth step from the top. Forensics also found a fingerprint in fresh blood on the inside of the door, close to the splattered blood. Although there wasn't enough blood to reveal a blood type, the print matched Simms' right forefinger. 'There is no doubt that there was blood on the finger when the print was left on the door,' a senior fingerprint officer said.

More jigsaw pieces were starting to fit. Remember the men's clothing found by the dog walker the morning after Helen disappeared? This was sent to the forensic laboratory at Chorley for routine analysis. At this stage, remember, there was no link with Helen's disappearance. These clothes, which had been found fifteen miles away, could have gone to any of the scientists who worked there.

In addition, the forensic lab was used by several police forces including Merseyside, Cheshire and Greater Manchester. Merseyside was the main force investigating Helen's disappearance, but the Hollins Green area came under Cheshire Constabulary while Irlam (which would also be involved) came under Greater Manchester. But, by complete chance (again, I thank St Martha), they went to the very same forensic expert, Dr Eric Moore, who had been called out to the George and Dragon the day before to search Simms' car.

Opening up the bag, he immediately spotted the sweatshirt

which was no longer inside out. It featured a distinctive Labatt logo. Then it came to him in a flash.

The George and Dragon was running a promotion of Labatt beer. There were posters behind the bar. Staff were wearing Labatt sweatshirts.

This find was crucial to the case. Had the clothes gone to any other forensic scientist that connection might not have been made. Thank God it was. Both Simms' wife, Nadine, and his girlfriend, Tracey, immediately identified the clothes as belonging to Simms. In fact, the police report said that, Tracey's reaction was dramatic: she vomited.

Tracey also confirmed the towels recovered with the clothes were similar to some used in the George and Dragon flat and the dishcloth was identical to one of two she had recently bought from the village store to use in the flat (this was also confirmed by the shopkeeper).

The distinctive light blue leather boots belonged to Barry Smith – a previous pub manager (and son of Mrs Smith, the cleaner), who had lived on the premises. When he'd moved out in September 1987, he'd left the boots behind. Simms had been seen wearing them.

And those muddy Supertuff-branded jeans? Simms had been issued with four pairs of them while working at the glass company Pilkington Brothers – known as Pilkingtons – as a process worker and, later, trade union representative. This was his job prior to taking over The Stone Barn restaurant and then the George and Dragon itself.

For twenty-four hours Simms insisted the clothes weren't his, that Tracey had been mistaken in identifying them. Then, out of the blue, and without being shown the clothes again, he admitted they had come from his flat but must have been taken by someone else.

Brick by brick, a wall of evidence was building up. Helen's

blood group was not known. However, by examining blood from both myself and Billy, scientists were able to establish the blood group she would have inherited from us. And they identified a one in 470 chance that the blood stains found on Simms' clothing, the flat and the car were consistent with a child parented by myself and Billy.

The DNA genetic fingerprint findings were even stronger. Newspapers reported how scientists concluded that the DNA make-up of blood samples recovered was 14,000 times more likely to have come from a child parented by us than a random person.

'The Crown submit that this is strong evidence that the person who bled onto the clothing was Helen McCourt,' said Mr Leveson.

With the sweatshirt, the findings were even stronger – at 28,000 to one. And with the jeans, they had increased to an astonishing 126,000 to one.

Mud was also recovered from the bracelet and two rings Simms had been wearing, leading the prosecution to declare he had been 'wrist-deep' in mud.

As we know, on Sunday, 14 February 1988, Simms was charged with Helen's murder. For more than three weeks, the search for her body continued.

Then on 3 March, a young gym instructor was shooting rats on the bank of the River Irwell, in Irlam – three miles away from where Simms' clothing had been found in Hollins Green – when he spotted a woman's dark blue handbag in the undergrowth. Assuming it had been stolen, he gathered up the make-up and personal possessions which had spilled out, then took the bag home. Inside, his dad found a Royal Insurance identification badge. His heart missed a beat on seeing the name and photograph: Helen McCourt.

'This is that missing girl from Billinge,' the dad had said.

Police searches recovered Helen's red purse five feet from the water's edge, while divers retrieved a black bin liner containing her coat, navy trousers, white knickers, mitts, maroon scarf, a right brown suede knee-length boot (the left has never been found) and her Superdrug shopping, submerged in the water.

Police also found a grey, zip-up cotton jacket, which Simms immediately recognised as his – a jacket he said he rarely wore because it was getting 'tatty'. Partially washed-out blood stains were found on the upper right front of the jacket and on both sleeves – particularly the right. Scientists identified the blood as human but were unable to group it as it had decomposed. Bullets found in the pocket matched bullets retrieved from the pub safe (Simms had been a member of Pilkingtons' gun club until twelve months previously).

The most disturbing discovery was a piece of electric flex or cable. It was made up of two separate pieces knotted together. A total of twenty-four strands of long, brown, tinted hair were caught in the knot and twisted around the cable. Simms admitted the flex had come from the pub. Indeed, close examination showed it was punctured with bite marks that matched the teeth of his Rottweiler, who had been playing with it that week. But he could provide no explanation for the hairs being caught in the knot.

We'll come back to this shortly.

Police also found two of the bracelets Helen had been wearing when she vanished – a snake bracelet set with a ruby, Helen's birthstone, and a triple bracelet, now damaged and pulled out of shape, while, they believe, being yanked off her wrist.

A candy-striped pillowcase, identified as coming from the pub, was also found. A microscopic examination of the black bin liner, which had held Helen's possessions, revealed that the series of holes punched near to the top edges, and the heat seals at the bottom, corresponded with the roll of bin liners at the pub.

Inside her red purse was the receipt from Superdrug, listing prices of all the items she'd bought that day with a five-pound note. Police matched up the receipt with all of the items found strewn inside the bin bag: shampoo, body lotion, nail varnish, mint and orange hot chocolate sachets and stockings.

However, one 49p item was missing. Returning to the George and Dragon, police carried out a fingertip search. There, in the back bedroom, they found a brand-new Superdrug toothbrush, costing 49p. 'Helen was always brushing her teeth,' I told the police. 'She'd brush them every time she ate, even at work. She was always going through them [toothbrushes] and could well have been buying a new one.'

For some reason, this evidence was not allowed in court, but it still had a dramatic effect on the investigation. Suddenly, police realised the significance of the noises that had been heard coming from the room above the restaurant the night Helen disappeared.

The room was emptied and searched forensically. One officer found a butterfly clip that matched Helen's broken earring. Police also found, between the bed and a chest of drawers, a blood stain and a clump of hair – they were long strands of tinted hair pulled out at the root.

Without a body, forensic experts really had their work cut out, but I thank God for how diligently they worked, gathering and analysing essential evidence.

Remember how, shortly after Helen disappeared, police had taken some strands of her long hair from her Velcro rollers? Examining them microscopically, they detected a gradual colour change from mid-brown near the root to a distinctive red-brown colour towards the tip from where Helen had dyed her hair.

While scientists examined the strands forensically, police made regular calls asking what shampoo and hair products she'd used. I'd answered as best I could, but it was clear there was still something flummoxing them. Something else they'd identified on her hair.

Something out of the ordinary.

Driving home from one of our Tuesday novenas, it suddenly came to me: 'Dettol!' I cried. 'That's it.'

Once a week, Helen had started giving her hair a final rinse in a very weak dilution of Dettol as she'd read somewhere that it prevented dandruff (not that she had it, she was just a stickler for keeping on top of that sort of thing). I told the police and they reported it to Dr Moore. 'Well remembered, Mrs McCourt,' was the response I got back. Apparently, it was the last substance they had been trying to identify.

Back to the hairs in the knotted flex. Under a microscope, scientists could see roots on these caught hairs, indicating they had been pulled forcibly from a scalp. But there was very little tissue that could be used to identify DNA. However, the police forensic scientist had examined these microscopically and detected a gradual colour change, from mid-brown near the root to a distinctive red-brown colour towards the tip – that is to say, they matched the hair found on Helen's Velcro rollers. The strands also matched Helen's in length.

Two hairs were retrieved from the boot carpet, eight from the left pocket of the grey jacket belonging to Simms, and one hair on the right sleeve. All indicated they had been pulled out at the root. They all matched Helen's hair.

Scientists also recovered 'a large number' – at least twenty – of human head hairs from Helen's coat. All had been 'forcibly plucked out'.

As part of their thorough checks, scientists examined hair samples from every woman who had been in the flat – including Tracey, Nadine and the partners of previous managers. Not one of them matched.

Simms had two dogs — a black Labrador which lived at the family home and a black and ginger Rottweiler guard dog called Oscar. On the Labatt sweatshirt found at Hollins Green, Dr Moore found black dog hairs similar in colour and microscopic appearance to the black hairs from both dogs, plus ginger-coloured hairs identical to the Rottweiler. Black and ginger hairs were found on the carpets in the back bedroom and the landing, one of the towels recovered from Hollins Green, the grey jacket belonging to Simms and the coat and trousers belonging to Helen.

'Whoever owned the Labatt sweater also had to come in contact with a dog with black and ginger coloured hair,' said Mr Leveson. He explained to the court that, in the same way that animals and humans shed hair and skin, fabrics like clothes and carpets shed tiny fibres which can be identified under a microscope.

The two piles of discovered clothes were all forensically examined, as were the carpets on the pub landing and back bedroom, and the interior of Simms' car.

Inside Simms' grey jacket, scientists found fibres from the Labatt sweatshirt (found at Hollins Green), showing the jacket had been worn over the top.

On the outside of the jacket, forensics found fibres from Helen's taupe coat, one green acrylic fibre which matched her mittens, and black and ginger dog hairs, which matched Simms' Rottweiler.

The landing carpet at the pub flat consisted of brown and grey acrylic fibres. On the Labatt sweater, forensic expert Dr Eric Moore found twenty-six brown acrylic fibres and nineteen grey acrylic fibres identical to the landing carpet; on the jeans there were six brown and five grey fibres, and yet more fibres were found on the blood-stained grey jacket.

Moving to Helen's coat, the experts found a large number

of both brown and grey fibres; Dr Moore stopped counting at twenty-five. And on the trousers, he stopped counting at twenty.

The carpet in the back bedroom was different in colour and texture – made up of mauve wool, mauve nylon and blue-grey wool. Again, these were all found on the Labatt sweater and jeans, and on Helen's coat and trousers.

Finally, they examined the blue-grey nylon carpet in Simms' VW car – and found two matching fibres on each of the blue boots found at Hollins Green.

The complex two-way transfer of fibres on Helen's clothes, in particular, led Dr Moore to conclude that her clothing had 'almost certainly' been in the flat. Scientists found matching fibres from her taupe coat on tape lifts from the mattress and carpet in the back bedroom and on the man's grey jacket and Labatt sweater.

Fibres from Simms' sweater were also found on her coat. And three wool fibres from Helen's taupe coat were recovered from the boot carpet.

There was also one more significant discovery. Close to Hollins Green you'll find Rixton Claypits – a former clay extraction site used by the nearby brickworks factory, now a nature reserve.

As the mud found on Simms' car was 'clay-like', police divers began to search the deep ponds – popular with anglers – for Helen's body. (Simms was found to have a fishing permit for those ponds.)

On 24 March, they recovered a spade from an eighteen-feet-deep pond. The previous owner of the George and Dragon, Frank Keralius, recognised it immediately. It was a distinct Spear and Jackson design with a worn label. He'd left it behind after selling the pub to Simms.

My head sank in despair when the court was told that, regrettably, someone had picked up the spade shortly after it had been found and began to dig with it. *That handle could have had*

Simms' DNA all over it – despite being in the water, I thought. *Now it's contaminated.*

Still, combined, the evidence was 'absolutely overwhelming', said prosecuting counsel Mr Leveson.

While opening for the prosecution, he had asked the jury to open up their folders and place the transparent sheets for hair and blood on top of the other diagrams, i.e. the pub, the car and the sites where clothes were found. Then he explained: 'Both blood and hair were found in the back bedroom of the George and Dragon, in the boot of the car and on Ian Simms' grey jacket found at Irlam.

'Blood group has nothing to do with hair colour. Can there be any doubt that it was Helen McCourt's blood and Helen McCourt's hair? Can there be any doubt that it was she who rested on the floor of the George and Dragon, bleeding, and her body which was carried away in the boot of Ian Simms' motor car?'

From these extensive discoveries, experts were able to build up a disturbing but accurate picture of what happened that night.

One newspaper reported how forensic scientist Dr Eric Moore 'concluded from the way her blood had been splattered that she [Helen] had probably been assaulted with fists or an implement'. The report continued: 'Dr Moore said he thought Helen had also been hit with the rear door of the licencee's flat in the pub then dragged by her arms along the landing carpet into the rear bedroom, where further bloodshed took place'.

Unless the first blow is of 'unbelievable ferocity', blood splashing occurs when part of the body already bloody is hit again, Mr Leveson had already explained.

I closed my eyes, thought of flowers, beaches … anything to block out the image of my daughter being struck.

'The victim of this attack is likely to be Helen McCourt because of the unusual nature of the fibres found in the flat,' continued Dr Moore. 'The victim may have been dragged along the landing and into the back bedroom, which would account for the large number of fibres and dog hairs found on that clothing and the damage. Possibly the victim was dragged along by the arms, which could explain why the lining of her coat was torn and split at the seams.'

Hearing these words, my whole body started to tremble.

Was she unconscious? Out cold? Or was she semi-conscious … wondering, 'Where am I? What are you doing? Why are you hurting me?'

When Dr Moore commented that both carpets were in a 'dirty condition' with 'thousands of dog hairs on them', I felt repulsed. The thought of my daughter being dragged, barely conscious, along a grubby carpet in the last moments of her life was unbearable.

'She was then placed in the boot of Simms' car and at some stage a piece of electric flex had been used as a ligature around her neck.'

Whoever committed the assault also drove the car, he added.

A hush fell as Dr Moore showed the flex to the court. The hairs, identical to those recovered from Helen's rollers, were broken, he said. Some had roots, indicating they had been pulled out by force.

Dr Moore had testified: 'This hair matches Helen's hair and this electric cable looks to me as though it has been used as a noose. The knot was tied with the hairs in situ as if it had been used as a ligature around someone's neck.'

As the flex was passed to the jury, some members broke down and cried. I wept too. *Oh Helen*, I thought, shaking my head sadly. From the moment she was born, people had commented on her crowning glory.

I remembered that beautiful mop of downy, newborn hair that the midwives had admired – 'Our own Bootle Beatles baby,' they'd called her. It had slipped softly between my fingers as I'd rocked her to sleep. Over time, it had grown into thick, glossy tresses that I'd tie in neat ribboned bunches for school photos. I'd shown her how to use a hair dryer herself, bought her heated rollers for Christmas. Now, a few sorry strands, yanked brutally from her scalp, were all that was left of her.

Like Helen's coat, Simms' jacket also showed signs of damage. There were thin smears of mud on the outside and inside – plus one large tear down the left side seam. Had this been caused by Helen fighting for her life?

The blood found inside the premises, in the car boot and on the clothes recovered at Hollins Green all originated from the same person.

At one point in the trial, the jury passed Justice Caulfield a note asking if they could visit both sites where clothing had been recovered – from Hollins Green (where Simms' clothes had been dumped) and the riverbank in Irlam.

Photographers snapped Justice Caulfield standing by the canal at Hollins Green and the jury studying their maps and overlays as they walked along paths. Journalists reported Simms apparently laughing and joking with wardens.

Finally, scientists had focused on the pale brown mud found on Simms' car, clothes and jewellery.

'Smears of mud were found on the lower inside part of the driver's door, on the driver's seat, sidesill, footwell and pedals. Mud was also found on the steering wheel, gear lever, fascia, inside the boot, boot lid and catch,' they said.

Dr Moore concluded that the mud was consistent with the car being driven forwards and backwards over muddy ground and with the driver being heavily mud-stained.

Simms' clothes had both mud and blood on them but scientists concluded the blood was definitely there first. The mud, which matched the mud found on the car, suggested the 'wearer had stood in liquid mud up to several inches deep and, at some stage, had either knelt or fallen in'. There were also four adjacent smears on the top of the driver's door – consistent with mud-stained hands pulling the door shut.

The colour of the mud found on his jewellery was similar to that found in his car and on his clothing and the distribution of mud on his bracelet and two rings, said scientists, was 'consistent with contact with wet mud of sufficient depth to cover all the surfaces', explained Mr Leveson, in his opening argument. 'In other words, Ian Simms has at least been up to his wrist in pale mud.'

I winced.

What have you done with her? Where have you put her?

Mr Leveson concluded: 'Simms' clothing and the car was "very, very muddy" – no doubt, alleges the Crown, because Helen McCourt had to be buried or lost where no one would find her.'

All in all, said the prosecution, the evidence was over-whelming. 'The Crown alleges that she [Helen McCourt] has been murdered and her body hidden so well that it has not been found, although very considerable effort has been put into looking,' Mr Leveson had said in his opening argument.

'The Crown further alleges that the person responsible for murdering her and then trying to cover up that murder is this man – Simms.'

The evidence was overwhelming. Yet Simms, who turned thirty-three during the trial, had pleaded not guilty. He was about to deny everything.

Chapter 8

The verdict

On the thirteenth day of the trial, Mr John Kay, barrister for the defence, rose to his feet. 'I call the defendant,' he declared.

The response was immediate. Journalists shifted in their seats. There was a brief flurry of paper as they flipped to fresh pages in their spiral notebooks. Behind me, I could sense the nudging of elbows, hear the wave of whispers and murmurs ... until they stopped suddenly.

One journalist reported how 'a stern glance' from Justice Caulfield was enough to restore absolute silence in court as Simms left the dock and was escorted to the witness box.

In opening the prosecution, Mr Leveson had said 'He [Simms] has never shifted from a resolute denial that he ever had anything to do with Helen McCourt's disappearance: the Crown submit that having at least to date successfully disposed of her body, he has created a story for himself which he has stuck to.'

Now we were about to hear it, straight from his own mouth.

Apparently, Simms' own counsel had advised against going into the witness box at all, but he'd insisted.

Bizarrely, dozens of people – including Helen's friends and colleagues – received an eleventh-hour summons to present at court the following morning as witnesses for the defence. They turned up, unhappy and bewildered. A handful were called to testify but it was clear that their testimony wasn't supporting Simms in the slightest.

Afterwards, it became very clear why Simms' 'good character' hadn't been laid before the court by the defence: it would have been ripped to shreds.

Finally, he was taking the stand, promising to tell the truth. A tiny part of me hoped that he would, finally, even at this late stage in proceedings, do the decent thing. So many times, I'd imagined him holding his hands up, looking across at me and confessing, 'It was a terrible accident. I didn't mean it to happen. Yes, I killed Helen. And here's where you can find her.' That's all I wanted; that's all I ever wanted. In time, I might even have been able to forgive him.

Within seconds, it was clear this wasn't going to happen.

We'd already heard from various police officers' testimonies that Simms had lied from the outset. The police report which went to the Crown Prosecution Service referred to Simms' accounts for the evidence being 'improbable to the point of absurdity' and 'repeatedly tainted with lies' so heaven only knew what he was going to come out with.

When first questioned at St Helens police station, Simms had signed a very lengthy witness statement insisting he had spent the entire evening of Tuesday, 9 February with Tracey. He claimed that after picking up his son from nursery and taking him home, he had returned to the pub, where he remained for the rest of the afternoon – doing his books in the first-floor office and 'getting his head down'. Later, after washing, he'd gone out, filled his car with petrol and returned to the pub at about 8pm. He and Tracey had dozed until nearly 11pm. After Simms checked on the pub, he'd asked staff to lock up. He and Tracey had gone to bed and she'd left in the early hours.

He denied visiting the garage at 8am the next morning – insisting he'd only got up at 9am to let the cleaners in. But examination of his car revealed a slow puncture in the very tyre that he'd been seen filling.

He said he had then left fifty minutes later for the cash and carry warehouse, before returning for lunch at the pub with Tracey.

After a break in questioning, however, detectives had returned to the interview room and said Simms was lying. He then changed his story, later complaining that police had bamboozled, tricked, threatened and confused him. He also insisted that he didn't realise it was a murder inquiry to start with – as if that makes lying to the police acceptable.

In his revised account he said that when Tracey revealed people had been overheard gossiping about their affair, he had decided to confess all to his wife before she heard it from someone else. He'd called at the family home with every intention of coming clean. But after playing with his young children, he couldn't do it. After five minutes he had left and driven to Southport – a special place for him and Tracey. There, if you remember, he had parked on the prom and cried over his marital situation for three-quarters of an hour – not telling the police, supposedly, for fear of being laughed at. Yet, he became confused about the routes he had taken and whether trees were down or not. And, as we'd already heard, despite the gale force winds, forensic examination of the car didn't reveal a single grain of sand from the beach.

What about the allegations of him reversing his car to the side gate at 5.45pm? First, Simms denied leaving the pub at all at that time. Then later, in police interviews he conveniently 'remembered' moving his car from his usual parking spot underneath the pub sign swinging precariously in the high winds as he was worried it would fall onto his car.

Yet, Simms never parked underneath the sign. His usual parking spot was at the front of the restaurant. And a concerned customer had only alerted him to the dangerous sign much later that evening – after 9.30pm. He had seemed surprised and concerned to hear about it, jumping onto a windowsill to peer out at the sign and declaring he would sort it.

In interviews, Simms denied panicking when police visited the pub on Thursday, 11 February – two days after Helen went missing. 'I was nervous because I said in my mind, "Well, this is it. Nadine is going to find out about me and Tracey,"' he'd insisted.

He denied point-blank that, on Tuesday evening, the snip was on the front door to the flat, preventing Tracey from gaining access: 'There was no difficulty getting into the flat through the door,' he said. 'I hadn't put any snip on the lock.' As part of their thorough investigations police had checked the lock on the door and it was in good working order.

His car, he claimed, was muddy from walking the dog at Carr Mill Dam, a local beauty spot, on Monday, 8 February – the day before Helen disappeared. But his car had been mud-free on Tuesday afternoon when he gave a lift to someone and forensic examination revealed that the mud on his car didn't match that location.

As for the earring found in his boot? Simms claimed several people had keys to his car and if, as alleged, it was seen at Hollins Green the morning after Helen went missing, someone must have taken it from the pub the night before and returned it the following morning. The jewellery, he said, had been planted there by someone or dropped by a legitimate passenger.

At one point in interviews he had said, 'There's something funny going on at the pub', implying others were gaining access with keys.

When police said blood had been found in the boot, Simms insisted it was caused by his Rottweiler injuring a paw while out on a walk. He said he put the dog in the boot to prevent him bleeding on the seats. When told the blood was human, Simms was unable to offer an explanation. It was at this point that he was arrested and his 'explanations' became more and more far-fetched.

Simms had resolutely denied all knowledge of the clothes found at Hollins Green – saying Tracey must have been mistaken in identifying them as his or the identification was as a result of 'police malpractice' or 'fear of' the police.

Then, after twenty-four hours, he admitted, out of the blue, that they were from his flat, but he'd been framed by someone who had gained access to the flat and stolen his clothes to deliberately incriminate him. This would have involved removing his jeans from where they were draped over a radiator and rifling through his bag of dirty washing for the sweater, socks and pants.

He used the same explanation for the flex and jacket which were found at Irlam: someone had planted them. He also told detectives that if he knew where Helen was he would have said because 'as a father himself' he knew what I was going through. He also hoped that her body would be found soon so that forensic experts could say that he had nothing to do with the killing.

Simms insisted the scratches on his body were caused by running with his dog at Carr Mill Dam on the Monday – even though he'd admitted he'd been wearing waders. The other scratches, he insisted, were caused by Susan when he pulled her away from Helen on the Sunday night.

But Susan denied this vehemently. Witnesses hadn't seen a single blow or scratch from her and no one saw any marks, scratches or injury to his neck and lip.

As we'd already heard, an expert who examined her fingernails declared them brittle and weak and unable to have caused those scratches. Helen, on the other hand, had long, strong fingernails.

Simms had slept with Tracey, as usual, on Sunday and Monday

night and she hadn't spotted a single mark on him until the Tuesday evening – hours after Helen vanished.

Simms' answer? He didn't want Tracey to know about the row in the ladies' toilets as she couldn't stand Susan. Instead, he'd used her make-up (he had used Tracey's foundation to cover a black eye after being punched by a customer three weeks earlier) to cover the marks since Sunday and had forgotten to apply the make-up after his bath on Tuesday evening.

And the blood found in the pub? Simms had claimed to police that blood had been spilt in his pub during various disturbances since he took over as landlord in March 1987. But police had traced those people and taken samples. None matched.

With regards to his feelings towards Helen, Simms denied hating her and said he had agreed he hated her to calm Susan down. He said he had got on well with Helen, they would confide in each other and he had never barred her.

I knew that Simms' attraction to Helen would be raised at some point – and dreaded hearing what he'd come up with. Some of his friends testified that he had boasted of once sleeping with a Helen. They hadn't asked him to clarify but all assumed he'd meant my daughter – even though there were three Helens who visited the pub regularly.

As a parent, I can't even begin to tell you how awful it was listening to this. There was no way she'd have looked at him. But you can't know everything about your grown-up children, can you?

During a break in proceedings a young woman in her twenties approached me. 'Mrs McCourt?' she began. 'You don't know me but I worked with Helen at the Royal,' she said. 'She was such a nice girl. I just wanted to say how sorry I am.'

'Thank you,' I said. Then I took a deep breath. I had to ask. 'Alison,' I said, lowering my voice, 'can you tell me something? I'd rather hear it from you here than in there.'

She nodded.

'Was there ever anything going on between Helen and that man?' I asked. 'I know he liked her, but is there anything I need to know?'

Disgust washed over her face and she almost spat the next words out. 'Never!' she said, vehemently, shaking her head. 'Never, Mrs McCourt. He was always pestering her and she didn't want anything to do with him. One night in the pub after he'd been talking to her, I could tell she was upset. I said to him, "Why don't you leave Helen McCourt alone? You know she hates you."'

In response, Simms had told her to mind her own f*****g business and get out of his f*****g pub.

I sighed with relief and reached out to touch her arm. 'Thank you,' I said. 'I can't tell you how much that means.' It was a huge weight off my mind.

Helen's friend, Brenda, also told me about a night out at a club when she and Helen had bumped into Simms. He'd kept asking Helen out, but the answer was no.

Knowing the truth helped me cope with the desperate lengths Simms was prepared to go to in explaining why the butterfly earring clip and coat fibres were found in the back bedroom.

When first questioned by police at the pub, he was adamant that Helen had never been into the living quarters. Later, at the station, he said that he hadn't wanted to mention it in front of Tracey, but, yes, Helen had been upstairs one night. I felt disgust as he told the court that during a stay-behind with other customers, one night in September 1987 he and Helen had ended up kissing and slipped off to the back bedroom, tiptoeing past the main bedroom where his mistress was fast asleep.

I tightened my grip on my prayer cards, bracing myself.

As the bed wasn't made up, he had pulled a blanket over them. While checking Tracey was still asleep, he said Helen had pulled a coat over herself to stay warm. I assume he was inferring that the coat was her own – to explain fibres found on the mattress.

Ridiculous, I thought. There was no way Helen would wear her winter coat on a mild September night, let alone carry it around with her all evening.

Also, if the butterfly clip had fallen off then as he was also implying, so would the earring, surely? Yet Helen had been wearing two earrings throughout winter – with a spare (which we still have) in her jewellery box, complete with butterfly clip.

Simms claimed they had kissed and cuddled before coming to their senses, realised what they were doing was wrong and returned to the bar.

It was absolute nonsense. But, of course, it was a dream for journalists covering the trial. Up in the press gallery, pens were scribbling away furiously. 'The Night I Got into Bed With Helen,' screamed the front page of the *Liverpool Echo* that evening in giant font. 'Kisses with Tragic Helen,' shrilled another.

My fury reached boiling point. How dare he? How dare he sully my daughter's reputation in a bid to wriggle out of a murder charge? So, I was delighted when Mr Leveson went straight for the jugular in his cross-examination: 'Would you agree you perfected the art of lying so that you could do it not only with ease and skill but also most successfully?' he asked.

'No,' Simms replied – only to then have to admit that he had, in fact, lied to his wife, the police and his girlfriend.

Mr Leveson suggested he'd delayed Tracey coming to the pub that evening because something had happened between 5pm and 6.10pm. 'This is the time you were killing Helen, isn't it?' he asked coolly.

Simms replied: 'No, it isn't.'

When asked how the blue ankle boots from his flat had ended up in his car, he replied, 'I haven't a clue.'

When asked why Helen's hair should be in the knotted cable,

which he admitted came from the pub, he replied: 'I think someone has got hold of it, put the hairs in it and tied a knot.'

Justice Caulfield peered over his bench: 'To fix you?' he asked.

'I know so,' replied Simms.

He admitted that he couldn't explain how a bundle of Helen's hairs ended up in the pocket of his jacket nor why there were blood splashes on the stairs leading to the flat and the car. And he insisted: 'I have not seen her since the Sunday night. I have never set eyes on her, I never touched her.'

Simms repeated his assertion that, had he done something like this, he would have either buried the clothes or put them in the boot of his car and set them alight, reporting the vehicle stolen.

John Kay QC, his defence barrister, went redder and redder in the face and shook his head so furiously that the ringlets on his wig jiggled.

'But you didn't,' said Mr Leveson, smoothly. 'That's exactly what you'd planned to do, isn't it, Mr Simms? If you hadn't been caught out by Mr Bannister's dog.'

The crassest comment came when Simms told the court that the scratches on his neck, arms and body were 'not much' and not marks that could be said to be made 'by a girl fighting for her life, are they?'

I closed my eyes and shook my head in disbelief.

Who on earth would make that sort of comment in a murder trial?

Shortly after this, John Kay got to his feet and asked for a recess so he could take instructions from Simms.

Outside, the court was still rammed with people who had been summoned to appear for the defence. I was told later that Kay's voice, raised in fury and peppered with expletives, could be plainly heard by those standing close to the wall of his room.

When the court resumed, Kay announced that the defence was resting its case.

So, that was it: his great attempt to prove his innocence.

With all evidence now concluded, it was down to the counsels to sum up the case. Mr Leveson began for the prosecution by insisting that Helen was dead and Simms had killed her.

'Consider for a moment how what I have told you could be explained otherwise than by Helen McCourt's death. If she was assaulted at the public house, if it is her blood on Ian Simms' clothes, if some of her hair was pulled out, if her blood and part of one of her earrings was in the boot of his car, if all her clothes and her belongings were found strewn on wasteland in Irlam, how could she still be alive?

'Put all that against the fact that neither her mother nor anyone else has either seen or heard of her since that evening and you are driven inevitably to the conclusion that she is truly dead and has been ever since that night in February last year.'

The mud found on Simms' jewellery was vital evidence, too, he added. 'This is not a case of somebody else wearing Ian Simms' clothing and jewellery – one of the rings would not even come off. This undeniably and incontrovertibly involves Ian Simms himself.'

He continued: 'The body of Helen McCourt would have told us a great deal but she has never been found and it may be the fact that she has not been found gives heart and hope to Ian Simms.

'The Crown do not have to prove how or why she died. Only two people know what happened at the foot of the stairs between 5.15pm and 6pm on Tuesday, 9 February last year. Only two people know why it happened. Helen McCourt is not here to tell us. Her attacker hasn't told us.'

He insisted Simms' guilt was 'overwhelming'. Simms' claim that he'd been framed reminded him, he said, of a Sherlock Holmes case called 'The Silver Blaze'.

'The other murderer would have had to get into his pub and carry out the murder without alerting Simms' dog,' he explained.

'Like the dog in the Sherlock Holmes story, the dog did not bark. It remained silent because it knew the murderer.' It was like a scene from a courtroom drama.

In defending Simms, John Kay QC urged caution over the forensic evidence and added that without the clothing, 'there is not the beginning of a conclusive case against this defendant'.

'The Crown say he parked his car at Hollins Green and walked along a pathway, where he stripped naked. But if he was there in the car there was a canal right alongside into which he could have thrown the clothes and been back in the car within seconds. The Crown say he did not have time to hide the clothing, and for some reason stripped off in the middle of the pathway. The defence say someone wanted the clothing to be found. That is why it was not hidden in the bushes.'

And in response to Mr Leveson's comment about the police being lucky in both sets of clothing being found, he added: 'Did the police have absolute luck or is it that someone is making sure they did have good fortune and luck?'

Justice Caulfield's summing-up of the case was dramatic. His words are still quoted to this day in stories about Simms. He opened by saying: 'If Ian Simms has murdered Helen McCourt, you might put him in the first division of cold-blooded murderers.

'If,' he added dramatically. 'If Ian Simms is the murderer, he had no respect for the corpse. Those who loved Helen McCourt are denied the tribute that they could have paid to her.'

He also referred to those precious strands of hair recovered by forensics, saying that was all that remained of her, if the jury believed the prosecution. But he used the words 'if' repeatedly, stressing that by using the word he was exposing the principle of our law that had to be obeyed. 'Notice the word obey,' he said. 'You the jury – and only you – decide whether the Crown has proved that Ian Simms did murder Helen McCourt. That is your responsibility; it is a heavy one but you have to discharge it honestly and truthfully according to your consciences as to how you view the evidence.

'The Crown – to succeed in this case on the count of murder – has to make you sure of the guilt of Ian Simms. If the Crown has not made you sure […] you should return to court and say not guilty. If the Crown has made you sure – on the whole of the evidence – that he is guilty […] you return to court and say guilty.'

His next instruction chilled me to the bone: 'Your verdict has to be unanimous. Forget about majorities. Unless and until I tell you to the contrary, strive to reach a unanimous verdict.'

The jury had to be sure of three essential factors: that Helen was dead, that Ian Simms unlawfully attacked her resulting in her death, and that he intended to kill her or cause serious bodily harm. Then, painstakingly, he went through every jot of evidence that had been covered in the trial: 'If ever there was a criminal trial where detail counted, where police investigation had to be thorough and searching, where every iota of evidence had to be examined with caution, this is the trial,' he said.

He added: 'It is not often that in a murder trial the body is not there to be examined by a pathologist. There is no body here … you have to decide how that hurdle has been dealt with by the Crown. You have to decide.'

At one point in his summing-up, he referred to me as 'poor Mrs McCourt', adding, 'I do so not to seek sympathy for her in preference to the defendant. She remains poor Mrs McCourt, whatever the verdict is in this case.'

I've been 'poor Mrs McCourt' ever since.

* * *

The trial had been expected to finish on the Wednesday but the judge finished summarising just after 12.30pm on the Tuesday – and sent the jury out to consider their verdict. Once again, a Tuesday was coming into play. I was wearing Helen's best plaid navy trouser suit. I'd lost so much weight, it was hanging off me but I felt close to her in it.

I'd wanted to un-nerve Simms by wearing her clothes but, once again, he'd refused to even glance in my direction.

The judge's parting words rang in my ears: 'You took an oath three weeks ago to give a true verdict according to the evidence. That is your task; not according to your sympathies, not according to your heart, but according to the evidence.'

Taking lunch into account, Justice Caulfield said he would take a verdict at any time after 2.30pm. The hands of the clock crawled around painfully slowly.

As each hour ticked by, my nerves grew. I twiddled the prayer cards in my hands.

What if they can't make a decision? I fretted.

If just one member of the jury was in any doubt at all, they'd have to find him not guilty. The thought of that monster walking free, back to the place where he'd murdered my daughter, to carry on pulling pints and women didn't bear thinking about – he could even go and dance on her secret grave.

I shook my head resolutely. I'd promised Helen I'd get justice and I was going to get it, even if it killed me.

Now, I'm just so grateful the jury took their time. Maybe if they had returned with an immediate verdict, the defence could have appealed on the basis that they hadn't considered the evidence properly, that they'd already made their decision.

Inside that room, they were so thorough – poring over every single piece of evidence. But all I could think was, *What's taking them so long? What's going on in there?*

Apparently, plans were already being made to adjourn, to put the jury up in a hotel for the night, when the mood changed. There was a flurry of black gowns along the corridors.

The verdict was in.

This was it.

John steered me to my seat. My knees knocked as I sank onto the bench. 'Please God,' I whispered, over and over, like a mantra. The jury filed in silently and took their seats. I gazed across, trying to read their faces but they gave nothing away. The next few moments would change my life forever – leaving me vindicated or destroyed.

As the clerk asked the foreman to stand, a woman rose to her feet. 'Madam Foreman,' he said. 'Please answer my first question either yes or no. Has the jury reached a verdict upon which they are all agreed?'

She paused. Then her voice rang out clearly: 'Yes.'

The clerk continued: 'Do you find the defendant guilty or not guilty?'

Time stopped. Those next two seconds went on forever. I held my breath. The silence was suffocating, all-encompassing, closing in on us. My heart was beating out of my chest.

In slow motion, her mouth opened. And there it was. One word. Just one word echoed around the court: 'Guilty.'

Gasping for breath, I slumped forward. 'Thank you,' I whispered. Around me, the place erupted. 'Yes!' some of my family cried, jumping to their feet. Someone started clapping and others joined in. Mum and my sisters and I were sobbing loudly. Tears were running down John's face and Michael's shoulders were shaking as he buried his face in his hands.

The clerk's next question was 'Is that the verdict of you all?' and the affirmative answer from the foreman was drowned out by the commotion.

The judge was livid. 'Order! Order,' he thundered. 'This is a court!'

I couldn't blame my family. From the word go, I'd stressed that this was about Helen – that we would show respect at all times. But they were hurting so much. They'd lost their beloved niece, cousin, sister, granddaughter. And they were so grateful that the jury had seen through Simms' lies and convicted him.

Also, because I'd remained resolute and dry-eyed after Helen's disappearance – so I could really focus and remember every detail – they'd all decided they needed to stay strong so as not to upset me. If any relative had turned up to the house weepy and tearful, they'd been bundled into the downstairs loo and ordered to pull themselves together before being allowed to see me. That verdict released a year's worth of bottled-up emotion.

I turned to look at Simms. He genuinely looked shocked. Journalists reported how he'd visibly paled and gasped at the guilty verdict.

Right up until that moment he'd been convinced that, without a body, he'd walk free. But he hadn't counted on brilliant detective work. Nor a determined mum who'd raised an early alarm into her daughter's disappearance.

Finally, the court was silent. 'I have something to say to this man,' said Justice Caulfield. 'Words I must say by law.'

Looking straight at Simms in the dock, he said: 'This jury, after long and grave deliberation, have decided that you took the life of this young, happy girl.'

I stifled my sobs into my tissue as he continued, pointing directly at Simms. 'Having taken her life, this jury has said that you have hidden or desecrated her body so her parents can never respect her corpse.

'You have cast her garments virtually to the rats.

'You have done that coldly and callously and shown no remorse. For some reason, which may be selfish to you and difficult to understand, this girl is no more.'

As he was about to be taken down, Simms turned towards the jury: 'I never seen the girl!' he bleated.

It was like lighting the touchpaper. One of Helen's cousins, Tony, lunged at the plastic partition separating the public gallery from the dock. There was no way he'd have got over the top of it, but security were on him in a flash. Then, like a bullet being fired from a gun, Michael shot to his feet. 'I'll get you, Simms!' he roared to Simms' retreating back. 'I'll wait for you!'

The guards hurried Simms down the steps with more urgency. Once again, the judge erupted: 'Is there no respect for this court?' he said. 'I know your grief, horrors and anguish, but you must remain quiet. There is pandemonium.'

With all due respect, I wanted to say, *you have no idea of our grief, horrors and anguish. Not only have we lost our Helen but we have spent the last year, and will spend years to come, digging for her body so we can lay her to rest.*

Michael was trembling like a leaf as I gently guided him back into his seat. To this day, he has no recollection of his outburst. A spontaneous reaction, straight from the heart, it just shows the enormity of feeling that consumed him in that moment. He had lost his beloved sister, his best friend, his mini-mum, who had always been there for him. She was the one who had put plasters on his scraped knees, kissed his tears and given him, as a terrified toddler, the courage to touch sand for the first time.

Both he and Tony had thrown themselves into the family searches, crawling into dark, dank, rat-infested tunnels with ropes tied around their waists, looking for Helen's body. Of course, they were going to lash out.

'Tell us where she is,' someone else wailed in anguish. It could have been any one of my family – they were all hurting.

Before retiring, the judge thanked those witnesses who had found Simms' clothes and Helen's belongings. And he singled out praise for the police: 'It was a difficult case brilliantly executed,' he said.

Some of the female jurors were openly crying as they filed out of the courtroom. Again, the family applauded. We couldn't help ourselves.

* * *

That was Justice Caulfield's last ever trial. In subsequent interviews, he commented on the uniqueness of the case, saying he had never heard applause in a trial before.

Emerging from the court, I was taken aback at the sheer number of journalists all waiting for me to speak.

'Mrs McCourt, how are you feeling?' someone called.

'I am happy with the verdict – if life means life,' I said. 'Hopefully, he will open his mouth now and tell us where she is. That is all we want to know – that is all we have ever wanted to know.'

Vowing to carry on searching, I said, in a shaky voice: 'I'm convinced she will be found one day. None of us accept that we will not see her again.'

Then, in a direct plea that I hoped would reach him, I stared straight into one of the cameras and said: 'There's nothing for you now. You've gone down for life. So please tell us what you've done with our daughter.'

I also urged Simms' wife and mother to get him to reveal where Helen's body was. 'As mothers, they can imagine how I feel. It's been bad enough trying to live with her gone, but not knowing what happened or where she is, has been the hardest to bear.

'Simms' wife, Nadine, must understand the anguish we are suffering and I am hoping she can put pressure on him to reveal where he put Helen's body.'

But I vowed I would not lower myself to beg: 'He is not human,' I said. 'He is a robot.'

Like the judge, I had to praise the police for helping me get this justice for my daughter. 'I cannot thank them enough,' I said. 'They have been brilliant throughout. We have adopted them all,' I added with a watery smile.

Then, in a final tribute to Helen, I said: 'In a way I count myself lucky. I had a beautiful daughter for twenty-two years. Many people have not been so fortunate.'

I was so proud of Michael for standing tall beside me and

giving his own statement. 'It's the right verdict and I'm happy,' he said. 'We have been waiting a year for this.

'With or without Simms' help, we are going to go on searching.' Then he turned to me. 'My mother has been superb,' he added. 'I do not think any of us would have got through this without her.' Tearfully, I reached out for his hand. My poor son had been to hell and back, but we'd get through this together.

In separate interviews DCS Alldred said police would be visiting Simms to implore 'for pity's sake, tell us where she is'. He explained he would be consulting with lawyers and counsel to appeal to his better nature.

'I will never rest until I have found Helen's body. Killers usually show some sign of remorse, but Simms has shown none and has gone to jail in a defiant mood. In this case the file on Helen McCourt will remain open until her body is found,' he vowed.

As reporters hurried off to the phone box to file copy to editors, I glanced at my watch: 'If we hurry, we can just about make 7.30pm mass,' I said to John.

The rest of the family went to the pub to buy the police a drink.

Slipping into our usual pew, I allowed relief to envelope me like a cloak.

'Thank you, St Martha,' I whispered.

It was over, he'd been found guilty. There was no point in staying quiet now – he'd been sentenced to life. Surely, he'd now say where she was so we could lay her to rest and start to grieve properly?

Surely.

Closing my eyes, I willed an image of a smiling, beaming Helen to appear in my mind and felt an intense surge of love.

Hold tight, Helen, I thought. *You'll be home soon, I promise. We'll find you.*

Chapter 9

Bring her home

Simms' conviction dominated the papers for days: 'Braggart Killer Takes Grim Secret to Jail' and 'Cruel "Missing Body" Killer Jailed for Life' were just some of the screaming headlines.

Editors went to town on details that were never revealed in court: how Simms was a Jekyll and Hyde character well known for his hot temper and violent outbursts. One pub customer who'd joked about Simms going bald on top ended up in hospital. I heard that a woman had walked into the empty pub one afternoon to find Simms on the floor astride a man, strangling him. After pushing him off (shrieking 'You'll kill him!'), she described him as suddenly 'coming to'.

'Sorry about that,' he mumbled, helping the lad up and asking if he'd like a pint.

Simms had been involved in small-time drug dealing and money lending. He once produced a gun and offered a customer a wad of money to put the gun in his own mouth and pull the trigger. When the man refused, a furious Simms had fired the gun into the wall – it was loaded.

Chillingly, he then boasted that he could kill the lad and

get rid of his body so well it would never be found or traced back to him.

Good God, I thought. *He's a monster.*

I felt vindicated at a double-page spread in the *Liverpool Echo* headlined: 'To Save His Skin, He Dragged Her Reputation Through the Mud' – dismissing Simms' ludicrous claim that he had lured Helen into bed in an attempt to explain her earring being found in his room.

Other stories reflected on the impact of the murder on Billinge and how our close-knit village would never be the same. As one local poignantly said: 'I don't think this tragedy will be over properly until Helen's body is found.'

Yes, Helen's killer had been caught and convicted, but this was far from over. Until my daughter was found, there would never be closure – for any of us.

* * *

My heart goes out to the naive, hopeful, pitiful Marie of those early days, hurrying to answer the doorbell or phone. She was so sure that, now he'd been convicted, it was only a matter of time before Simms did the right thing and ended this misery. She imagined him requesting a meeting with his wife, his mistress or his lawyer – or even his mum – then he'd take a deep breath and tell everything.

At some point, he might ask for a map, or a pencil and paper. Turning the paper this way and that, he would draw a crude diagram. There would be arrows, scribbled instructions and references to landmarks such as third lamp post along, high stone wall or tall oak tree – all leading to one dominant spot. 'She's here,' he'd finally conclude, circling a definite area.

I'd see myself, watching from a distance, as forensic searches got underway. I'd listen out for a cry or a shout, indicating a positive find. Then I'd fall to my knees in gratitude and grief.

Thank God.

I even visualised Helen's coffin, sprinkled with holy water and bedecked with yellow roses gently, and with the dignity she deserved, being lowered into consecrated ground.

(Back then flowers were a luxury we couldn't afford. Very occasionally I'd buy a cheap bunch to pop in a vase. But neither Helen nor I had favourites. However, I've always loved her in yellow and that vibrant shade would become the theme of the campaign I would fight in her name. And roses are beautiful. Like my daughter.)

Burying a child is every parent's nightmare, but it was a dream that spurred me on for the next three decades. It was to become an obsession. A compulsion.

First, however, we needed to show our gratitude to those who had snared Simms. We delivered a case of whisky to Merseyside Police and a box of spirits to the forensic team.

Many of the police officers and forensic experts, who received commendations for their work, became lifelong friends. They've attended every memorial service I've ever had for Helen and to this day, Paul Acres sends a bouquet on the anniversary of Helen's murder.

We bought beautiful magnifying glasses, in presentation boxes, for prosecuting counsel Brian Leveson and Bryn Holloway and also gave 'thank you' gifts to the two men who had stumbled across, and alerted police so quickly to, crucial evidence dumped by Simms.

In one post-trial article forensic expert Dr Moore said that the only way Helen's body would now turn up was if Simms confessed or she turned up by accident.

'Or we find her,' I added determinedly.

And so, on Sunday, 19 March 1989 – just five days after the trial had concluded and on the same day that Tracey Hornby was telling readers of a Sunday tabloid how she would 'always love sex brute killer Simms' – we resumed our searches.

Two days later, I was back in church, saying my Tuesday novena to St Martha for Simms to do the right thing. He was refusing to allow police to interview him in his cell but he couldn't hold out for ever. Could he?

Ten days after the trial, an officer rang with news: 'He's appealing, Marie,' he said. 'On the grounds that the verdict was "unsafe and unsatisfactory".'

Was this some sort of sick joke? The man was guilty as hell.

My knuckles turned white as I gripped the phone. 'He never once looked at me during the trial,' I said, in a trembling voice. 'Not once. They are not the actions of an innocent man.'

It was a pathetic charade of innocence but it meant police had to wait until the appeal had been dealt with before requesting prison cell visits.

Yet another story, under the headline 'Bully Boasts: I'll Not Crack' chilled me to the bone. While on remand Simms had, apparently, boasted to Tracey: 'I've withstood seventy-two hours of questioning, but they couldn't break me. And they never will.'

Deep inside my very being, a maelstrom of emotions swirled – disgust, determination, fury. And resolve.

'We'll step up our searches,' I vowed. 'We'll find her with or without his help.'

With my brother Tez at the helm we became a formidable team, using all the evidence from the trial. We thought forensically, logically, poring over Ordnance Survey maps and placing ourselves inside Simms' sick, twisted mind.

Slight as Helen was, he wouldn't have been able to carry her over a long distance. 'We need to focus on secluded laybys where you could pull a car in close to a gap in woods or a fence …' Tez reasoned. 'And he's not going to bury her in the middle of an overlooked field or picturesque spots where dog walkers go. We're talking remote well areas away from houses. Canals, bridges, sewage pipes, clay pits.'

Simms had been missing from 6pm to 10.30pm on the evening Helen went missing (apart from brief glimpses at the family home and pub). I have no doubt that when he reversed his car up to the side gate, it was to load Helen's body into the boot.

Years later, a car passenger came forward, saying he'd seen a man outside the pub loading a roll of carpet into his boot. Suddenly, he'd exclaimed a horrified, 'Good God!' Hanging out of the carpet was a human hand. By the time they'd turned around and driven back, the car was gone.

'My friend said I must have imagined it, but I know what I saw,' he insisted. For some reason he hadn't come forward then but it had troubled him for a long time and I was grateful to him for telling me.

After Tracey had left Simms' bed at 1am, he was alone again until being seen back in Billinge at 8am. So, he'd only had a limited time to dispose of her body.

Where had he gone? What had he done with her?

Searching was to be a huge task. Billinge was an old mining community. As early searches revealed, the land beneath, and for miles around, was honeycombed with mining tunnels and shafts, flooded tunnels and quarries.

Simms was into fishing and shooting so he knew the countryside like the back of his hand. One local said he knew more holes and warrens than the rabbits. He'd openly boasted of being able to hide a body so well, it would never be found. Plus, a network of motorways on our doorstep means he could have driven a fair distance in a short time. We ended up covering a huge area – as far west as Southport and all across Lancashire. There was no internet or Google maps in those days. It was all done with pen and paper and Ordnance Survey maps.

During the week, we'd pore over new information before

deciding on an area for the following Sunday. We'd don water-proofs, industrial gloves, wellies and steel-capped boots (I always wore Helen's favourite jeans) and pack Thermos flasks, giant teapots and enough sandwiches to feed a small army. John's mum, bless her, would bake trays of flapjacks to keep us going.

We'd start at first light (John and I always went to mass first) and only stop when it was too dark or cold to carry on. Week in, week out, we toiled through torrential rain, thick fog, swirling snow, bone-numbing cold and blistering heatwaves.

Divided into groups, we'd probe and sift every square inch of ground for disturbed earth, unusual dips and mounds, trampled vegetation, heavy footprints or discarded clothes (Helen's upper garments and one boot were still missing). Simms had been covered in scratches so sharp, brambles or thickets always caught our attention.

My heart would jolt at a flapping corner of polythene (bin bags?) or a flash of metal reflecting the sunlight (an opal earring?). It was always a plastic bag or tin can.

The challenging terrain meant we quickly upgraded from our basic broom handles and spades. A foreman at John's work devised an innovative tool – a sturdy, strong pole with a hand-like metal claw welded onto the end.

Our 'scratchers' became essential – and we still use them to this day. As well as breaking up clay and levering us over uneven ground, we'd drag them through soil in the hope of snagging Helen's missing necklace. Even the police asked to borrow them.

We used sharp billhooks for cutting back shrubs and branches and hired industrial strimmers to clear long grass. John and some of the lads would head to a site the day before to prepare it for a search. Once, Tez even hired a boat to accompany Michael as he waded through deep water, checking under-water branches.

In the early days, an officer would accompany us. Many joined us on days off, roping in their families to help. Over time, the force couldn't always spare an officer but if we needed help, they were there in a shot.

Soil samples played a huge part. Forensic experts had concluded that if we could find an exact match to the mud found on Simms' clothes and car, we might well find the body. We managed to obtain some tiny samples to use as a control. Then we devised intricate analysis charts and grid references to cover our search areas.

With every step, we'd scoop a sample then dry it out, back home on the windowsill. I would spend hours scrutinising each tiny grain under a microscope. Occasionally, we'd grow excited and speed off to the forensic laboratory, breathlessly asking them to examine a sample.

'It's close, but not exact,' they'd say, kindly.

It never was.

Although they were bleak, sad times, we grew ever closer as a family. Helping each other over stiles, sharing the digging, passing around cups of hot tea. As well as the frustration, anger and exhaustion at this relentless task, week in, week out, there was also encouragement, compassion and even humour. If there was a pond to topple into, a tree root to trip over, or a slope to tumble down, poor John was guaranteed to find it. We'd listen out for the tell-tale sound of a cry and a heavy splash or dull thud as he hit the ground. He's a tall, well-built man so he didn't do it quietly.

Another time, the men were busy digging into the banks of a pond when I asked what me, Pat and Margaret could do.

'You girls go over there, round the outside,' Tez instructed.

My sisters and I looked at each other. Our brains synchronised. Quick as a flash, Pat began to sing: 'Buffalo gals go round the outside.'

It was a well-known hip-hop song by Malcolm McLaren

that had topped the charts in the early eighties. Margaret and I dropped our shovels and joined in.

'Round the outside, round the outside,' we chorused, clapping in time.

The lads leaned on their shovels and grinned. For a brief moment, we were carefree, without a worry in the world. I lived for those moments when reality was suspended and all was well, even just for a nanosecond. Helen would have found it hilarious.

And then, as our voices trailed away, we picked up our shovels and carried on digging. It was such a macabre task but the searching was almost like a therapy. We were doing something practical. And if I focused exactly on the task in hand, running my gloved fingers through blades of grass, picking my way through brambles, it was almost possible to forget what we were actually looking for: my daughter's body.

While the others went back to their jobs each Monday morning, I continued to delve.

I'd never returned to work following my whiplash injury. Now, it was out of the question. How could I think of anything but finding Helen? Yes, we struggled financially – especially forking out for search equipment hire and petrol. Over seven years, I estimated we spent £25,000. So, while the rest of the family worked, I'd pore over all the paperwork and cuttings from the trial, checking we hadn't overlooked anything vital.

I'd drive to new building sites and implore foremen to keep their eyes peeled for human remains while digging foundations. I grew used to the sudden flash of horror reflected back at me in their eyes before they promised to co-operate. I imagined them shaking their heads in disbelief and thinking, 'Poor woman' as I walked away.

Holding out a photo of Helen, I'd ask landowners and farmers if they'd noticed something – anything – and ask permission to search their land on Sundays. They were all so amenable.

I regularly appealed in the local papers for dog walkers, hikers, joggers and workmen to look out for disturbed ground. And I begged Simms' childhood friends to rack their brains for dens or secret hiding places he might have told them about. I went back to witnesses from the trial, working out Simms' timings of movements to the last nanosecond. Through painstaking research, I pinpointed which old mine shafts and clay pits were being filled in at the time of Helen's disappearance and made careful notes to share with the team.

I acted on every single piece of information that came to me. I learned that, in one area, a massive underground drainage system was constructed at exactly the time my daughter went missing. During building work, it was under constant surveillance. But, afterwards, while being filled in, it was unmanned between shifts. Did Simms know about it? Could he have disposed of Helen there? The company gave us permission to use a JCB and dig down fifteen feet – all we found was rubble.

Over time, we embraced new search methods. Merseyside Police trained two dogs: Benny, a Springer Spaniel, and Gyp, a Border Collie, especially to help in our searches. They went on to become a permanent part of the force.

A local dog training club also offered the services of their dogs. We'd spend hours punching holes into the ground to release scents.

After appealing for help on dowsing rods, a retired expert from Leeds – who had been about to sell his equipment – donated his best rods and gave me full training.

'You're a natural,' he said, when I picked up tiny shavings of gold he had buried in his garden.

I'd insert something personal of Helen's – a strand of hair from her hairbrush or a baby tooth I'd kept – into the little boxed chamber near the handle. I'd then walk along holding the rods out, horizontally, in front of me. If they detected a similar substance, underground, the rods would cross. So many times, the rods would jerk and cross dramatically and we'd eagerly start digging.

Early in 1990, we were exploring a stretch of canal in Woolston when a man called down from the bridge: 'Why haven't you got gloves on?' he asked John. 'Have you never heard of Weil's disease?

'A deadly disease?' he continued, seeing our blank faces. 'Carried by rats in water?'

Pointing to a cut on John's hand – an entry point for infection – he insisted that John down tools and go straight to the local hospital for blood tests. 'But if you have got it, you'll be dead by the time the results come through,' he added.

Brian Houlton, a Manchester Ship Canal expert, scrambled down to introduce himself. From that moment, he came on board. In addition to his invaluable knowledge of tidal flows, he was also an expert dowser. We spent hours exploring sites together.

There were so many efforts, so many hopes – which all came to nothing. There is old video footage of me, walking alone through fields, biting my lip in concentration. You can see I'm desperately trying to pick up signals, anything, that would reveal where she was.

Each Sunday evening, as the sun started to sink, the despair and disappointment I'd kept at bay would start to wash over me.

Another week without her.

Driving home in silence I'd catch glimpses through curtains of families tucking into a late Sunday dinner – ordinary families living ordinary lives. Just like we used to. The raw envy would almost choke me. While they were pouring gravy and tucking into steaming roasties, I was out searching for my daughter's body.

Later, with our filthy clothes on a hot wash and our sodden boots drying out on newspaper, we'd dab ointment onto insect bites and scratches and wearily update our maps and records.

Helen's bosses were brilliant – donating an old computer and filing cabinets so we could keep proper records.

Our dining room came to resemble a police incident room. Huge maps on walls became criss-crossed with string and peppered with coloured drawing pins. We devised intricate indexes and references.

Since that first morning following Helen's disappearance, tuning into the local news became a vigil. Even today, it's the first thing I do on waking and the last thing I do before going to bed. I strain my ears for just one story: has a body been found?

Sadly, it happens more times than you'd imagine. On each occasion, my heart literally stops beating. With trembling hands, I'll dial the number of the officer in charge of the case and I'll remain on tenterhooks until they call me back. It can take hours, it can take weeks, depending on how long the body has been there. But the answer is always the same: 'Sorry, Marie, it's not Helen.'

Once, torrential rain prevented us from continuing a search at a local lake called Pennington Flash in Leigh. Later that day, while driving, I almost crashed the car on hearing the news that the body of a young woman had been found by fishermen that afternoon. It wasn't Helen. I thanked God for sparing me from finding that poor, poor girl – and then I cried for her family.

On one dig in 1995, I almost fainted when we unearthed bones. But expert analysis identified them as animal, rather than human.

As a devout Catholic, I'd always dismissed the idea of mediums or psychics but my desperate need to find Helen opened up my mind. After all, I believed in the afterlife and heaven. Was it really so far-fetched that Helen might try to send a message to help me find her? And if she did, how could I turn my back on her? If anyone approached me with any information, I listened to them – mostly.

Back in the early stages of the trial, a woman approached me outside the packed courtroom.

'I know where she is,' she said quietly. 'I know what he did with her.'

I stared at her, bewildered.

'She's in the incinerator,' she continued. 'At Billinge Hospital. He worked there for years, he's still got a key.'

It took a few seconds for her words to fall into place. Nausea swirled in the pit of my stomach. I shook her hand off my arm and backed away, wide-eyed.

'Can you get me into the court? I just need to look into his eyes and I'll know for sure,' she continued, earnestly. 'But she's there,' she said, louder now. 'He put her in the—'

I clapped my hands over my ears. 'No,' I cried. 'Don't. Don't! I don't want to hear it.'

In a flash, Mum was steering me away.

'What's going on?' she cried.

I was too upset to tell her.

That rumour, along with others, cropped up again and again. Simms had worked there as a chef before moving to Pilkingtons but police assured me the incinerator had been checked thoroughly, only allowed for 'small items and medical waste', was securely locked and the ashes were stone-cold. Plus, I reasoned (when I was finally able to think about it rationally), he'd have burned the evidence, too. It made no sense to get rid of his victim's body so well, but scatter her possessions and his own blood-stained clothes in a panic.

Over the years, countless mediums have provided information. Jean Cull, from the Midlands, who had been instrumental in locating the body of Black Panther kidnap victim Lesley Whittle in an underground drainage shaft, in 1975, assisted the early police official searches.

She sensed there were chains and an item connected with

Helen in Fiddler's Ferry Lock, a stretch of the St Helens canal between Widnes and Warrington. Police divers investigated and found chains and a bedsheet. Unfortunately, while being recovered, the dripping bedsheet somehow ended up in the fast-flowing River Mersey, which ran adjacent to the canal. In an instant it was gone – along with all the clues it might have held.

The police officer involved in that search, Mike McDermott – another wonderful officer who became a close friend – was convinced the lock was key. But I couldn't see it. Why were Simms' car and clothes caked in mud if he'd simply immersed her in water? Would he really risk dumping her in a busy canal when there was a chance she could float to the surface? Also, while searching for Helen, police had recovered two bodies from the same canal. If they were found, why wasn't she?

In October 1995, police investigated a stretch of the Manchester Ship Canal at Woolston after a chance conversation a local police officer had had with a workman on holiday. The workman had mentioned that, while laying pipes at this site, in February 1988, an area of land had been disturbed overnight.

I remember holding my breath, watching the metal claw of a JCB bite effortlessly into the soft banks of black silt – like a knife through butter. Was this it? Was our search over? Again, disappointment followed. After three days, the search was called off.

We explored every inch of a dank tunnel near a disused railway after being led to it by a local medium. Yet another, from London, asked me to take, and send, photos of an area she felt drawn to.

She returned them with intricate instructions. Standing on a high point of a field and using background landmarks, I called out instructions to the team – 'Left a bit, right a bit' –until they were on the exact spot she had circled. 'Stop!' I instructed. 'You should be near a metal grid leading to a draining tunnel.'

I ran across to find a stunned Tez standing on a metal grid, which led to a drainage tunnel. Each time, hope – excitement even – would flare inside us all. Our hands would tremble as we set to work.

Could this be it? The spot where Helen was?

Afterwards, we'd go over the clues again and again.

Could the message have been mixed up? Was it the wrong field? Were we desperately close?

There were times when the disappointment was just too much. One Sunday, one of the sniffer dogs ran excitedly into a pond, barking furiously.

We spent an entire day emptying it – scooping out gallon upon gallon of stagnant water. I worked feverishly, encouraging everyone to keep going – I had a good feeling. Finally, as dusk fell, the muddy bottom came into view. In the fading light, my eyes darted around for the shape, the outline, of a body. I was still looking long after the others had stopped. John tried to coax me out, but a wave of despair consumed me. Suddenly, I was on my knees. As cold mud seeped into Helen's jeans, I lifted my face to the sky. And I wailed.

John raised me to my feet and steered me away. I couldn't look at anyone – couldn't bear to see the pain on their faces. No one uttered a word as they packed up miserably.

It was gruelling physically, too. Looking back, I'm horrified at the danger we put ourselves in every single week. One weekend, we nearly lost my nephew, Tony, in a river.

On another, Michael insisted on inspecting an old mine's 25ft-deep ventilation shaft that we had spent three weeks clearing. I watched, uneasily, as ropes and harnesses were clipped around him and a helmet secured under his chin. As he sank into the dark hole, terror struck.

I've lost one child. I can't lose another.

'Michael!' I cried instinctively, trembling. He was mortified at the emotional reception he received on emerging. 'Mum, you have to let me do this,' he insisted, later. As much as I wanted to protect him, his need to find Helen was just as strong.

Then there was that risk of Weil's disease in all that dirty water we found ourselves in. Thankfully, John was fine. But it was yet another example of the awful lengths we went to in order to find Helen. Simms could have ended it at a stroke – he chose not to.

Looking back, I'm staggered we continued for as long as we did. 'But we could all see what it meant to you,' Tez said recently. 'Your face lit up each Sunday morning when we congregated. It was a passion for all of us – we were all so determined to find her and bring her home.'

And it wasn't just family. On dark nights with a full moon and high winds, just like 9 February 1988, police officer Mike McDermott would venture out alone to remote places – hoping to stumble across the spot. He would walk around by torchlight, imagining himself in Simms' shoes.

What was going through his head? Where did he take her?

As DCS Eddie Alldred told one journalist: 'A lot of police officers have become emotionally involved with the family and they feel the job is only half done. They're as keen as anybody else to find Helen's body.'

We have searched so many places over the years, but we've always been drawn back to one place – Rixton.

Prosecutor Mr Brian Leveson had told the court that, out of more than 600 samples of mud taken by forensics, those from Rixton had come closest to matching the mud found on Simms' clothes and car – 'There were still differences, but find the site and it could well be that the body of Helen McCourt will also be found,' he'd said.

No matter how awful the weather was, when we arrived there, the rain would dry up and the sun would struggle through the clouds. And, after a long day's searching, when someone suggested packing up, a gust of wind would suddenly swirl around us from nowhere – almost urging us to stay.

Is that you, Helen? I'd ask, gazing across the sprawling wetlands. *Is this where you are?*

Yes, it was such a shame that the spade, recovered by divers, was mistakenly picked up and used for digging – contaminating any evidence it might have revealed. Initially, I was distraught and furious in equal measure. After all, without a body even the tiniest amount of evidence is like gold dust.

Over time, I learned to let it go. We are all human. Anyone can make a mistake. It's what we learn from mistakes that counts. I have nothing, I repeat, nothing, but praise and gratitude for every single person who helped secure Simms' conviction and who helped in the search for my daughter.

Eventually, by 1997, we were running out of places to search. The landscape was also changing beyond recognition. Tiny saplings were becoming sprawling trees. Housing estates were springing up. But to this day, we still go out if new information arises.

While writing this book, I came across stacks of old videos from news programmes and documentaries. Watching them all again was heartbreaking.

You can see the pain etched in my still-young face: 'I need Helen to be found,' I told one reporter. 'It's part of the grieving process. Until I have that, how can I begin to start getting over this? How can I begin to get on with my life?'

Then, with a helpless shrug, I answer my own question: 'I can't.'

More than thirty years on, nothing has changed. I'm three decades older but still living a perverse, awful Groundhog Day. Every morning, I wake to the same, tortuous questions: Will it be today? Will I find Helen today?

In other tapes, we're all gathered in my conservatory,

earnestly chatting and sharing photos. We could be discussing our next family holiday. Instead, we're talking about next week's search.

There's my poor mum being shown how to look into a microscope and examine close-up samples of clay that came from Simms' jeans.

'Do you see the tiny pieces of clinker, Mum?' I'd explain patiently. 'If we can find the exact match of clay, we'll find Helen. See?'

In another interview, I reveal: 'The search is constantly going on. It's going on in my head twenty-four hours a day. I wake up and realise I've spent all night searching in my dreams. Once, I dreamed we had found her. Someone shouted, "We've found her. She's over here." That's a dream I hope will come true.

'Another time, I dreamed she was still alive. But that was in the early days. I don't dream that anymore.' My voice trails away sadly.

In another film, there is Margaret and my youngest brother, David, both digging. Both are long dead now – I don't think either ever got over Helen's murder.

The camera pans back to me: 'Until I find Helen, this is my life,' I say simply. 'People have asked me not to go out searching. They say, "She is safe in heaven. It's only her body and that doesn't really matter."

'But it does to her mum.

'When you have laid a loved one to rest,' I explain, 'you can talk to them in your heart. But I can't do that.'

More footage shows us unblocking a tunnel at the end of a stream, inspecting a drain overflow, scouring the arches beneath a railway bridge. It's horrible, relentless work, but it's what we did, over and over.

Then the camera zooms in on Mum. It's a pitiful scene that chokes me to this day. Oblivious to the cameras recording her, she is totally engrossed in the job at hand. Jabbing and scraping at the ground with one of our tools. Trying to find the body of the granddaughter she adored.

Chapter 10

Learning to live without her

'She won't go, you know,' I heard Mum say as I opened the living room door.

She was inside with John, who was clutching an envelope and looking slightly wretched. 'Who won't go where?' I asked blankly.

'You, love,' Mum said. 'John's bought tickets to Rome, but I've said he's wasting his money.'

John sighed, defeatedly. 'I was trying to get you an audience with the Pope …' he began. 'But it's OK, I'll try and get my money—'

'We'll go,' I said, interrupting him. They both looked stunned. Apart from the searches, I was refusing to leave the house – let alone fly to Italy.

But a chance to tell Pope John Paul II about Helen? His prayers would make a difference surely.

It was September 1989. Helen had been dead for nineteen relentless months. In a way it seemed like she had been gone forever. There was a huge chasm in our home, our lives, our hearts. And, in another way, it was no time at all. Sometimes, I could imagine her in the next room, pottering about, singing to herself. The realisation that she was out of our lives and never coming back would hit me like a sledgehammer. Sometimes, it left me doubled up, struggling to breathe, clutching my chest to ease the physical, unbearable pain. I missed her so much but there had been no more visions, no more dreams. For me, at least.

On Helen's first anniversary, in February 1989, we'd had a house mass for all the family. On arriving, my Aunty Maro (short for Mary – our family was full of Marys!) had darted straight into the downstairs toilet. In her rush, she hadn't closed the door properly and could only watch, helplessly, as it slowly yawned open. Praying no one would decide, at that moment, to come out of the living room, she looked up and then froze.

Helen, her great niece, was walking down the stairs towards her, smiling, with one hand trailing on the banister. 'She was as real as you are to me now, Marie, girl,' Aunty Maro had told me later in a trembling voice. 'And then she was gone.'

Aunty Maro, who was elderly by then, died shortly afterwards. Was Helen letting her know that all would be well?

I envied Aunty Maro her encounter with Helen. The only time I ever saw my daughter's face now was when she gazed back at me from the pages of newspapers. To my great relief, journalists were still eager to keep covering the story of my quest to find Helen. I gave countless interviews, pleading for help in finding her.

In the months after Helen's murder, the George and Dragon had become a boarded-up eyesore – a constant, grim reminder of the horrors that had occurred within its walls. But in the summer of 1989, the brewery announced a £250,000 revamp and reopening.

'I've always accepted that the pub would have to reopen again,' I told reporters pragmatically. 'It's not the pub that was evil and wicked, but the landlord – and he's now locked up.'

Simms had only had the pub for eleven months before killing my daughter. Why should villagers be deprived of a pub that was decades old? Besides, Helen had loved that place. She'd had drinks there for her eighteenth and twenty-first birthdays while I got the party buffet and cake ready at home.

I did ask for a name-change and appearance alteration, however. The pub reopened at the end of August as The Pavilion. Over thirty years, there have been numerous revamps – it's currently The Billinge Arms.

I'm pleased to say that we've always had a really good relationship with the landlords. When we or the police have approached them to double-check something, they've always bent over backwards to help.

* * *

Seeing village life go on while my daughter was still missing was hard so the trip to Rome couldn't have come at a better time. My brothers promised they'd continue searching while we were away.

Our parish priest wrote to the English College in Rome to request an audience with the Pope. They couldn't promise anything, but would try their best. 'Just being there will be wonderful,' I assured John. My novena candles were the first things I packed.

Checking into our hotel, the concierge handed over a thick, creamy envelope. As John opened it, his face lit up. 'These are better than Cup Final seats,' he grinned, holding out two tickets for a Papal Audience.

Our hotel was close to St Peter's Basilica. Stepping into the cool interior, I was drawn like a magnet to Michelangelo's Pietà – the statue of Christ's body draped in the arms and lap of his grieving mother after his crucifixion. I gazed at it, taking in every tiny detail, feeling Mary's raw heartache. It shames me to admit it, but I envied her saying goodbye to her dead child. Even if we found Helen tomorrow, I'd never be able to wrap my arms around her, kiss her sweet face and tell her how much I loved her. The most I could do now, as her mother, was bring her remains home and lay them to rest in consecrated ground. Determination rose within me: by God, I would do that.

A few days later, we were ushered into the Vatican audience hall, and my heart sank at the sheer number of people assembled. I learned afterwards we were one of 15,000 people who had attended that day.

'We're never going to get close to him,' I despaired. Excitement rippled through the room as Pope John Paul II appeared in the distance. Just knowing we were in his presence was an honour.

Craning our necks, we watched him make his way up one side of the giant room, greeting people and shaking hands, before starting on our side. We were on the front row so had a good chance but as the minutes ticked by, I grew more jittery: 'He's not going to reach us,' I fretted.

As he blessed a newly-wed couple – still in their finery – I remembered with a pang that I would never see Helen as a beautiful bride, or a flushed, new mum holding out her newborn to show me. Simms had stolen so much from us.

Pope John Paul II was two feet away, one foot away … My knees quaked, my hands trembled.

Suddenly, an ambassador next to us – who had blanked our greeting when we first sat down – launched forward, blocking my view. The back of his head bobbed as he gabbled earnestly. The Pope listened patiently, shook his hand, tried to move on – but the ambassador was having none of it. He continued to hold the Pope's hand, talking ten to the dozen.

Pope John Paul II had now focused his attention on John and me but the ambassador was still hovering, still jabbering. Finally, the Pope slipped his hand away and rested it on mine. It felt warm, dry and safe. In official photos, you can still see the ambassador hovering, grinning inanely, looking for a moment to re-join the conversation (John had him airbrushed out when we got home), but I didn't notice.

Gazing into the Pope's gentle, questioning face, I was in an absolute trance. I swear I could hear choirs of angels singing. John nudged me and gestured to the photo I was clutching of Helen.

'Father,' I began, falteringly. 'This is my daughter. She was murdered. Her killer is in prison but he won't say where she is. I pray every day to find her so I can lay her to rest.'

His brow furrowed in concentration. 'But how? How can there be a murder conviction without a body?' he asked in beautifully accented English.

'Forensic evidence and DNA, Father,' I explained. 'They found her blood. The police proved it was him.'

As comprehension filtered through, Pope John Paul II nodded. My voice cracked. 'All I want, now, is to find my daughter.' Understanding, empathy, pity all flickered across his face. Then he reached his left hand and tenderly cupped my face. It was like coming home. I wanted to stay like that forever.

He blessed Helen's photo. Then, taking John's hand so we were all connected, he said gently: 'We will pray, together, for your daughter to be found.' He closed his eyes and his lips moved as he prayed silently. Then his piercing, soulful blue eyes gazed into mine. He patted my hand and then he was gone.

I sank into the chair, stunned. Helen's photo had been blessed by the Pope! Our Holy Father had prayed for her to be found. Tears ran down my cheeks as I grabbed John's hand and kissed it. 'Thank you,' I whispered. 'Thank you for doing this for me. And for Helen.' I literally floated out of that room – I'd gone as high as I possibly could in asking for prayers that Helen would be found.

My faith has not only helped me over the years, it has saved me. Without it, I wouldn't be here. I'm not sure I would ever have deliberately harmed myself, taken my own life. But without my faith, my beliefs, who knows?

What I could easily have done so many times, particularly during the 'No' year, was given up. Laid down and never got up again. I could have refused water and food. The life would have left my body and all this pain would have been over. But where would that have got me? Helen would still be missing. I was her mother, it was my job to find her. That meeting with the Pope helped me come to terms with the life I was now leading. Over the years, I came to see my quest as a mission – a calling, even.

Every evening in Rome, after dinner an opera singer would open the piano and sing. On the evening of our audience with the Pope, he serenaded me. I closed my eyes, thought of Helen and let the music wash over me. It was like that scene in *The Shawshank Redemption* when opera plays over the loudspeaker and Morgan Freeman describes it as 'something so beautiful it can't be expressed in words and makes your heart ache because of it'.

John also hired a car and drove miles to San Giovanni Rotondo so we could visit the shrine for Padre Pio, the Italian stigmatised priest (he had developed Christ's crucifixion wounds) who was made a saint in 2002. When Helen was thirteen, she'd accompanied my mum on a church pilgrimage trip there. I desperately wanted to walk in her footsteps.

We arrived just in time for mass. Afterwards, we went to the back of the church and knocked on the door. The priest who had cared for Padre Pio answered. When we explained our reason for visiting, he took us down to the crypt and the cell where Padre Pio lived and prayed. Standing in the gloom of this holy, blessed place, I could feel Helen all around me. She had stood in this very spot just a few years ago.

That trip, and another to Lourdes, revived me; they gave me the strength to keep going through that long, yawning winter. That second Christmas and New Year without her was actually harder than the first. At least then we'd had hope that Simms would confess at the trial.

I remembered Christmases past with Helen coming home laden down with yet more gifts and scurrying upstairs to hide them. 'Just a few little extras,' she'd say when I queried the cost.

I still went to midnight mass on Christmas Eve. Outside, I ached, watching parishioners place festive wreaths on graves – they had no idea how lucky they were.

The lack of sleep was also taking its toll. Evenings would find me struggling to keep my eyes open, but the second I crawled wearily into bed, my brain fizzed into life.

Where are you, Helen? I'd think. *Send me a sign, anything.*

And then the guilt would creep in. How could I lie on fresh sheets, under a soft duvet, when my daughter was out there somewhere in the dark and cold? What sort of mother was I? Was she calling out to me but I wasn't listening well enough? I'd fine-tune all my senses and strain every sinew to hear a whispered word, a clue as to where she was. My brain would roar with effort. Nothing. Wearily, I'd slip back downstairs to pore over the search folders again, hoping to uncover something overlooked. If all else failed, I'd put the TV on quietly and stare blankly at an old black and white movie.

Every morning, I gave a jolt of surprise at my reflection in the bathroom mirror. Was that really me? Dead behind the eyes, lines of misery spreading like giant hogweed around my sunken eyes and mouth. One day, I put my hand up to my hair: it had gone brittle and grey, just like that.

Helen would have applied a deep conditioning treatment, encouraged me to get it coloured. But Helen wasn't here.

Simms, on the other hand, was always there, always on my mind.

* * *

John once persuaded me to have a day out in York. While checking the map, I realised that if we kept on the M62, we'd reach Hull where I knew Simms was in jail, temporarily, until space became available in a secure unit. In a flash, I'd turned to John: 'I need to see where he's being kept.'

Having to buy essentials for an impromptu overnight stay in York was worth it to satisfy myself that Simms' new home was miserable. I don't know anyone else who has done this, but I have been to see every single prison he has ever been in bar one (Long Lartin, in Worcestershire, was too remote).

Full Sutton was far too bright and modern. And Garth didn't look too bad, either. However, Hull, Wakefield and Wormwood Scrubs – bleak, sprawling, Victorian prisons – were decidedly grim.

The grimmer they were the better, I felt.

We checked into a little hotel, clutching brand new underwear and toothbrushes in a plastic bag. Heaven only knows what the staff thought of us. We still use the term 'overnight carrier bag' rather than a case or holdall.

Simms' first application for leave to appeal, in October 1989 (funded by legal aid, no doubt) was thrown out by a single judge sitting in private.

Our relief was short-lived. He could still apply again – to a full court. And he did so.

The appeal was adjourned again and again. Finally, at the eleventh hour, we learned from Merseyside Police that it was going ahead on Monday, 8 October 1990 (back then, families were the last to know about that sort of thing). We paid through the nose for train tickets to London.

I clutched my prayer cards as we entered the High Court. If the three judges sitting today agreed with Simms, they could order a retrial or even quash the verdict completely. Simms wasn't allowed to be there but his junior barrister David Turner put forward the case. He conceded that Simms had been linked to the killing by a 'brilliant scientific investigation' and 'at the end of the day, the jury could have had no doubt that he was involved in the disposal of her body'. However (here we go), even though Simms had instructed his legal team to seek an acquittal, Mr Turner argued that the trial judge should have directed the jury on the alternative and lesser verdict of manslaughter.

At the word 'manslaughter', my mouth fell open.

Simms, he continued, was physically strong and an expert in Thai boxing. Miss McCourt was slight. It could be that he never intended Miss McCourt really serious harm.

I gasped in disbelief as he explained that an argument had developed inside the pub. He had hit her once, then hit her again … the fatal blow.

I was trembling like a leaf. *He was admitting it: he'd hit her. And he'd killed her.*

Mr Turner continued. There were factual errors in the judge's summing-up and his address to the jury was 'too colourful', he claimed.

After just a brief hearing, the judges ruled that there was nothing 'unsafe or unsatisfactory' about the jury's verdict.

Thank God.

I'll never forget the response from Lord Justice McCowan: 'You lawyers want to have your cake and eat it,' he said sternly. 'At no time during the trial did you bring the issue of manslaughter into the courtroom. You know very well that had the trial judge done what you have just put to us, you would have immediately asked for a retrial on the grounds that manslaughter had never been put forward.'

The grounds of appeal amounted to pure speculation, he continued. Simms had never run self-defence or provocation as a defence and for the judge to have given the jury directions on manslaughter would have positively harmed the defence case.

Shakily, I left the court, clutching John's arm. It was over – Simms could go no further, in an English court, at least, with his ridiculous appeal. There were always the European courts, but even he must see it was futile by now. Surely, now he would tell us where Helen was.

Once more, I was leaping to answer the door or phone convinced that Simms had finally cracked. But as each day passed, without news, my despair intensified: it was unbearable.

Helen's case was so unique that it continued to attract the attention of journalists and TV producers. Two weeks after Simms' appeal was turned down, in October 1990, the BBC broadcast a film based on her murder as part of its respected *Indelible Evidence* series. Presented by the late Ludovic Kennedy (later, Sir Ludovic), it looked at cases where forensic evidence played a crucial part.

Crews had descended on Billinge to film the reconstruction section, even hanging a George and Dragon sign on the new pub. Through newspaper interviews, I urged viewers to watch the programme entitled 'Murder In The Wind'. I wanted any doubters to see just how guilty Simms really was. And I also hoped it might trigger new information on Helen's whereabouts.

We watched in stunned silence. Ludovic made it abundantly clear he was in no doubt at all about Simms' guilt (I later learned from a reporter that Simms was allowed the use of a prison video recorder so he could view the programme).

After midnight, we were still discussing the episode. *Maybe right now, someone is picking up the phone to Merseyside Police with crucial information*, I wondered hopefully. Suddenly, a loud crash from the front of the house had us leaping out of our seats.

'What the—' John cried, racing to the front door. Someone had smashed the rear windscreen of his car. They'd done a thorough job – lobbing a large stone and two house bricks.

Neighbours reported seeing two men dressed in black running away. Merseyside Police investigated and guarded the house for a few days but the perpetrators were never caught.

It had to be connected to the programme. A small part of

me felt hurt. I was the victim in this. My daughter had been murdered and yet someone had deliberately put bricks through the window of a car on my drive. Another part of me felt a flicker of fear: what would they do next time? But more than anything else, I felt incandescent with rage: 'How dare they?' I fumed.

If Simms' cronies, or whoever they were, thought I was going to crawl away quietly, they had another thing coming. This was just the start. Until he told me where Helen was, I would keep shouting from the rooftops. The longer he stayed silent, the louder I would become.

'I will not be frightened off,' I insisted to reporters.

I'd always vowed I would not lower myself to ask Simms where Helen was. But, as his cruel silence continued, I became more desperate. As the third anniversary of Helen's murder approached, an awful realisation started to form: 'I'm going to have to write to him,' I blurted to John.

I could see the surprise on his face. 'I know I said I wouldn't,' I admitted. 'But this is the stage I'm at. This is what he's driven me to. The searches are too dangerous and I'm terrified for you all. I can't go on like this.'

He agreed. Over the next few weeks, helped by my good friend, Kath Moodie, I made countless drafts. I scribbled words out, then put them back in. Flashes of inspiration would come to me in the night and I would sit up to scrawl a new line. Finally, I was copying out my last draft. I struggled on how I should address him. He might balk if I just put 'Simms' but he certainly didn't warrant a title of 'Mr' – I settled on Ian Simms.

I started off by telling him how much I loved my daughter and how it was almost three years since I'd seen her smiling face and heard her infectious laughter. I tried to empathise, saying that the night of her murder had marked the start of a nightmare for both me and him. I could even understand why he was insisting he was innocent – as he was worried his girlfriend would stop visiting him if he admitted what he'd done.

I pointed out that the love for my daughter, and the fear for my family's safety on our dangerous searches, had driven me to write to him:

> As a mother, I beg you to end this nightmare for both
> of us, now, before it's too late. Please let me give Helen
> a Christian burial for both our sakes.

He was serving a life sentence, I said, and would never be free until he showed remorse and admitted what he had done. And I warned that until he did, he would 'never be free of me':

> I will not allow either you or Helen's case to be forgotten.

Finally, it was signed and sealed. Merseyside Police arranged for me to hand deliver it to the Governor at Wakefield Prison. The *Sunday Express* offered to take me there. John couldn't take time off work so I accepted gratefully.

Walking up to the prison entrance, I introduced myself: 'I am Mrs McCourt. I have a letter for the Governor,' I said. The envelope trembled in my hand.

The guard recognised me. 'Ah yes, would you like to come in, Mrs McCourt?' he asked. On seeing the photographer, his expression hardened. 'But you can't,' he said brusquely. 'And put that camera away.'

Holding the door open, he waited patiently. I stared down at the ridge that the doors slotted into, and my breathing quickened. I'd imagined myself striding in, head held high, handing the letter over, seeking assurance that it would be given to Simms immediately. I willed myself to take just one step, but it was like standing in quicksand. The monster who had killed my daughter was in this very building. For all I knew he could be watching me right now. My legs were shaking so much, it was all I could do to stay upright. I felt like a waterfall – all my energy pooling into a puddle around my heels.

'I— I don't want to go in,' I stammered. 'Please. Will you promise me you will give this to the Governor.'

He nodded and took the letter from my hand. 'He's in his office waiting for it to be delivered,' he told me. 'I'll take it to him straight away.'

I turned and walked away unsteadily. The ball was in Simms' court now. A story about my letter appeared in the weekend papers. All I could do now was wait, hope and pray.

* * *

Before this point, I hadn't met anyone else who understood my pain, but that changed when I went to Manchester to be interviewed. Weeks earlier, I had gone to Manchester to be interviewed for a TV news programme on the impact of a child being murdered.

Two other mums – Ann West and Winnie Johnson – were also being interviewed. Both had lost a child, in the most brutal way, to Ian Brady and Myra Hindley – the so-called Moors Murderers.

Winnie's son, Keith Bennett, twelve, was on his way to his gran's when he was snatched by the evil pair in June 1964. Six months later, ten-year-old Lesley Ann Downey – daughter of Ann West – became the fourth and youngest victim.

The murders sent shockwaves across Britain, which are still felt to this day. Lesley Ann, a pretty little thing with jet black curls and a rosebud mouth, was lured from a fair on Boxing Day 1964. Shockingly, the evil, twisted pair recorded her pleading for mercy and calling for her mother as they tortured and killed her. The harrowing sixteen-minute tape reduced jurors, hardened police officers and even the judge to tears in the trial in 1966.

On being introduced, we embraced instinctively. I had seen these mums so many times in newspapers and TV news bulletins. I'd wept reading their painful words and seeing their tearful pleas. Now, I joined them on their platform.

As we stood, talking, it was as if our very souls were communicating. Finally, *finally*, here were two mums who could feel my pain and understand my need to keep searching for Helen's body.

Both knew what it was to lose a child and not be able to lay them to rest.

Tragically, to this day, Winnie's boy, Keith, is still lost on the moors. And even though Ann was able to have a funeral for Lesley Ann (her body was the first to be recovered on the Moors in October 1965), she still never found peace. She devoted her life to keeping a supposedly coerced Hindley behind bars and later, during the same year I met her, endured the desecration of her daughter's grave for the third time. (John and I attended the internment to a new secret resting place in 1992.)

We swapped numbers and agreed to meet up privately. That TV programme marked the start of two very special friendships.

* * *

Since delivering that letter to Wakefield,, I'd been like a cat on a hot tin roof, pacing the floor, staying inside, waiting for a reply. Finally, on Thursday, 14 March 1991 I couldn't stand it any longer and agreed to meet with them both. I visited Ann first, then headed to Winnie's.

I can still see Winnie now, sitting by the fire, smiling up at me sadly, as I entered. That familiar black and white picture of Keith adorned the mantlepiece. My heart broke for her.

We drank tea and spoke for hours, comforting each other, encouraging each other. Even though her health was failing, she, too, went out searching for her son's body. 'Don't give up,

Winnie,' I urged. 'He will be found. You just need to keep the publicity going. That's the one thing that keeps driving me.

'I'm determined that Helen's case will not be forgotten. Keep doing interviews, keep doing stories with the papers. I'll keep mentioning you. We can help each other.'

Finally, I was pulling back onto the drive at home. It had been a surreal day. I couldn't believe I was now in the same awful position as poor Winnie Johnson.

Stepping into the hall, I stopped. There was a fist-shaped hole in the kitchen door.

Michael was sitting at the table with a face like thunder.

With a shaky hand, he held out three sheets of handwritten paper. On the table lay an opened envelope stamped HMP.

Simms' reply.

The papers trembled in my hand as I scanned the childish writing.

Was this it? Was he finally going to tell me?

'Mrs McCourt & family,' it began. 'For more than three years now, you have haunted me. Not me. You.'

My hand flew to my mouth in disbelief. I looked at Michael. He was gripping the kitchen table, his knuckles white.

I turned back to the page to read a diatribe of ridiculous, appalling lies. Simms accused me of lying in my statements, swore he was innocent and offered to send me a dossier of new evidence. He also accused me and my family of threatening a pregnant member of his family and hitting a seventy-five-year-old man.

'I cannot and will not forgive that,' he said. 'The lord [sic] says an eye for an eye and a tooth for a tooth.'

He said I must stop 'playing to the gallery' (that is, talking to the press) and repent my sins as he had repented his.

On and on, he went – telling me to read depositions, accusing one of the experts of lying in court.

In his next line he urged one of my brothers to repent his sins

183

next time he was in church. 'He will repent when I see him,' he added menacingly.

He insisted I look at the case papers and once again pleaded his innocence, adding: 'The time is almost here. Let there be peace or there will be grief.'

He concluded: 'God forgive you for accepting payments from the media for each article (£2,000 isn't it?).

'I won't,' he added, smugly. For his concluding line he vowed: 'On my release I will have justice.'

The word 'justice' was underlined three times.

Appalled, I sank into a chair, speechless.

As an afterthought, or PS, he'd even added: 'BMW isn't it?' – in a barbed reference to the plush car I was supposedly driving, bought with media payments.

Something else in the torn envelope caught my eye. It was the original envelope I'd enclosed my letter to him in. He had crossed through his address at Wakefield Prison and chillingly, written beside it, 'not for much longer, Mrs McCourt. Everything is about to come out. I have been quite [sic] for much too long.'

John arrived home from work to find us both sitting there, in a shocked stupor.

To this day, I thank God that I was out when Simms' reply came. I'm not known for violent rages but I may well have smashed the house to smithereens.

I think we got off lightly with a punched door. It was only the second time in his life that Michael had lashed out over what had happened to his sister (the first was his outburst in court).

I needed help in dealing with this. An expert from Ashworth High Security Psychiatric Hospital, a Mr Grey, agreed to visit me at home.

In silence, he read the letter.

'How do you feel about this?' he asked gently.

'It's nasty and threatening and I can't believe he's written it,'

I replied. 'People keep telling me to keep writing and see if it will break him down but it was the hardest letter I've ever had to write. And I don't ever want to write to him again.'

'Why?' he asked.

I grappled for the right words. 'I feel that he would be like a cat playing with a mouse,' I said, finally.

He nodded. 'That's exactly what he will do,' he said. 'Go by your feelings.' Then, as an afterthought, he added: 'You do know he's a psychopath?'

I'd suspected it, but it was reassuring to hear it from an expert.

'If you do change your mind and want to write, wait another seven or eight years – when he's approaching his tariff review. If you'd like my advice, please ring and ask for me,' he told me.

I did ring a few years later for advice. His wife was lovely. 'I know all about it,' she said kindly when I explained why I was calling.

Sadly, Mr Grey had died eighteen months earlier.

* * *

Two months after receiving Simms' letter, I almost fainted on seeing the front page of the *St Helens Reporter*. 'I Pray Helen Will Be Found,' screamed the headline. He'd only written to the editor of a local paper, who had made it the 'splash' for that week.

'I want her found more than, or as much as anyone else, and have prayed every day for the last three years for her to be. But god [sic] knows that I don't know. I am not responsible for Helen McCourt's disappearance.

'I am no killer and certainly not evil.'

I drove straight to the office and confronted the editor. 'Have you any idea how hurtful this is, what that man is putting me through?' I stormed. 'You didn't even give me the right to reply.' He was very sheepish and had no idea how to answer me.

Years later, I would mention this incident when I gave lectures to journalism students. It was important to me that reporters were aware of the huge impact, both good and bad, that stories can have on victims' families.

In 1995, I befriended Seamus McKendry, son-in-law of the then missing, presumed murdered, IRA victim Jean McConville, and founder of the pressure group Families of the Disappeared in Northern Ireland. Seamus very kindly wrote to Simms 'beseeching him' to end my torment: 'Would it not be better to be remembered as someone who offered a little compassion rather than callous silence?' he asked. 'Helen's death came from a moment of weakness. It is now time for courage.'

In his reply, Simms made even wilder denials and accusations about my supposed behaviour. 'I am an innocent man,' he declared dramatically, adding that he had been subjected to treatment that the public would be 'horrified to learn about'. He also included a poem railing angrily against the judicial system and 'democracy'.

'Have you ever had your heart ripped out for something you know nothing about?' he wrote. 'Listen to my story for it could happen to you.'

'Oh, where is the justice?' he clamoured. 'Could anyone show some to me.'

Years later, I learned that the Mother Superior of the Carmelite Monastery in Birkenhead, where Aunt Bibby (who became Sister Mary of the Angels and Trinity five months after Helen's murder) was a nun, also wrote to Simms. The nuns would all collectively pray for Helen whenever I visited.

I never got to see his reply; no one did. All we knew was that it was 'so distressing' she sent it to the Prison Governor, insisting Simms never be allowed to contact her again.

'Marie, please don't write to him again,' Aunt Bibby begged. I didn't.

Top: Always smiling: Helen's first Christmas, aged five months old. The giant teddy bear, a gift from her paternal grandmother, is still sitting in her bedroom 55 years on.

Below left: A beaming Helen, aged two, dressed up for Easter – complete with matching bonnet and gloves. I loved buying and knitting new outfits for her.

Below right: Helen's first school photograph. She wore her best candy-striped dress (from Marks and Spencer) and her bunches were tied with matching ribbons.

Left: Helen, aged five, with her brother Michael, three - after she'd helped him overcome his terror of sand! They found everything funny.

Below right: Helen, Michael and I dressed up in matching snazzy waistcoats. Even then, Helen and I loved wearing similar outfits.

Below left: Helen, aged seven, making her First Holy Communion. It was such a proud day.

Right: One of my favourite photos of a teenage Helen. Seconds after this demure picture was taken, a snowball fight broke out.

Right: Tucking into Birthday cake with a ladle. Helen loved nothing more than making us laugh.

Below left: One of my favourite family photos with Helen and Michael as teenagers. We were such a tight little unit and look so happy.

Above right: Helen loved driving. Here she is, as proud as punch, aged 18, with her first car.

Left: This shot of Helen and Michael at their cousin's wedding illustrates just how close they were... best friends as well as siblings. She always looked lovely in yellow.

Left: Bubbles at breakfast for Helen's 21st. I woke her with a bottle of champagne and two glasses! Such happy memories of me and my girl.

Right: This is exactly how Helen appeared to me on our church altar shortly after her murder. It's an image I treasure.

Left: This was our last New Year's Eve together – Helen's favourite night of the year. Just five weeks later, she was taken from us.

Left: A burly Simms following his first appearance at St Helens Magistrates Court charged with Helen's murder. My petite daughter didn't stand a chance.

© *PA Images / Alamy Stock Photo*

Below: Thousands thronged to Billinge to help search for my daughter – leaving the village grid-locked.

© *Liverpool Echo*

Left: I begged Simms to tell me where Helen was. This was included with his reply.

Right: United in our search for Helen. From left to right: John, my brother Tez, sister Pat, me, Michael and my late mum, Sarah.

Left: 'We will pray for Helen'. Meeting Pope John Paul II in September 1989 – 18 months after Helen's murder – brought me such comfort.

Right: Michael and I unveiling Helen's marble seat, with the tribute 'Loved Every Minute, Missed Every Day' in 2008. Until we find Helen, it's the closest we'll come to having a grave.

Left: Me (far right) with my Pilates class members wearing their Helen's Law campaign T-shirts. The support from family and friends, every step of the way, has been astounding.

Top: Presenting our petition for Helen's Law to Downing Street, in February 2016. From left to right: John, Michael, me, my niece, my MP Conor McGinn and journalist (and co-author of this book) Fiona Duffy. © *change.org.*

Below left: John and I on one of our many trips to Parliament seeking justice for Helen. Credit: © *Mirrorpix/Reach Licensing.*

Below right: Still looking for Helen. More than 30 years after her murder, here I am with search expert Peter Faulding.

Helen. This unique canvas of my beautiful daughter – incorporating photographs and media cuttings from over the years – was created by Liverpool artist Anthony Brown. © *Artwork by Anthony Brown.*

Chapter 11

The victims' champion

It was becoming crystal clear that Simms had no intention of telling us where Helen was. So, if he wasn't going to speak, I'd have to make him – by any means possible.

Soon after the conviction, in March 1989, I made an appointment with a barrister who specialised in family finances.

'Can I sue him?' I asked.

Let me stress here that I did not, under any circumstances, want a penny from Simms. But money was his God. He was renowned for being mean. This was the man, remember, who would remove the door handle from the pub's stockroom so no one else could gain access.

And on the afternoon of Helen's disappearance, he'd torn a strip off his manager, Ken Booth, for not alerting him when the Labatt representative arrived at the pub. He'd told the court that he was 'steaming with' Kenny 'because he had not told me about Labatt's which meant a loss of money'.

So, I reasoned, I could reach him through his pocket. Hard. However, I was conscious that his wife, who had now filed for divorce and moved back to her childhood home, had two small children to bring up. They were victims in all of this, too. I wanted to ensure they'd be OK financially.

* * *

Nadine's mum looked stunned to find me on the doorstep.

'I haven't come here to cause bother,' I assured her.

She invited me inside to speak with an equally surprised Nadine.

'I've been advised to sue your husband but I want to make sure you're OK, first. He's going to be in prison for a long time and you've got the pub to sort. Can you just do me a favour and let me know when you're sorted? That's all I ask.'

She nodded. Then she said quietly: 'I'm so very sorry. I wanted to go out searching at the time. I felt I should, but ...'

I was touched. 'No, no, you didn't have to do that,' I said.

'One of the reasons that stopped me was that I thought your family might not be happy with me being there,' she added.

I shook my head firmly. 'My family are easy-going. There wouldn't have been anything like that.'

She nodded. 'But it could have been a distraction you didn't need,' she continued.

I thought about it: she was right.

'Thank you,' I told her.

She wrote to me afterwards thanking me for considering her and the children. Later, I heard that she had moved away from the area and remarried. I gather both of the children took their stepfather's surname and neither visited their dad in prison.

A few months before that chat with Nadine I'd paid a visit to Simms' mum – and mistress. In May 1989, I was driving home from Friday evening mass when I saw Tracey Hornby's car parked outside Simms' mother's house. Before I had time to think, I'd pulled over and knocked on the door.

A tall lady answered.

'Mrs Simms?' I asked. 'I'm Helen McCourt's mother.'

She gave a nod. 'I know, Mrs McCourt,' she said. 'Won't you come in?'

I don't know where I got the strength but I stepped inside. Tracey was sitting on the couch. The television was on.

'Take a seat, Mrs McCourt,' his mother said, gesturing to an armchair, but I remained standing. 'Mrs Simms, I have only come to ask you one thing,' I said. 'Please, please, will you tell your son to tell me where we can find Helen's body. The evidence against him was overwhelming.'

She looked down. 'I believe some of the evidence was biased,' she said. 'And some of it was lies.'

'Who told you that, Mrs Simms?' I asked, politely. Then I pointed towards Tracey, who was watching TV – or at least pretending to. 'Her?' I spat the word.

Tracey turned her head but said nothing.

'Because she wasn't even in court to hear the evidence,' I pointed out.

'No, but my mother was there,' piped up Tracey.

'Oh, yes,' I said coldly. 'We all know that your mother and sister were there.' (According to Tracey's post-trial tabloid exclusive her younger sister, Jane, had had an affair with Simms first.)

I turned back to Mrs Simms. 'All I want is for him to tell me where my daughter's body is so I can give her a proper funeral.'

She nodded. 'Oh, I will, Mrs McCourt.'

'Thank you,' I said, then added, 'If he refuses, tell him that I will be seeking a barrister to sue him for every penny he's got.'

She blinked.

'There's no money,' she said.

'Isn't there?' I asked. Then I held my hands out dramatically to gesture the room we were in. 'You have this, don't you? And I won't wait too long, either.'

As I headed for the front door, she followed me.

'I'm so sorry, Mrs McCourt,' she said.

In that moment, she looked stricken.

I sighed; the fight had gone out of me. 'It's all right,' I said, wearily. 'But please tell him I am not going to wait much longer.'

The following week, there was a 'For Sale' sign outside the house.

(By 1991, Tracey was still visiting Simms in prison, still telling newspapers what a 'kind man and wonderful lover he is'.)

The next time I heard about Simms' mum was in sadder circumstances: the probation service rang to say she was gravely ill. Would I agree to him attending her funeral?

What – while he continues to deny me my daughter's funeral?

I chose my words carefully. 'He can visit his mother while she's ill,' I said. I knew more than anyone the importance of saying goodbye. 'But no, I do not give permission for him to attend her funeral.'

When I heard that his mother had died, I rang the prison. 'Will he be attending the funeral?' I asked.

They sounded surprised. 'We didn't even know she was ill. Are you a relative?'

'No,' I replied. 'I'm the mother of his victim.'

There was a long pause. 'He hasn't applied to visit his mother and as for her death, we know nothing about it. Can we get back to you?'

Later, they rang and said: 'We've had no requests and, in any case, it's too late to arrange. So, no, he won't be attending.'

I gripped the phone. 'I hope what you are telling me is true,' I said. 'Because I know where the service is and if I see any sign of a prison van, I'll be straight on the phone to the press to get down and take pictures.

'I don't want to do that,' I added. 'Her family have the right to have a quiet funeral, but I also have the right to bury my daughter. A right that he has denied me.'

There was no need for any intervention. He didn't attend the funeral. Nor, apparently, did he visit her while she was ill. I've often asked myself, what sort of person doesn't go to see their sick mother?

I'd already decided that suing him would be a last resort. I didn't want his blood money, I just wanted him to say what he'd done with Helen.

Well-wishers urged me to give up the searches. 'It's too upsetting for you,' they'd say. 'Your daughter's in heaven. Let it go.'

I'd shake my head firmly. They'd never understand. How could they? How could I go about my life knowing the child I'd brought into this world was lying dumped in an unmarked grave somewhere? Bringing her home was more than just an urge now. It was a primeval need, an instinct, that became stronger by the day.

A professor in bereavement explained it to one journalist: 'When a body can't be seen, a person is unable to come to terms with the fact that a death has occurred,' she said. 'Searching becomes a substitute for grieving.'

I refused to go on holiday, or even a day out. 'I can't – this could be the day we find her,' I'd plead. Every morning, without fail, my first whispered words were: 'Please God, let it be today.'

By now, equipment hire, maps, photocopying and petrol had pushed the cost of our searches to £40,000. 'But I will sell my house if I have to,' I vowed.

Local solicitor, Robin Makin, read about my plight and suggested I apply for criminal injuries. At this, I bristled. 'I don't want money, thank you,' I said coldly. 'I want my daughter.'

'But you could be entitled to it,' he persisted. 'And surely it could go towards your searches?'

He was right, I wasn't in a fit state to work. And I could hire more equipment, put it towards her funeral … when it finally happened.

The hearing was at the Customs House in Liverpool. John couldn't get time off work so I went alone. While Robin Makin put his case, I wasn't permitted to speak. I started to prickle. Didn't they want to know how this was affecting me? How a part of me had died on 9 February 1988?

'Thank you, Robin,' I said during a break. 'I think you put the case extremely well. However, I don't think you're going to win.'

He tilted his head. 'I think we have a pretty good chance,' he said.

I shook my head and sighed. 'From where I was sitting, they're going to say no.'

I was right: they said no. Because Helen was over eighteen, unmarried and still living at home, we weren't entitled to anything. Her life had no value. I've since heard of families who haven't been able to afford a funeral for a murdered loved one because they weren't entitled to compensation.

As we left the building, angry tears stung my eyes. I'd put myself through that humiliating ordeal for nothing. Hot blood coursed through my veins.

'Are you all right, Mrs McCourt?' Robin asked, as I strode up and down the car park, eyes darting wildly around. 'Have you lost something? What are you doing? Can I help?'

'What am I doing?' I retorted wildly. 'What am I doing? I'll tell you what I'm doing! I'm looking for a good heavy brick to throw through their lovely window.'

Alarm, quickly followed by confusion, flashed across his face.

'That way, the police can come and read me my rights,' I continued hysterically, jabbing my chest forcefully. 'Because right now, I have none. None! I haven't broken the law. I haven't killed anyone. But I have no rights whatsoever. It's all there for the criminal to escape conviction or punishment! And it's not fair!'

By now, people were openly staring. I took a deep breath. As quickly as it had engulfed me, the blind rage evaporated and ebbed away. 'I'm sorry,' I mumbled, wearily.

In more than thirty years I have never received a penny

from the state to either fund searches or fight decisions. Simms, however, has been granted legal aid countless times.

* * *

That outburst lit a fire in my belly. Simms had been given a sixteen-year tariff, which meant that in 2004, his case would be up for review. If he hadn't told me the truth by then, it was up to me to ensure he stayed locked up.

'We need new laws,' I argued. 'How can killers get away with this? They should be made to reveal the location of their victims' remains. And the longer they remain silent, the longer their sentence should be.'

I'm a naturally shy, unassuming woman. The thought of calling for change and approaching figures of authority to highlight what was wrong with our justice system terrified me. But if I didn't do it, who would?

Other women, other mums, would help, surely? Kath Moodie put me in touch with the head offices for the National Federation of Women's Institutes, Soroptimist International Great Britain and Ireland, and the National Council of Women.

I'd summon my courage, take a deep breath and start talking: 'Hello,' I'd begin. 'My name is Marie McCourt.' From that point on, the words flowed – either from my mouth or my pen. They all agreed to support me.

Every anniversary, Christmas and birthday, journalists contacted me to cover the story. I was so grateful to them.

I wrote to HM The Queen, to my MP, John Evans, and Prime Minister John Major.

The Queen wrote back and said although she sympathised, she couldn't intervene. She forwarded my letter to the then Home Secretary, Michael Howard.

Winnie Johnson, Keith Bennett's mother, supported my campaign. I arranged for us both to travel to London to be interviewed about our plight on a BBC daytime news programme. 'No one else understands our pain,' I said. 'If killers know they will never get out until they co-operate, they might well end this nightmare.'

Learning about an ancient English common-law offence of preventing a burial spurred me on. For some reason it was rarely used. But why?

There were other offences, too – obstructing a coroner, hiding a corpse, not to mention perverting the course of justice.

So why hadn't Simms also been charged with these offences? Initially I was told they were only used in cases of manslaughter and not murder – a bizarre answer which didn't make any sense to me.

Then in April 1994, paedophile Robert Black was convicted of the kidnap and murder of three beautiful little girls, Caroline Hogg, Sarah Harper and Susan Maxwell, between 1981 and 1985.

It was a horrific case and my heart went out to the families of those little girls. But my eyes widened when I read that Black had also been charged, and convicted of, three counts of preventing a lawful burial. It was the first time I'd heard of this charge being used.

If these offences had been used against Black, surely they could be used against Simms too?

However, it wasn't as straightforward as that.

A barrister advised me that although I could try to have him charged with preventing Helen's burial he doubted it would go anywhere. Simms had already been found guilty of murder – one of the gravest crimes there was – and was already serving life.

In the eyes of the law, Simms had been convicted. He was banged up. A dangerous killer had been taken off the streets. There was no way he would be brought back to court for additional charges.

I'll never forget his words. 'Every time it came to the top of the pile of paperwork it would be put straight to the bottom again,' he said. 'There are simply too many other cases for them to focus on.'

Only, for me, and Helen's family, this was far from over. Yes, he'd been convicted of my daughter's murder. But if I was ever to move forwards from her tragic, needless death, I needed to be able to bury her.

I'd fully intended to take out a private prosecution once I was sure that Simms' wife, Nadine, and the children were sorted.

But the costs involved were astronomical. I could literally lose everything – with no guarantee of a successful outcome.

Besides, we were all still under the illusion that Simms would never be released without saying where Helen was. And I genuinely believed it.

Robin Makin also helped me take my case to the European Court of Human Rights. It was a lengthy process and went on for more than a year, from 1994 to 1995. We got to the final stage before it was thrown out. We appealed – and lost.

That was it, the end of the road: you can't appeal after an appeal.

* * *

Fighting for a change in the law was my only option. My plight was continuing to get lots of coverage in the media. 'If I can prevent one more family from going through this torment, something good will have come from Helen's death,' I said.

Producers began inviting me on to news shows to talk about my predicament. I'd quake with terror as the cameras lit up, but this was something I had to do – for Helen. While appearing on the TV programme *Kilroy* in 1992, I finally got to meet Diana Lamplugh, mum of missing estate agent Suzy Lamplugh, twenty-five. Suzy had vanished in July 1986 while showing a man around a London property.

Diana had sent her support when Helen went missing and now we hugged instinctively. My heart went out to her. At least the monster who had taken Helen's life was behind bars. It was another two years before Suzy was even declared dead, in 1994. Her disappearance remains a mystery to this day, but it's believed she was murdered by convicted sex killer John Cannan.

We sat side by side – two mums searching desperately for their daughters – and, afterwards, continued to support each other. (Sadly, Diana died in 2011 – still not knowing what had happened to her daughter.)

Later that year (ironically, on Friday, 13 November 1992), a Channel 4 documentary called *Short Stories: Still Missing*, focusing on Helen's disappearance, was watched by 2.7 million people. Afterwards, a neighbour called me into her house to listen to a message on her answer machine. 'Sorry for calling on this number,' said a male voice in a Liverpudlian accent, 'but I have a message for Marie McCourt. I have information that could help her. Can you get her number and I'll call back for it?'

My heart leapt. I waited excitedly, but he never rang. Both I and the police issued an appeal, urging him to come forward. Nothing. Did he change his mind? Did someone talk him out of it? Sadly, I'll never know. But if he, or anyone else, is reading this now and has information that could end more than thirty years of misery, please, please contact me through the email at the back of this book.

I was astonished at the letters of support I received from people who said they would back my campaign.

'We need to do this,' I said to John.

Ever since Helen had failed to come home, he had been a tower of strength. I don't know what I'd have done without him.

I often think back to when John and I met in 1985. Did he have any idea what he was about to get into? The death of a child, let alone the murder of one, can take a huge toll on a couple. I can see now how easily they can be left splintered and hurt, coping and surviving in their own separate ways.

After Simms had lost his bid for an appeal, I rang Kevin Conroy of Merseyside Police.

'When will I get Helen's things back?' I asked.

There was a silence.

'You've got them, Marie,' he replied.

I shook my head. 'No, I haven't,' I insisted.

More silence.

'John picked them up after the appeal was finished,' he finally admitted.

When John arrived home from work that night, the smile on his face froze when he saw my expression.

'Have you been and got Helen's things?' I asked in a clipped voice.

He turned a distinct shade of grey. Mortification crept across his face.

'Where are they?' I asked through gritted teeth.

His answer horrified me.

'In the loft?' I screeched. 'You've put her clothes up in the loft?'

I went berserk, absolutely berserk. It's yet another example of how irrational your thinking becomes when tainted by grief. Helen's clothes had been torn off her and scattered on a rat-infested riverbank for the best part of three weeks. They had been scrutinised under microscopes, presented as evidence, pored over in court. Yet the thought of them being secretly squirrelled in our loft hurt more than any of that.

'Helen would never have put her things in the loft,' I said furiously. 'I want them down. Now!'

The ladder rattled as he disappeared into the attic and passed down two big brown evidence bags. Without a word, I carried them into Helen's bedroom and closed the door. I knelt down, tenderly reached into the crinkly bags and pulled out her precious, crumpled garments, one by one. There was her lovely coat, her maroon scarf, the soft, green mitts that had protected her small hands on wintry mornings … After spreading them out on the floor, I sobbed over them. I paused, stooped closer and inhaled deeply, only to cry even more – they didn't even smell like her.

Then, as my eyes fell on her lower garments, a thought so awful it took my breath away erupted inside my brain. It was like being hit by a bolt of lightning.

Simms had hurt her.

He had hurt her in the most awful way and I hadn't been able to protect her.

Her clothes from the waist-down had been found. Her trousers, her underwear.

He had wanted my Helen and when she turned him down, he took her by force.

He'd raped her. And then he'd killed her.

'Oh, Marie, you can't think like that,' my appalled sisters insisted when I confided in them. 'He killed her and hid her, that's all. He didn't have time to do anything else.'

I could understand their reasoning, the truth was too horrible to contemplate. 'But if he killed her by accident, why drag her upstairs to the bedroom? Why not just put her in the car boot there and then? It's obvious.'

Now, scooping the clothes she had worn so proudly into my arms, I rocked back and forth as the tears flowed.

Oh, Helen! What did he do to you?

Finally, exhausted and spent, I folded the items up carefully, returned them to the bags, then placed them on a shelf in Helen's wardrobe. They were still her clothes, the clothes she'd left home in that day. She'd want me to look after them.

I walked downstairs, fired up with a new sense of determination. It was more essential than ever for me to bring my daughter home. Her last few moments on this earth had been filled with terror and violence. I needed to put that right, to let her know she was safe now and no one would ever be allowed to hurt her again.

Downstairs, I sat next to a stricken John.

'I'm sorry,' he said. 'I thought I was helping. I wanted to put Helen's coat into the dry cleaners so they could replace the buttons and sew the tear up. It was really upsetting for you to see it like that.'

My heart went out to this wonderful, thoughtful, considerate man. 'That's how they were found,' I said, gently. 'We need to leave them as they are – for evidence, if nothing else. But thank you.'

Then I kissed his cheek. I don't think I'd ever loved him more than in that moment.

When Helen went missing, we'd immediately shelved our wedding that we had planned for April 1988. Over the next few years, John would occasionally suggest getting married quietly, without fanfare.

'No,' I'd always said, dismissively. How could I even think about my own happiness while my murdered daughter was missing?

It's something only those who have lost a loved one to murder will appreciate. Suddenly, joy is something you are no longer entitled to. You survive, you go through each day, but you can't imagine ever feeling happy again. Those feelings are gone forever.

'Go,' I'd say. 'Leave. Find someone else who can make you happy. Because I can't.' Being without him would have killed me, but I was hurting so much.

But, one day, he gave me an ultimatum: 'Marie, I don't know where I am,' he said, anguished. 'I want to marry you, but ...' Then his voice trailed off. 'I'm going to give you to the end of this year,' he continued. 'If the answer is still no, I'll do what you keep telling me to do. I'll leave you and get on with my life.'

I stared at him, horrified. Then I felt a crushing sensation around my heart.

Please, I've lost Helen. I can't lose you, too.

'You don't mean that,' I said, shocked.

'Yes, I do,' he said, determinedly. I'd never seen him like that.

I gripped his hand. I loved this man and I wasn't going to lose him. 'I will marry you, John. But abroad, not in this country.'

I couldn't bear to see 'Tragic Mum Finds Love' stories in the papers. Articles needed to focus on Helen and nothing could detract from that.

He smiled.

'Done,' he said.

There was one other condition: 'I won't change my name,' I told him. 'To keep Helen's name alive, I need to have the same surname.'

John, bless him, offered to change his name to McCourt, but I refused. 'When your sons have families, your grandchildren will want to know why Grandad doesn't have the same name.'

We slipped away and wed quietly abroad in July 1992, agreeing to keep our separate surnames. Declaring my vows to this man, I felt safe and loved. He had come into my life just when he was needed the most. He was the glue that held our heartbroken family together and he has been my rock ever since. We celebrated our silver wedding anniversary in 2017 and it was one of the proudest moments of our lives – I only wish Helen could have been there with us.

Sadly, Helen's murder took its toll on our family in other ways. I firmly believe the stress killed my baby brother, David, in March 1992. Just thirty-four, he left a widow and three young sons Helen had adored. After the murder he spent so much time worrying about me – ringing up or popping round to check how I was. And he was devoted to the Sunday searches. But one Saturday night, he went to sleep and never woke up.

The coroner concluded that he was a healthy, very strong young man and his epilepsy was under control. But, at some time during that night, his heart, inexplicably, had stopped beating.

Stunned and heartbroken, we gathered at his home to plan the funeral. David's father-in-law wanted to hire a fleet of funeral cars for everyone, which my brothers thought unnecessary.

'You can send a car if you like, but we're not getting in them,' someone said. I stared at the carpet.

'Now, hold on a minute,' someone intervened.

Hurt, bickering voices swarmed around my head like insects. My breath quickened. I couldn't stand it. I grabbed my car keys, leapt up from the chair and ran from the room.

My mouth was set in a furious, thin line as I turned the ignition key and the engine roared into life. Veering onto the motorway, I pressed my foot on the accelerator until it hit the floor. How I didn't end up killing myself or someone else I'll never know, I was like a woman possessed.

Blue signs flew by and suddenly I was taking the turn-off for Irlam, thirty miles away.

It was where Helen's clothes had been dumped.

Choking back tears, I scrambled out of the car, then slipped and slithered my way down the dirty, muddy bank through the sharp gorse and thick trees. Just short of the water's edge, I sat down heavily, panting for breath. Cold, clammy wet seeped into my clothes. Then I opened my mouth and wailed like a banshee. I hung onto the cry until it wavered before petering out into a weary croak, then I took a deep breath and roared again. And again. It felt like the gates of hell had been opened and four years of pent-up, knotted pain, hurt and agony were finally unfurling.

Once I'd started, I couldn't stop. It was an uncontrollable reflex, like the way your abdominal muscles contract over and over during a bout of food poisoning until there is nothing left to expel. Finally, the waves subsided. I've no idea how long I sat there, exhausted and drained, as dusk fell. Up on the road, behind me, street lights snapped on, one by one.

'Hello?' someone called, breaking the silence. 'Are you all right down there, love?'

A few minutes later, there were more voices. My concerned good samaritan had gone to the nearby fire station for help.

'Come on, love,' a man's voice said, kindly. 'You've been here a while now, your family's going to be worried.'

I think they must have recognised me from pictures in the papers. They knew exactly why I was sitting there, crying.

Tentatively, they approached. I allowed them to lift me to my feet and help me up the bank and into the station. The bright lights made me wince. A hot cup of tea was placed in my hands, a blanket draped around me.

'I'm so sorry,' I mumbled. 'Putting you to this trouble.'

Despite their protests, I managed to persuade them that I was OK to drive home. As I pulled onto my drive, the front door was flung open. They all poured out – Mum, with her arms outstretched, followed by Pat, Margaret, John and Michael. I could see the terror tinged with relief etched on their pale faces.

'She's here, she's here!' I could hear them calling to others in the house.

'I'm sorry, Mum,' I whispered. 'I had to get out. Our David's *having* a funeral ...'

She rocked me gently. 'I know, love. I know,' she soothed.

I've no idea how we got to the church for the service but I know that there was never a cross word over funeral planning, or any sort of gathering ever again.

To this day, I can't abide hearing about fall-outs over who's going to attend, sit where or inherit this or that trinket. Being able to lay a loved one to rest is a privilege not all of us are fortunate to have. Please don't ever take it for granted.

The only place I could go that day, to feel close to my beloved daughter, was the dirty, litter-strewn riverbank where the rats run. I had nowhere else to go. Nowhere.

Chapter 12

Twisting the knife

S till the searches went on. It was relentless, exhausting, soul-
destroying.

Sometimes, the urge to sell up, move somewhere new and start
afresh where no one knew us was overwhelming. Shortly after
the trial, I'd gone as far as putting the house on the market. We'd
had valuations done and brochures designed before I suddenly
thought, *Wait, how can I move? Helen loved this house. And I want to
bring her home.*

I told the estate agent I'd changed my mind. Moving wouldn't
change a thing. In fact, it would make the searches even harder.

'This is my job, my duty as Helen's mum,' I told journalists
when they asked how I could bear to keep going. 'I brought her
into the world and I need to see her out of it, too.

'Besides, she'd be upset at the thought of no one looking
for her.'

Winnie Johnson and Ann West, mothers of the Moors' victims
I had befriended, were the few people who really understood.

Yes, we would always be within painful distance of the murder site. I grew used to averting my eyes whenever I had to pass it. It was like wearing invisible blinkers.

Time crawled by. We had the fifth, then sixth anniversary. With no grave to tend, to buy flowers for, all I could do was light candles and place them around her portrait.

One day, Helen will have her own resting place, I'd tell myself. *One day …*

Until then, all we could do was carry on looking for her.

Occasionally, John would insist on a few hours out, a drive somewhere. But even then, I would scan fields as we passed.

'Wait! Stop!' I'd urge. 'Did we check there? Or what about there?'

* * *

In 1994, police found the body of a man in a sewage pipe in Blackburn. It was awful news and my heart went out to his family, but in a macabre way those discoveries revived me, kept me going, gave me more ideas. I'd urge the public: 'If you know of any disused pipes on your land, any remote hiding places, please let me know.'

We always knew that 1995 was going to be a difficult year. Helen should have been looking forward to her thirtieth birthday in July. We should have been celebrating with a huge family party, maybe even a wedding – she'd planned to marry at thirty. Instead, I was arranging another memorial mass, with her portrait gazing back at us all from the front of the church.

On the last Sunday in January, a local journalist rang: 'Erm, I wondered if you had any thoughts on the article in today's *Independent on Sunday* magazine?' he asked, tentatively.

'What article?' I wanted to know.

Intrigued, John ran to the shop to buy a copy. And there it was, a lengthy four-page article by journalist Bob Woffinden, who specialised in investigating possible miscarriages of justice. He had examined the cases of A6 Murderer James Hanratty, Sion Jenkins, who was eventually acquitted of murdering his step-daughter Billie-Jo, and White House Farm murderer Jeremy Bamber, to name but a few. And now he had taken on Simms.

Under the headline: 'Burden of Proof', he asked, 'Is Simms Innocent?'

With a growing sense of horror, I read how, for the last four years, Woffinden had been visiting Simms in Full Sutton Jail in York – ever since he'd contacted him insisting his case was, *that's right*, a miscarriage of justice. And this article was the result.

Woffinden questioned the forensic evidence that had convicted Simms and suggested that an ex-drinking crony of Simms, or someone with a grudge, could have framed him for the murder. He argued that Helen would drape her coat over the bar stools, on visits, and occasionally pet Simms' dog (in an attempt to explain fibres and dog hairs) and also claimed that, according to passengers on the bus, her coat was already torn under the armpits.

Most shocking of all was the line: 'Although one would not wish to offer Mrs McCourt empty hopes, Helen may not even be dead. After all, hundreds of people in this country simply disappear.'

He recounted a statement from a witness (there were hundreds in response to police appeals) who said Helen had sat opposite him on a train heading south and pointed out that an entry in her diary read 'February: Barcelona'.

'I don't believe it,' I whispered. The police had already scotched this ridiculous rumour before the trial. Yes, Helen had been planning a holiday to Spain with her friend Hilary. They might have been considering Barcelona. But her passport was still in her desk, for heaven's sake.

At one point in the trial the defence had played up the word 'Inasun' that had also been written in her diary, pronouncing the name Inasuan, to make it sound like a person. Had she run off to meet a man by this name, they questioned. I'd wrung my hands in frustration. She meant Intasun, a low-budget holiday company – Helen was looking to book with them.

To imply that Helen had abandoned her family and run off to Spain with a non-existent lover was preposterous, hurtful and downright cruel.

Woffinden described a 'gathering groundswell of support among the community in Billinge, where former friends and associates are openly sceptical about whether justice was done'.

What?

'In prison,' he said, 'Simms felt the pressure of being a constant target of vilification. Twice, when arriving at a new prison, he was beaten up by fellow prisoners who believed the court verdict – routinely regaled by the tabloids – that he was the vilest of murderers'. However, 'it seems that, once he has established himself, he is a popular inmate, known for his straightforwardness'.

Woffinden himself found Simms 'when not unutterably depressed, good company, forthright, opinionated and engagingly droll'.

He described how I'd spent several weekends digging up the countryside looking for her.

Several weekends? Try seven years!

Incandescent with rage, I contacted my MP John Evans. He had been supporting me for many years. In fact, it was thanks to him that I'd received a letter from Home Secretary Michael Howard assuring me that Simms would never be freed without showing remorse.

Local TV news channels covered the story. They came to the house to film me reading the article. 'There is nothing here any different to when he was found guilty and convicted of my daughter's murder,' I said flintily. 'The best thing that could happen is for Simms to say, "Yes, I did it – and this is where Helen is."'

That evening, I tuned in. There was John Evans stressing that he hadn't been approached by a single person raising concern about the conviction – and arguing that this action was unfair both to Simms and, even more so, to myself.

'He is giving false hope to Simms that he is going to be released from prison or have a new trial,' he told the interviewer. 'He has twice been refused leave to appeal. I don't think it would be granted on the third application either.'★

Forensic experts at Chorley said they had complete confidence in the evidence given to the court.

And then, suddenly, there was Bob Woffinden himself on a screen speaking to the presenter in the studio.

'I have no wish at all to increase the burden of Mrs McCourt's grief,' he said. 'I realise that this is a very distressing day for her. What I would like to do is to alleviate her grief.'

My mouth fell open in disbelief.

'I am aware of the campaign she has conducted over the last few years and how determined she is to discover the whereabouts of her daughter's body, if indeed her daughter has been murdered, which we must presume.

'I would like to help her in her quest. And it seems to me, that, at the moment, she is not going to discover the truth about this case because, quite frankly, everybody has been headed down the wrong road.'

I gasped. The audacity of the man! I longed to pick something up and hurl it at the TV screen.

On and on he went: 'Ian Simms wrote to me from prison and said, "Could you look at my case. It's a miscarriage of justice."'

Yes, Simms wrote to me as well – pages and pages of abuse and threats.

★ Simms' first application was turned down but his second was granted and John and I were there to see it rejected by judges.

'I had a superficial look at it and wrote back saying, "Well, I'm sorry there seems to be an awful lot of evidence here." But to his credit, he persisted and I looked at the case more closely and was indeed convinced because I then realised that however convincing the forensic framework was, when you scrutinised it closely, it actually fell apart because it didn't make sense. There was no coherent scenario there for what was supposed to have happened.'

The interviewer interjected: 'Or is it that Simms is a convincing liar?'

Bob Woffinden bristled. 'I've met Simms on several occasions. I think he is a generous, warm-hearted person...'

'You have got to be joking!' I retorted.

'... I've got a great deal of time and affection for him and quite frankly, the idea that I've been duped is just ludicrous. I have been following these cases for some years now and I can assure you that no cases are taken up where there is any doubt about the rightness of the appeal.'

I couldn't take any more. Grabbing the remote, I jabbed a button and the screen went blank. I was shaking like a leaf.

'How dare he?' I raged.

For seven years we had lived with this torture only for a do-gooder to come along and claim the conviction was unsafe.

And so began an upsetting and exhausting four-year legal roller coaster which I could have done without.

Astonishingly, a week later, the day before the seventh anniversary of Helen's murder, I received a letter from Woffinden. Not only was his timing appalling but he sent it to an address in a road where Simms used to live. It was forwarded by a resident.

In it he wrote: 'I was deeply saddened to read your remarks but sometimes you have to make a judgement whether to contact the bereaved or not.'

So, in one sentence he acknowledged I was indeed bereaved. And in the next, questioned if my daughter was actually dead.

He offered to meet me.

I did not reply.

After Mr Watts raised the issue in the Commons, the Home Office banned Woffinden from visiting Simms without giving an undertaking not to write anything. Woffinden refused. Simms argued the ban breached Article 10 of the European Convention on Human Rights (which was being incorporated into British Law): 'the right to freedom of expression'. He applied for legal aid (which was granted, naturally) and, jointly with another prisoner who had been denied visits by a BBC producer, sought a judicial review of the decision.

They won their case in December 1996. I was so sickened, I was unable to organise a mass on Helen's anniversary the following February.

The Home Office appealed. John and I travelled down for the hearing in December 1997. Due to train delays, we arrived too late to hear the case but it was all over: Simms had lost. I punched the air! The court had ruled that prisoners, as part of their punishment, lost the right to freedom of expression. It was a victory for common sense.

'Justice has been done and the right result was gained today,' I told reporters. 'Ian Simms claimed [...] an infringement of his human rights. But what rights does a murderer or rapist give to the victim?

'I am so relieved that this chapter is over and hopefully one day Simms will show remorse by telling us where Helen's body is and giving us the human right of giving our daughter a Christian burial.'

Heading into a nearby café for a much-needed cuppa, I stopped in my tracks. There, just a few feet away from me, was

Mr Woffinden himself. John spotted him too – a fraction too late to stop me marching towards his table.

I'd have loved to have known what was going through his head as this furious middle-aged woman bore down on him, the ominous click-clack of heels on the hard floor growing ever louder.

Reaching into my handbag, I pulled out Helen's passport and slapped it onto his table. 'Mr Woffinden,' I said in an icy tone. 'Here is Helen's passport. It was one of the first things the police looked for when she went missing. So now you can stop writing that her passport was missing and she has gone abroad. Because if you do,' I said through clenched teeth, 'I will take it further.' Snatching up the passport, I turned and marched away.

He never said a word. I can still picture the stunned expression on his face.

Yet again, Simms appealed (again, funded by legal aid, no doubt), taking his case to the House of Lords. In July 1999, more than four years after this debacle had begun, they found in his favour – concluding the ban was unlawful and a contravention of basic human rights. Watching from the public gallery, I became so distraught that our new MP David Watts had to take me into a nearby office so I could calm down.

I was livid and hurt, but realised I had more important things to focus on. (Interestingly, even though he'd won the right for Woffinden to visit him in prison, I'm not aware of a single further article being published about Simms' supposed innocence.)

First, Simms had asked the newly founded Criminal Cases Review Commission (CCRC, which was set up to investigate possible miscarriages of justice) to examine his conviction.

Once again, I had to hand over every bit of evidence relating to the case – from Helen's soiled clothes to her private diary.

Second, we were still focusing on the searches and appeals to the public. The discovery of a body always had me sitting bolt upright. Each time, my heart leapt with hope and then broke for those poor girls and their families.

* * *

In August 1997, we came agonisingly close to thinking our quest was about to end when amateur divers discovered the body of a woman in Coniston Water, Cumbria. Aged between twenty and thirty, with dark hair, she had been wrapped in bin bags and weighted down.

Could it be Helen?

Merseyside Police sent off Helen's dental records. All I could do now was wait.

The papers ran stories about my hope: 'Mother Waits for Lake Body Probe ... "Is My Agony Over?"'

When the phone finally rang, I snatched it up. Closed my eyes. Prayed. And then slumped at the words, 'I'm sorry, Marie ...'

It was as if someone had punched me in the solar plexus. For a few seconds, I felt completely winded and had trouble breathing. My heart felt like a dead weight hanging in my chest, pulling me down, making me stoop.

'I don't know how much more I can take,' I wept to reporters. 'I really thought this time it would be Helen.'

The case, however, did raise awareness of the plight of missing murder victims. The woman was identified as mum of three, Carol Park, thirty, of Barrow-in-Furness, who had disappeared in 1976. Her husband, Gordon, hadn't reported her missing for six weeks – claiming she had run off with another man.

Initially charged with murder, the case was dropped in 1998 – only to be revived in 2005. Gordon Park was found guilty. He lost an appeal in 2008 and killed himself in prison, two years later.

Those poor children, I thought. Even then, that still wasn't the end. One of the children launched a posthumous appeal to the

CCRC on behalf of their father, but a judge dismissed it in May 2020.

Until now, everyone had argued that such cases were extremely unusual. They rarely happened, they were an anomaly.

'Don't you see?' I told reporters. 'They do happen. It's just that the killers hide the body so well they, literally, get away with murder.'

Once again, I thanked my lucky stars that I'd raised the alarm so quickly on Helen's disappearance. With another few precious hours, Simms might have covered his tracks completely. Helen would, forever, have been another missing person.

The more we discovered, the more compelled we felt to keep shouting and help others caught up in our misery.

It had all started at the mass for what should have been Helen's thirtieth in July 1995. Her friends and colleagues had all poured into the church. I took bittersweet delight in their engagements, their weddings, their pregnancy bumps and babies in buggies while a thought, on a loop, went round and round in my head:

That should have been Helen. That should have been Helen ...

Later that year, taking part in another news programme, I was introduced to Pat Green – a Liverpool mum whose teenage son, Phillip, had been killed in 1991.

After filming, she sought me out. 'There's very little out there for parents like us,' she said. 'I'm setting up a group for people who have lost a child to murder or manslaughter. I'd love it if you were involved.'

But I shook my head. 'No, I need to find Helen first,' I said. 'That's all that matters. Once I've found her and can give her a burial, then I can start to think about myself.'

But as another twelve months passed, my thoughts changed. The searches were becoming so much harder. Landscapes had changed beyond all recognition. We were all older and less fit.

And we were in a constant battle with Mother Nature, fighting her sprawling brambles and razor-sharp thickets.

Returning home wet, cold and despairing after yet another fruitless search, I rang Pat Green: 'Let me know when your next meeting is,' I said before adding, 'I'm only coming the once, mind.'

Inside the community hall, the air was thick with anger, frustration and bitterness. Some people had only recently lost their children. You could see the pain etched in their faces.

It took an age for me to be able to recognise the difference between them and me. One night, it came to me. We had all suffered a terrible loss but, unlike me, they had seen the body of their loved one. They had gazed, sadly, down on them in a morgue or held them closely as they took their last breaths. They had organised a funeral, laid them to rest, scattered earth or petals onto their coffin. Now, with that ritual behind them, they were working their way through the countless stages of grief – shock, anger, guilt, blame, denial. Eventually, they would come to acceptance and learn to live again.

I would never reach that stage.

Years later, grieving mum Sheila Dolton – who had also devoted her life to searching for her missing son, Jonathan, killed by a work colleague – summed it up brilliantly. She said: 'When you lose someone you have to fall apart to put yourself back together again, stronger and more resilient. But without a body, without a funeral, that's impossible. We are trapped in this "constantly falling apart" stage.'

I felt like a needle on a stuck record. In my heart, it would always be 8 February 1988.

* * *

The new group, Support After Murder and Manslaughter (SAMM), wanted to do wonderful things.

'We should help,' I suggested to John on the way home.
He nodded.

We agreed to join as volunteers for one year. More than twenty years later, we have still never missed a group meeting. John went on to work for the charity full-time as business development manager and we've both chaired the group over the years.

Members were passionate about making a difference. Steering committees sprang up, official agendas were followed, grants applied for and fundraising programmes released. Within twelve months there was a helpline up and running. We all took it in turns to man the phone – day or night – and set up a round-the-clock rota for supporting families in need.

On hearing of a local homicide, we'd brace ourselves, knowing our help would be needed. The police would pass on our details with the message that, at some point, in the early hours, in their darkest need, they could pick up the phone and speak to someone who understood exactly what they were going through.

Volunteers would visit them in their homes, talk them through the judicial process, walk into court with them, accompany them to inquests, support them through appeals and parole hearings. We listened while they vented their anger, frustration and pain and then, when there were no more words, we offered our shoulders for them to cry on.

For a long time, I thought it was a one-way system. Then, out of the blue, it came to me: *You idiot*, I thought, incredulously. *This is helping you just as much.*

It was keeping my mind focused, giving me something worthwhile to do. Also, it helped me realise that something good had come out of Helen's death. Yes, her life had been taken, but other people were being helped. That thought comforted me.

Stepping up our mission, we reached out to the CPS, probation services, the courts, the police, journalists, the Government. We gave presentations and told our stories to new recruits and trainees.

In December 1997, I joined hundreds of other families whose lives had been destroyed by murder in a rally at Trafalgar Square, organised by Mothers Against Murder and Aggression (MAMA). We marched to Downing Street to hand in a 'life should mean life' petition. Afterwards we lit candles and released white balloons with loved ones' names on.

At every opportunity, I shouted about the need for legal changes in cases of missing murder victims. For these heinous crimes against both the victim and their family to be recognised. But it was like playing a game of rugby on your own. I'd clear a part of the field then make a strong pass – only to find there was no one there to catch the ball. I could only watch, dismayed, as it soared through the air, hit the ground awkwardly, then rolled pitifully out of play.

The game was over.

There was no social media in those days, no way of getting your message out to thousands of people at the click of a button. I was making myself hoarse and getting nowhere. Little did I know, with the tenth anniversary of Helen's murder approaching, all that was about to change …

Chapter 13

'Tell me mum I'm here'

Suddenly, in the blink of an eye, Helen had been gone for a decade. Ten endless, tortuous years.

The idea of holding a memorial service came to me after one of my Tuesday novenas. Simms had denied us her funeral but he couldn't stop us celebrating her short, happy, life.

I designed Order of Service books, selected readings, asked a soprano singer to perform and arranged a buffet in the church hall for afterwards. The only thing we didn't have was a coffin.

I was so touched when more than 400 people who had known, loved and remembered Helen came along. Schoolfriends, Girl Guides, colleagues … they were all there, along with the friends I'd made through my work with Support After Murder and Manslaughter Merseyside and various championing groups.

The priest gave a lovely sermon: 'This isn't the final chapter of Helen's life, which is still unwritten, but the penultimate one,' he said.

As moving renditions of 'Pie Jesu' and 'Ave Maria' floated up to the rafters, I remembered the singer who had serenaded me in

Rome, more than eight years earlier. I'd been so sure we'd have found Helen by now.

Finally, it was my turn. I stood nervously, smoothed down my dress and then walked onto the altar. After taking a deep breath, I cleared my throat, then began to read. The unforgiving microphone amplified every jitter in my voice but I was determined to read this poem 'God's Lent Child' without breaking down:

> I'll lend you for a little while
> A child of mine, God said.
> For you to love the while she lives
> And mourn for when she's dead.
>
> It may be six or seven years
> Or forty-two or three
> But will you, till I call her back
> Take care of her for me?
>
> She'll bring her charms to gladden you
> And, should her stay be brief,
> You'll have her nicest memories
> As solace for your grief …

Glancing up, I could see hundreds of eyes glistening in the gloom. Mouths were twisted and lips bitten in the effort of holding back tears.

> Now will you give her all your love
> Nor think the labour vain
> Nor hate me when I come to take
> This lent child back again?

I poured my heart and soul into the final few lines – the response from the grateful parents, accepting this gift from God:

> We'll shelter her with tenderness
> We'll love her while we may
> And for the happiness we've known
> Forever grateful stay.
>
> But should thy angels call for her
> Much sooner than we planned
> We'll brave the grief that comes
> And try to understand.

As the last word died away, you could have heard a pin drop. The page crinkled softly as I lifted it from the lectern. 'God bless you, Helen,' I whispered. Then I slowly made my way down the steps and returned to my seat. Family members reached across to pat my arm or squeeze my shoulder.

Every member of the congregation had been given a candle to hold. Now, as lit tapers were distributed, 400 wicks were brought to life. One by one, pews were lit up by rows of flickering, joyful, tiny tongues of fire.

For sixty long seconds, as the flames danced, we remembered Helen. Precious memories flashed through my mind – her first day at school, tearing up her L plates, blowing out the candles on her twenty-first, twirling around in a new work outfit …

Afterwards, in the church hall, I thanked everyone for coming. Family photos of Helen appeared on a screen and songs from her favourite artists from the eighties were all played. She'd loved the Human League, Blondie, Spandau Ballet and Paul Young. Sadly, she'd only ever been to one concert – to see David Bowie in Manchester.

It all went so well. I'd hoped it would close a chapter in my life, enable me to move forwards.

But who was I kidding?

That night, I lay awake. Tears soaked the pillow as I realised I could hold as many memorial services as I liked but it changed nothing. My murdered daughter was still out there, somewhere. And until I found her and brought her home, I'd never rest.

Journalists had all covered the 'Ten Years of Pain' story. One local freelance writer placed my story with a women's magazine called *Bella*: 'An editor will ring you for a chat,' she said.

And so, a few evenings later, my phone rang. It was Fiona Duffy. 'Sorry to trouble you,' she said. 'I'm going through your story and just need one or two more details, please?'

We chatted for three hours. Fiona remembered my story from working on the *Liverpool Echo* a few years earlier. During a discussion of stories at an early morning news conference when the name Marie McCourt was mentioned, a colleague had whispered, 'Her daughter was murdered. She goes out digging to try and find the body.'

She told me, 'I was lost for words – appalled that in this day and age, a grieving mother was being left to search for the body of her murdered daughter, alone.'

Fiona moved to London soon afterwards to get married and start a new job. Now, three years on – and by a bizarre quirk of fate – my story had landed on her desk for editing. Once again, I thanked St Martha. 'I'll help you,' she said. That promise marked the start of a close friendship that is still going strong more than two decades later, resulting in the book you are reading now.

The magazine did a sterling job. A brilliant researcher called Kim Jones waded through the legal confusion around these ancient burial charges; why they were used in some cases and not others.

The CPS told her that it would 'not be in the public interest' to bring a prisoner serving a life sentence back to court for further charges.

'Says who?' I raged. 'Who are they to decide what's in the public interest or not? Why don't they ask the public?'

Kim also wanted to know why serial killer Robert Black had been charged with these crimes in addition to murder and kidnap. A former deputy chief constable involved with the investigation explained that, 'although it was easy to connect Black to where the children were taken and where their bodies lay, it wasn't cut and dry that he'd be found guilty. Additional charges were brought so that if he had got off the murder charges on a technicality, at least we had him on the other counts'.

It was, as far as I could see, a prosecution tactic – to ensure a conviction. I have no argument with that – they should throw the book at these evil killers. But surely they should be applied in all homicide trials where the body hasn't been found? The article in *Bella* triggered sympathetic letters from readers and a dramatic new development which would dominate our lives for the next thirteen years.

Rita Rogers – the favoured medium of the late Diana, Princess of Wales – had a column in *Bella* magazine. In 1999, a year after my story appeared, she invited me to her home – she was receiving information from a young woman that she needed to pass on.

An impressive thick cloud of raven-black hair framed her face and she gazed at me with dark, piercing eyes. She spoke for hours.

Some of the details were hard to hear. 'He lured her to the pub,' Rita said. 'He hit her. He dragged her upstairs. He raped her. And he strangled her. Afterwards, he wrapped her up in a carpet and put her in the boot of his car.'

I listened avidly. She was confirming everything I'd suspected.

'There was a grave open at the time, in a local churchyard,' Rita continued. 'Someone had been in the grave for a long time and another member of the family was due to be buried there two days later.

'She's telling me "He knew the grave was open",' she continued, recounting Helen's words. 'He knew it. He stove in the lid of the coffin and threw me in. I'm a second-hand Rose, I haven't even got me own grave.'

Rita's dark eyes twinkled. 'She's a bit of a character, your daughter, isn't she?'

Over two separate readings, Rita described the location of this grave and even the surname and initials on the headstone. 'She's there, she's there,' she insisted.

Merseyside Police agreed to look into it. There *was* a local grave open at the time. It had been dug on Tuesday, 9 February 1988 – the day Helen went missing – all ready for the funeral on the Thursday.

As pub landlord, Simms would have heard all the local gossip. Did he set out to kill Helen that day, knowing he had the perfect hiding place?

Naturally, the family who owned the plot (I gave my word that I would not identify either them or the grave) were shocked and upset, but wanted to help and agreed to co-operate with investigations.

While Fiona Duffy researched the next steps we'd need to take, John insisted I needed a holiday. After years of refusing to have a day out, let alone a vacation, from 1997 we'd started spending New Year abroad in Goa. New Year's Eve was Helen's favourite night of the year and I always found it so hard to cope with. It became our annual sanctuary, a place of peace from the relentless stress of trying to find my daughter.

Our only other holiday had been to Tunisia with Ann and Alan West. But there was a heartbreaking reason: Ann was poorly with cancer. We went to support them on what would be her last holiday.

My overriding memory is of Ann and I sat in the back of a speedboat, legs dangling in the water as it flew across the azure sea. We were having a ball until I spotted a shoal of glittering jellyfish.

'Lift your feet up!' I squealed.

I can still see her now, peeling with laughter as we clung to each other, yanking our legs out of reach. The sun was shining and the wind whipped her blonde hair. It was a precious, precious moment.

Sadly, Ann died the following February, in 1999, aged just sixty-nine. She was laid to rest beside Lesley Ann in her new secret grave.

I'd seen, first-hand, the pain Ann had endured right through to her dying day – campaigning to keep her daughter's killers, Myra Hindley and Ian Brady, locked up until they died. Thankfully, she had been successful.

Now, as the Millennium approached, more than ever I wanted to shut out the world. There was so much excitement over the dawning of a new century but, for me, nothing would change. My daughter was still murdered. And still missing.

* * *

As New Year's Eve celebrations rang out across the planet, John and I were thousands of feet in the skies, returning to Goa.

Earlier in the year, my sister Pat on her own visit there had heard about a psychic called Di who lived in the mountains. People travelled from far and wide to consult with her. She was renowned for finding long-lost items.

'Could she locate a dead body?' Pat asked.

A lovely woman called Fatima offered to take us to visit her. As we sat down on the stone floor of her house, I saw John's mouth twitch and shot him a warning look: 'Take this seriously, please, John,' I warned. 'No messing about.'

John was a bit of a sceptic so it was rewarding to see his eyes and mouth widen in astonishment as the reading progressed.

A translator explained my murdered daughter was still missing. Di, an elderly woman wearing traditional clothing, nodded before pacing up and down the flagged floor, barefoot. Then she started speaking.

'The man who did this is in prison,' said the translator.

I nodded. 'She has mentioned a man behind a desk. A big man smoking a cigarette. He made this man do it …'

John and I have mulled over this information so many times. Was someone else involved? Is this why Simms had refused to speak for all of this time?

Still, Di paced. Up and down, up and down. Her skirts swished, her feet softly scuffed the stone. Pad, pad, pad … She described our village with its traditional stone walls. A church at the top of the hill, a graveyard.

My breath quickened. I knew exactly where this was going. 'There was a grave open,' she said. She described the exact location; the row it was in, how many plots along. 'That is where your daughter has been hidden,' she concluded.

We left too stunned to speak.

Back at home, I returned to this particular cemetery, stowing my dowsing sticks discreetly inside my coat. Checking no one was around, I got them out and started dowsing. As soon as I approached the grave, the rods swung together dramatically as if attracted by magnets and crossed over right above the grave.

Another medium from the Isle of Man also brought us to this grave. And shortly afterwards, a young man in his twenties also travelled for miles to tell me about a recurring dream: 'It's a really windy night and I'm walking along with my head down. Suddenly, I can hear a girl's voice calling, "I'm here, I'm here."

Right at that moment, the pavement under my feet cracks open and a chasm appears.

'As I look down, there's a young woman deep down in this hole looking up at me.' Then he turned to meet my gaze. 'It's your daughter. I've seen the photos and it's your daughter,' he said. 'She's sitting up and wearing a long black skirt.'

I was baffled … until I remembered the bin bags that had gone missing from the pub. Had he wrapped her in them? Did they resemble a skirt?

'She's saying to me over and over, "I'm here",' he continued. '"Tell me mum I'm here."'

'I think it's a family grave,' he continued, as the blood in my veins turned to ice. He offered to show me. I found myself looking down at the exact same grave the three other mediums had led me to.

By now, my hopes were soaring. These were all signs. My daughter was there, she had to be. All we had to do now was get permission to look inside the grave.

* * *

While Fiona Duffy continued to consult experts in geophysics and ecclesiastical law, there was a separate issue I needed to raise with Jack Straw, Home Secretary.

The Human Rights Act, incorporating the European Convention on Human Rights into UK law, had gone onto the statute book in November 1998 and was due to come into force in October 2000.

Ever since Simms had been convicted, I'd written to the Home Office. I'd begged them to charge Simms with these other criminal offences, urged them to intervene, to change the law.

If you remember, the previous Home Secretary Michael Howard had assured my MP, John Evans, that Simms would never be released without showing remorse and revealing where Helen was. But, in the light of these new laws, how watertight was this promise? At some point, parole judges would start to look at his case in readiness for his eligibility for parole in 2004.

John and I had pored over the Home Office website regarding the release of lifers, searching for the word 'remorse'. It wasn't there. Anxiously, I'd fired off a letter to Jack Straw, asking for an urgent meeting. He responded, inviting me to a meeting in August 1999.

He listened to my plight and extended his sympathy. I also handed over a video recording of a BBC2 documentary on bereavement called *The Long Goodbye* that Michael and I had just taken part in; he promised to watch it.

'Simms won't be released until he shows remorse and says where your daughter is,' he said confidently.

I sat forward in my chair. 'But where does it say this in the law?' I asked. 'Please show me.'

He repeated his assurances.

Eventually, he stood up and edged his way towards the door. The meeting was clearly over. Defiantly, I remained seated.

'Mr Straw,' I repeated. 'Please show me where I can find the word "remorse" – or a word like it.'

'Mrs McCourt,' he said, slowly and determinedly. 'Simms will not be released until he shows remorse. And showing remorse means saying where your daughter's remains can be found.'

At this point, he opened the door. I gathered my handbag and walked towards him, determined to have one last try.

'Mr Straw,' I attempted again. 'You keep using this word "remorse". But where will I find it?'

He tried to hide his exasperation. 'Mrs McCourt, I have told you. Unless he shows remorse and tells us where your daughter's remains are, he will not be released.'

Then, for good measure, he added: 'He will die in prison.'

Reeling at the bluntness of his answer, I stared at him for a few moments, then nodded. 'Thank you, Mr Straw,' I said, satisfied. 'That's all I needed to know.'

I travelled back to Billinge cloaked in reassurance: until he did the decent thing, Simms was going nowhere.

* * *

A few weeks later, a letter arrived from Jack Straw's office thanking me for my visit. However, there was no mention of the topic we'd discussed or that vital word 'remorse'. Alarm bells started to ring.

I don't blame Jack Straw, I think, at the time of our meeting, he genuinely believed that the Home Office still had these powers to grant or refuse release. But the Human Rights Act was having huge implications on our laws. In just three years' time, in 2002, following a ruling by the European Court of Human Rights, the High Court would strip the Home Secretary of two powers: to set minimum terms and to overrule a recommendation by the Parole Board to release a lifer.

It would mean the unthinkable was about to happen: Simms would be eligible for parole. And it was only a matter of time before he got it.

Meanwhile, the grave highlighted by the mediums was taking up all our attention. Witness statements placed Simms close to the graveyard. There were no other graves open at the time. The gates had been open, allowing access for a car. Simms' clothes and car had been muddied. And a spade from the pub had been dumped.

By poring through research, we came across a case that heartened us in our bid to seek permission to investigate. In 1997, members of an indigenous tribe in Australia had arrived in Liverpool, demanding the return of a 150-year-old skull belonging to their ancestral leader.

Almost two centuries earlier, Yagar had been murdered by an

Englishman and his head taken. After years of searching, it had been traced to a grave in Everton.

Astonishingly, by using sophisticated Ground Probe Radar (GPR) equipment, experts managed to locate the head, remove it without disturbing any other bodies in the grave and return it to the rightful owners.

Through speaking with experts and professors involved with the case we found a sympathetic specialist willing to help.

Peter Simkins, of Oceanfix International in Aberdeen, agreed to travel down with his GPR equipment and 'scan' the grave for signs of an extra body. The device would travel across the grave and give readings directly to a laptop.

'We should know there and then,' he said.

Getting all the necessary legal agreements, permission from the family and supervision arrangements with the police took an age, but eventually, we were good to go. And then disaster struck.

On studying photos of the grave, Peter realised there was a raised border which would limit how far the machine could 'travel' to give an accurate reading. The chances of success had plummeted. At the crack of dawn, one morning, before anyone was awake the operation still went ahead but, as predicted, Mr Simkins couldn't 'see' inside as he'd hoped. However, conditions were ideal for an endoscopic camera to be inserted via a small borehole, he said. This would give us a definite answer either way, but as it involved penetrating a grave – even in a very small way – it was far more complicated. We needed the approval of the Church of England.

It took the best part of a year just to gather the information and evidence needed to apply to the Consistory Court of the Archdiocese of Liverpool, an ecclesiastical court. I was told the chancellor – a retired judge – would consider my application and make a decision.

Everyone we had to approach was in favour. The Home Office granted an exhumation order in June 2001.

The coroner gave written permission. The family, once again, gave written permission and the police were happy to oversee the project.

I'd been dreading the display, for a whole month, of a public notice at the back of the church with full details of our application, including my name. The court insisted this had to be done to rule out any possible objection. Surely, someone would read this and put two and two together? But no one noticed, objected or alerted journalists.

The court also suggested I have legal representation. *Bella* magazine paid for a consultation with a specialist barrister, who was happy to represent me. 'There has to be a good and proper reason acceptable to right thinking members of the public for an investigation or exhumation,' he said. 'Focus on factual evidence rather than the mediums,' he advised.

I had to provide a whole bundle of information from over the years: Simms' various appeals and his current application to the CCRC, my letter to him and his appalling reply, maps, details about the grave itself, permission from all parties, articles demonstrating my anguish. Finally, the date came through: 18 December 2001 – a week before Christmas. At the eleventh hour, we learned the cost of legal representation was far higher than we'd anticipated.

I had to either pull out or go ahead, representing myself. It was a terrifying prospect, but the court office assured me it would be informal. And I had my team behind me.

Come on, Marie, girl, I told myself, *you can do this.*

* * *

The hearing was held in the church itself, with tables and chairs set up just in front of the altar. The church was freezing – we all kept our coats on.

The Chancellor introduced himself as Judge Richard Hamilton. 'You can address me as "sir",' he said.

So much for informal.

Then he invited me to introduce my case. I'd had it all prepared but as soon as I mentioned Helen's name, I started to cry. 'It's the need to give her a burial and have a headstone to say who she was, that she lived and that she died,' I said tearfully, fumbling for a tissue. 'I need to find Helen's body or her remains … That's all they would be now,' I added sadly. 'And give her this last, final human dignity. It's the only thing, as a mother, I can do for her now.'

I explained there were rumours that Simms had placed my daughter in an open grave and how he'd boasted of hiding a body so well it would never be found.

Then the questions came. I answered them as best I could, but I'd never needed a barrister more. For a while, I sensed the Chancellor skirting around the issue. And then we came to it.

'How many mediums have you consulted with, Mrs McCourt?' he asked.

My heart sank. I'd wanted to concentrate on the actual evidence behind our application, but I had to answer honestly.

I hesitated. Did he mean those who'd had dreams? Those who called themselves healers? Clairvoyants, psychics? Did he mean in person, over the phone or by letter?

He was waiting for an answer. I honestly didn't know. There had been countless approaches over the years and I didn't want to underestimate.

'Erm,' I stammered. 'Thirty to fifty?'

I tried to read the expression that flashed across his face. Surprise? Disbelief? Disappointment? All I knew was that we were off to a bad start. And things were about to get a whole lot worse.

Judge Hamilton then suggested I call my first witness. This was ridiculous. We were in a chilly village church, not the Old Bailey.

I listened hopefully as Peter Simkins, then Detective Super-intendent Nick Housley, who was now involved with the case, stepped forward. They were brilliant, offering information and answering questions in detail.

Yes, the camera would give an accurate answer. Yes, the family who owned the grave were in favour. And, yes, the only way of knowing once and for all if Helen was there was for Simms to confess or the grave to be looked into.

We were all shivering so much that the Chancellor suggested moving to the back of the church, where it was warmer. But no sooner had we started up again than another interruption came: the choir needed to practise their carol singing.

In the church.

After some discussion, it was announced that, after lunch, the hearing would reconvene – in a local pub.

I stared in disbelief. Was this a joke? Did he realise my daughter had been murdered in a public house just a few hundred yards away? Before I could object, a barrister for the church then stood up. 'What is the likelihood of Helen being buried in the grave?' she began. 'Mrs McCourt would say several reasons …'

I looked around incredulously. It was like a barrister addressing a jury in a trial. And the person in the dock was me!

'We do know Helen's blood was in the car. Why would it be there unless she was moved after her death?' I turned to look at DS Housley in despair.

Why was she going over all this old evidence?

Judge Hamilton then read out a statement from a cemetery expert, who we had been led to believe would be present.

'Physical evidence militates against the body being there,' the Chancellor concluded.

I spent the lunchtime adjournment consulting frantically with my team: 'Where can I get a copy of that statement? Have I missed anything out? What do I need to add?' I asked. I also questioned the suitability of the hearing resuming in a pub, but was assured it was a private room and quite suitable.

It wasn't. The entire floor of the pub was open-plan. In the next bar, the clear clunk of pool balls on baize indicated a game was under way. Pints were pulled, jokes made.

There were also times when complete silence fell. When every word being uttered in this supposedly confidential court was crystal clear. I shifted anxiously. This was sensitive information involving a convicted murderer. Names were being freely mentioned. What if anyone overheard? What if word got back to any of Simms' cronies?

After a lengthy analysis of soil from the judge, I was invited to give my closing statement. By this time, I was a nervous wreck – I just wanted this to be over.

'I do believe that the circumstantial evidence warrants this action, not just for my sake but for the family the grave belongs to. This needs to be looked into so that once and for all, our minds can be put at rest. Thank you.'

I sighed with relief: we'd done it. I waited for him to tell us that he was now adjourning and would come back in time with a judgment.

To my surprise, he opened up a laptop and fiddled with an old-fashioned tape recorder. A copy of the *Big Issue* appeared on his desk.

'I am now going to deliver my judgment,' he declared.

What?

He then proceeded to read out a lengthy statement. (I was sent a copy afterwards. It was three pages long.) He couldn't possibly have written this during the adjournment. It meant that he had arrived at this court with his mind made up and simply added a line or two over his lunch.

'If I were to say this was one of the most remarkable cases ever to come before a consistory court no one would accuse me of exaggerating,' he pontificated. 'It arises out of a murder case which was in itself remarkable, in that the defendant Ian Simms was convicted of murder upon circumstantial evidence because the body was not found.'

I reeled as if I'd been slapped.

Remarkable? Try 'horrific', 'awful', 'tortuous'.

I imagined him holding court at his next dinner party: 'Do you know I presided over the most remarkable case recently ...'

And 'the body'?

'That's my daughter,' I wanted to scream. 'Her name is Helen McCourt. And her murder has destroyed me.'

On he continued, going to extra lengths to cast doubt on Simms' conviction: 'If Ian Simms was not guilty of the murder, there is no telling where the body of Helen McCourt is.'

What did he mean, 'if he's not guilty'? *I'm not here to question how safe the conviction is, I'm here to find my daughter's body.*

From then on, he referred to Simms as Mr Simms. Since being convicted, my daughter's killer had only ever been referred to by his surname. It's well known that convicted criminals lose their title so I objected to hearing him called 'Mr'.

At one point, he broke off to fiddle with his tape recorder before continuing.

It was clear that he was unhappy that we'd already carried out a GPR investigation on the grave, even though we'd been granted full permission from everyone concerned.

'For the benefit of future cases,' he said. 'I am going to suggest that any investigation of graves on consecrated land should take place through a specific field of the consistory court.'

That's us told.

Finally, with relish, he came onto mediums.

'This is a case which comes linked with the evidence of a medium. And that's a very important matter for a court such as this to consider.

'I was surprised to learn from Mrs McCourt that she has consulted no less than fifty mediums in the past apart from Mrs Rogers.'

My blood pressure rose.

I said thirty to fifty – and only because you pushed and pushed for a figure.

'I am not going to set out any diatribe against mediums,' he said, but then proceeded to do exactly that, referencing the Fraudulent Mediums Act 1951.

'I have found no case which suggests that the evidence of a medium is properly to be received by an ordinary court of law, and the very fact of that criminal act, still on the statute book, suggests that I should not do it.'

On and on he went. 'I was interested to read this month in the *Big Issue* a review of Rita Rogers' latest book, *Mysteries.*'

I was so distressed at this point that I can't remember if he actually opened the magazine or continued to read from his screen.

'The reviewer says,' he quoted, '"either she is a charlatan or mentally deluded in some way or – here's the biggie – it's true. Hmmmm."' Then he gave a theatrical pause. 'I think that puts it very well,' he added.

I looked around, bewildered.

Puts what very well?

Misery welled up inside me. I couldn't hold it back any longer, I started to cry. Behind me, someone placed a hand comfortingly on my shoulder. Now the tears had started, I couldn't stop them. As I breathed in, I gave a loud involuntary sob – my heart felt like it was breaking.

In his opinion, the judge concluded, there was a 99 per cent chance or probability that Helen's body was not buried in Billinge and suggested that allowing my application would 'open the floodgates' for others who might want to look inside a grave or a coffin.

I slumped forward in the chair, my head hanging despondently.

Please – make it stop.

'Except for the very strongest reasons and very solid prospects of success, such applications cannot be granted. It is with great regret for Mrs McCourt's situation that I […] cannot allow her petition here, which is dismissed.'

Graciously, he added that there would be no costs for me to pay. And then he was switching off his radio, packing up his laptop.

I remembered my manners so I tried to pull myself together. 'I'd – I'd like to thank everyone for their help today,' I sobbed, then I buried my face in my hands. Around me, chairs and tables were scraped away.

I'd never felt so small, so belittled. We'd been thrown to the wolves.

Informal hearing, my backside! Where was his compassion? Call himself a Christian?

The judge's words rang round and round in my head. How dare he compare my plight to that of someone curious to find out if a trinket had been buried with their great-aunt? I'd put myself through hell – and for what? He had already made his mind up before even walking into the church that day.

* * *

We had just fourteen days to appeal. Christmas was one week away. My head was spinning. Would we appeal against the decision or the circumstances in which the hearing was held? I didn't know.

Fiona trawled ecclesiastical law websites. We found countless other cases where full exhumations had been granted (not just endoscopic cameras inserted) and lists of pro bono barristers, community legal teams, public law projects.

I can do this, I can do this, I told myself, preparing to fire off letters.

And then I looked up at Helen's portrait and crumpled. 'I'm sorry, love,' I sobbed. 'I'm so, so sorry.'

The strength which had kept me going for years abandoned me. I felt like a puppet whose strings had been mercilessly cut. My throat constricted so tightly, I lost my voice completely. I could only whisper hoarsely.

John insisted we go ahead with our planned holiday to India and concentrate on getting me well. He nurtured me, made me rest, prepared nourishing food and coaxed me back to health. Finally, I was well enough to consider this properly but we were well out of time. And the longer we left it, the more our chances diminished. Plus, another chancellor, or even the Appeal Court, could come to exactly the same decision. I couldn't put myself through that again. Besides, it could cost me a fortune.

Reluctantly, I came to the decision: this had beaten me. For now. But this wasn't over. Not by a long shot.

Chapter 14

My faith is sorely tested

The humiliating rejection from the Consistory Court knocked the stuffing out of me, physically and emotionally. I felt as if I'd just done ten rounds with Mike Tyson. Long after my voice weakly returned, my emotions were still bruised and my nerves exposed. (Which made it even harder to learn, more than twelve years later, that it could all have been solved so simply, with kindness and understanding.)

Since Helen died, I have been blessed to meet with some considerate, compassionate people high up in our legal and political system. I have also encountered others who were, unfortunately, at the back of the queue when those qualities were being given out.

If I can urge one thing from my story, it is this: be kind and be fair. Show a little empathy. Please understand that when grieving families challenge judgments or laws we are not acting out of spite – to create extra work or flag up mistakes. We are highlighting that the hell we find ourselves in is being compounded by a serious wrong that needs righting.

A decision to challenge a law or judgment is not taken lightly. It is harrowing, daunting and costly in so many ways. But we do this because we have to. Not just for ourselves but for anyone else unfortunate enough to follow in our footsteps.

Put aside past judgments and case law. Simply ask yourself, 'Is this situation right or wrong? Is it fair or grossly unfair to the average law-abiding person in the street?' And if it's wrong and grossly unfair, let's put it right and make it fair. For all our sakes. Believe me, we will all benefit. You never, ever, imagine that something like this can happen to you. But we are living proof. It can, it does and it will.

Slowly, gingerly, I picked myself up and carried on, starting with a task I'd been putting off for ages – Helen's bedroom. It had become a shrine, untouched for so long now. When I needed to feel close to her, I'd sit on her bed and gather her dolls (including Emma Kate) and soft toys into my lap, or I'd rearrange her little statuettes or drawer of pretty soaps. Touch the things she once loved.

But no matter how much I vacuumed and dusted, the baby blue and cream décor that she'd so excitedly chosen now looked dated and tired: we needed to decorate.

Her clothes are still in the wardrobe and Emma Kate is still propped up on Helen's pillows, all these years on. But now the room is a fresh pastel green, with pretty curtains and cushions that I know she'd have loved.

It's still Helen's room, it will always be Helen's room.

I also continued to keep the closest of tabs on him – her killer. This is another thing that only families in our situation understand. Much as you want to shut out, turn your back on, never give another thought to the one person who has caused you so much pain, you can't. They will always, always be there. Either lurking on the periphery of your life, or when times are particularly bad, taking centre stage.

You are on constant alert, looking out for updates on their appeals, their misbehaviours, their applications for parole. Where are they now? What are they up to? Who are they befriending, filling with poison and lies? It's draining and it's exhausting.

I'd heard on the grapevine that Jane Hornby, the younger sister of Tracey who had had an affair with Simms first, was visiting him in prison. I also heard that Simms had produced two oil paintings while taking part in prison art classes.

One he'd given to his mum. The other – of a young woman dancing – to Jane, who hung it above the fireplace in her shared flat.

'Please try and get a photo of it,' I begged my source. 'There might be some clues in it as to where Helen is.'

They did better than that. Twelve months later, when I'd forgotten all about it, there was a knock at the door.

'I've got the painting for you,' this person said.

Apparently, Jane had moved out, leaving the painting behind. Her flatmate didn't want it either.

'It's yours,' my good samaritan said.

There was no way it was coming into my home. I carried it into the garage then balanced it against the wall. With trembling hands, I peeled back the old sheet it was wrapped in.

It was a fair-sized canvas – twenty-four inches across and thirty inches high. I peered at the picture, making out an image of a woman dancing the can-can. It was a direct copy of the iconic Toulouse Lautrec painting of dancer Jane Avril at the Moulin Rouge.

Beneath the painting was a mini portrait of an evil-looking man and the inscription 'Simo' – that's what Simms used to be known as among his cronies.

Focusing on the woman's face, a chill crept up my spine. As recognition dawned, I gasped. It was Helen, as plain and as clear as looking at a photograph. He'd given her brassy, blonde hair, but there was no mistaking the face – the piercing blue eyes, the full lips.

As my eyes took in the rest of the image, I clapped my hands over my mouth in horror. One stockinged foot was high-kicking into the air. But on her other foot there was clearly a shoe.

Only one of Helen's boots was ever found.

Had he recreated on canvas his last image of Helen?

As my heart quickened, I leaned against the wall for support, taking deep breaths. Then I noticed purple and red markings under the dancer's right eye. *Are they smudges?* I wondered, fetching my glasses. As the image became clearer, my stomach turned: they were blood and bruises.

Forensic evidence had indicated Helen was hit at least twice in the face, causing blood to splash onto the walls. Bile churned in my stomach. 'No, no, no ...' I said. Grabbing the sheet, I covered up this monstrosity then turned it to face the wall. *There*, I thought. *That's what I think of you and your sick painting.*

I vowed it would never, ever come into my house. But as well as disgust, I felt a sense of triumph – power, even – in now having this. Only Helen's killer would have known these details – the injury to her face, the missing shoe. He'd confessed on canvas.

When loading his brush with paint he could never have imagined his 'masterpiece' ending up in the garage of his victim's mother.

Shakily, I went inside and phoned Paul Acres, who had been Senior Investigating Officer on Helen's case: 'There's something you need to see,' I said. When he arrived, I directed him to the painting, then waited for him in the living room.

I scrutinised him as he walked in a few minutes later, trying to read any reaction in his face. For a split second his eyes flicked up to Helen's portrait on the wall before turning to me.

I knew it.

'It's Helen's face, isn't it, Paul?' I asked.

He nodded.

Simms might have given her brassy blonde hair but there was no mistaking that face.

I've had that painting analysed over the years; first, for clues as to where Helen could be. And, second, for my submission to the Parole Board that this man should never, ever be released.

You see, by 2001 – three years before he even became eligible to apply for parole – we learned that the Parole Board's Mandatory Lifer Panel would shortly be looking at Simms' case to consider lesser security and eventual release.

I wrote to the Parole Board, begging them not to release Simms until he revealed where my daughter was. Looking back at a *Daily Mail* interview, I'm shocked at my strength of feeling and the words that poured from my mouth.

'Don't Let This Killer Out to Dance on My Daughter's Grave,' was the resulting headline. It's a macabre, but powerful quote that I have used many times since.

As mentioned earlier, Simms had already applied to the CCRC, an independent body set up to assess whether convictions were safe. He was contesting the DNA evidence and claiming police told lies. However, from where I was standing, Simms hadn't exactly been behaving in prison. The police were still trying to make regular visits to Simms to ask where Helen's body was, but he was refusing to see them. Again, wouldn't an innocent man at least try to co-operate?

In the late nineties they were told that a planned visit to Wormwood Scrubs was unable to proceed due to 'a disruption' on the wing. Ian Simms had attacked a female prison officer, 'rendering her almost unconscious', police told me. I'll never forget those four words. As a result, all female staff had been removed from the wing and Simms transferred to Long Lartin prison in Gloucestershire – and he would never again be guarded by a female officer.

Then, in June 2003, an article appeared in the Scottish edition of the *News of the World*, saying Simms had attacked a fellow inmate in Durham's Frankland Prison in a row over which TV programme to watch.

He had slit the prisoner's throat so badly with a homemade blade that he was 'almost decapitated'. The inmate required eighty stitches and five pints of blood.

In a panic, I rang probation services: 'If other prisoners retaliate and attack him, I might never find out where Helen is,' I said. 'He'll take his secret to the grave.'

They investigated and reported back that the story was wrong – it wasn't Simms who had carried out the attack but another prisoner.

White-lipped with fury, I rang the *News of the World* editor: 'You want to be careful what you are putting in your paper,' I said flintily.

But his answer floored me: 'I can assure you we have no problem with that story, Mrs McCourt,' he said. 'We know what happened and every word is true.'

Again, probation services promised to investigate. A few days later, I learned that Simms had been moved to another prison. That told me all I needed to know – *it was him all right.*

That same year, I learned that Simms' application to the CCRC had been thrown out. Not only were there no grounds for referring his case to the Court of Appeal, but as a result of rechecks, the forensic evidence was now even stronger.

Back at the trial, the odds on the strongest samples of blood recovered from Simms' clothing, in the pub and car, were 126,000 times to one more likely to have come from a child parented by myself and Helen's father. These odds now stood at 9.5 million to one. (Later, in 2016, they would become a staggering billion to one).

Despite all his approaches to courts and investigative journalists, his claims of having dossiers and evidence that would clear his name, Simms had never once been given even permission to bring a claim.

'Maybe now he will come to his senses and realise that the only way to be released is to tell me where my daughter is,' I told journalists.

Simms, however, had other ideas. His solicitor released a statement saying, 'There is no limit to the number of applications that can be made to the commission and my client is as passionate and determined as he ever has been to prove his innocence.'

Here we go again, I thought.

* * *

Over the years so many people have asked, 'Why? Why won't he say?'

Who knows? Or why indeed? Maybe he feared reprisals from inmates or worried about the reaction from his family when it became clear he'd been lying for so long. Maybe he swore blind innocence for so long that he truly came to believe it. Maybe he was hoping to get compensation for wrongful imprisonment if the body never turned up. Maybe he was covering up something even more sinister. More bodies, perhaps?

Let's remember that Ian Brady and Myra Hindley denied they had killed Keith Bennett and Pauline Read for more than twenty years before finally confessing to their murders. What made them keep quiet all that time? Murderers who hide bodies are not normal people. Who knows how their brains work?

In 2004, Simms became eligible for parole. Back then, families weren't routinely informed as they are now (although some would argue that there are still huge improvements to be made) but I eventually learned in June that it had been a paper hearing and he had been turned down. Two months later, I was shocked to learn that he had asked for an oral hearing with the entire Parole Board.

Oh, has he now?

I've no idea whether that even happened. There's a lot of confusion around those early parole dates because he was applying to the CCRC at the same time arguing for an appeal. Looking back, I didn't know whether I was coming or going. I gather that in 2005, his second appeal to the CCRC was turned down and, in November 2006, a scheduled paper parole hearing was due to take place. I had to wait a week to discover that it hadn't gone ahead as there weren't enough officers available. Heaven only knows what that meant. In 2007, I gathered that yet another paper hearing had been turned down. He wouldn't be eligible to apply again for at least another two years. Once again, I hoped and prayed that this would be the catalyst for him – it wasn't.

Still, I campaigned, told my story and helped victims. Soon afterwards, a woman called the SAMM Merseyside helpline informing me that I had been nominated for— 'Can I stop you there,' I interrupted. 'This is a helpline for bereaved families. You are preventing a needy call from getting through.'

'No, wait, please,' she said. 'I'm genuine. You've been nominated for an award.'

I was stunned to be told I'd been shortlisted for the Inspirational Woman of the Year award run by Wellbeing of Women (a women's health research charity) and the *Daily Mail*.

Tears ran down my face as she read out John's entry. 'She deserves this award for the work she does with victims' families – despite her own loss with Helen – the amount of time she gives to other families in a similar situation and for the unstinting twenty-four hours a day she will be there for others.

'She helps people see there is light at the end of the tunnel. She is my strength as well.'

John and I went to a gala dinner at the Dorchester in London for the final. I didn't win overall, but I was presented with the North-West Woman of the Year award by Dame Esther Rantzen. And I won £100 vouchers to spend in Marks & Spencer. It was years since I'd been shopping. I'd stopped after losing Helen …

I've gone on to win more gleaming glass plaques over the years – including an Outstanding Achievement award from the *Liverpool Echo*; a Victim Care Award from MAMA; a Pride of St Helens Award from the *Liverpool Daily Post* and, the one I'm most proud of, The Queen's Award for Voluntary Service (the equivalent of an MBE) which was presented to SAMM Merseyside. John and I have also attended two of the Queen's garden parties both for my work with SAMM Merseyside and my campaign for Helen's Law. On each occasion, dressed in our finery, John has taken great delight in hailing a black cab outside Euston Station and saying 'Buckingham Palace, please' to the driver!

Still we went on campaigning, searching, hoping, living as best we could. Helen would have been delighted to see Michael settle down, marry and have two beautiful children. They have brought such joy into my life.

For years, I hadn't even put a tree up at Christmas. But suddenly, we were erecting a giant, light-up Santa on the garage roof especially for the little ones. The neighbours must have thought I'd gone mad.

SAMM Merseyside's annual memorial service in Liverpool Cathedral was also a well-established December feature. Hundreds of families came along to hear their loved one's name read out and see a candle lit in their honour. It was a lovely way to remember them at such an emotional time of the year. We tell all our families, 'There's a land of the living and a land of the dead. The bridge between them is love. It is our only survival.'

The following year, 2008, marked the twentieth anniversary of Helen's murder. I went to see our parish priest with a special request and was thrilled when he granted permission. Simms might have denied me Helen's funeral but he couldn't stop me putting her name in the churchyard where she belonged.

For Helen's birthday that year we unveiled a marble seat in St Mary's churchyard. Carved from a single block of marble granite, it's beautifully simple, with an inscription on the back:

*In Loving Memory of Helen McCourt, died 9 February 1988,
aged 22 years.
Loved Every Minute Missed Every Day.*

The company made no charge for the delivery or installation all the way from China. The young man who ran the firm remembered Helen from his school days. It was such a touching gesture.

The seat was both a memorial to my daughter and a thank you to the villagers who had searched for her and supported me. Now, when they visited the graves of their loved ones, they would have somewhere to sit and think about them.

Hundreds came to the unveiling and blessing ceremony. As the sun shone down from an azure sky, we released forty-three balloons, one for each of her birthdays, and five white doves to symbolise her spirit soaring to the heavens.

Twelve years on, I'm still touched to see parishioners pat the marble fondly on their way into or out of mass.

Flowers and tributes would appear on its smooth, cool surface on special occasions. John and I started putting up a little Christmas tree each year with fairy lights next to it.

Coming out of midnight mass, the first thing I'd see was her tree twinkling in the darkness. 'Happy Christmas, Helen,' I'd say, leaning down to kiss her photo.

That service gave me courage to prepare for the biggest parole hearing, yet, at Garth Prison, Leyland, Lancashire, in April 2009 – twenty-one years after Helen's murder. Changes in parole laws meant that I could now attend and read out a Victim Impact Statement (VIS) to parole judges – one of the first people to do so.

'I'm going to confront him and ask, "Where is my daughter?"' I told reporters.

Of course, I didn't get the chance. Simms refused to attend. 'He's a coward and a bully,' I declared afterwards. As far as I know, Simms could have been present whenever I spoke. He has always chosen not to be there.

Despite having my statement for weeks, his legal team objected to one passage in my statement – just ten minutes before I was due to read it. I had to strike it out or face not being allowed to give my statement at all. Even now, I'm shocked and disgusted that they did this.

Reading out a VIS is already incredibly traumatic. It revives all that pain. Reopens that wound. Objections and upsets are the last things you need. Two weeks later, I was notified he'd been turned down.

Thank God.

The year 2009 was also the year we lost Mum. She died, broken-hearted, that her adored granddaughter had still not been laid to rest. Only recently a medium told me that Helen had been there, smiling with arms outstretched, to welcome her as she passed over. That thought comforted me.

Still, all I wanted was to bring my daughter home. Occasionally, we'd have flashes of hope. In February 2011, on the very anniversary of losing Helen, I turned on the radio to hear a woman's body had been found by workmen on a building site.

Greater Manchester Police confirmed that Helen McCourt was on their list of possible names.

My hopes soared even higher on learning the body had been wrapped in carpet. Isn't that what Rita Rogers had said? What that car passenger had seen?

This could be it, I thought. *Finally, we could be bringing her home.*

I'd still carry on with my voluntary work supporting other families but now I could lay my daughter to rest. Tend her grave, start to live again … sleep soundly.

DNA tests and dental record comparisons seemed to take forever, involving trips to Scotland Yard.

Finally, the phone call came.

'Yes?' I asked.

I held my breath and closed my eyes.

'I'm so sorry, Marie,' said the voice. 'It's not Helen.'

I doubled over, winded. It felt as if an ice-cold vice had been clamped around my heart – and now it was squeezing … slowly and cruelly.

'Thank you for letting me know,' I managed to whisper. Gently, I placed the handset back in the receiver. Then I cried. I cried for myself and that poor girl's family. Yes, they'd be distraught. Grief-stricken. But they had her back, she was home.

Over the years, more families had joined Winnie Johnson and me in this purgatory. We knew our loved one had been murdered but we couldn't lay them to rest.

When I learned Winnie had cancer, I urged her to have a memorial service for Keith, as I had done for Helen. 'It will help you and keep publicity going,' I said.

I was among the 300 people who attended the service at Manchester Cathedral. We watched as she was helped to the cathedral lectern to light a candle next to her son's photograph. Then she wept as she told us: 'I'm Keith's mother. I've lived through this life knowing he is on those Moors. I just want him back.

'I'll do anything, go anywhere for him. As long as I know

one day, I'll be grateful. I hope he's found before I am dead. All I want out of life is to find him and bury him. I just wish he is found before I go.'

Every heartbreaking word resonated with me.

Afterwards, I asked cold case police (officers who focus on an unsolved criminal investigation that remains open) to focus on finding Keith before focusing on Helen: Winnie's need was greater. Meanwhile I continued to mention Winnie and Keith in every interview I gave.

On Saturday, 18 August 2012, while on a country walk with friends in Yorkshire, my mobile rang. It was a reporter asking for a quote, 'following the sad death of Winnie Johnson last night'.

John heard me gasp and caught me as my legs gave way.

'No, no,' I moaned softly.

I knew she was gravely ill but the news knocked me for six. 'That poor, poor woman,' I cried. Going to her own grave without finding her murdered child had been her greatest fear. And now, forty-eight years after Keith was murdered, it had happened.

I cried even harder when I realised: 'That's me. That's my fate.'

I hope Winnie and her family can understand that I simply wasn't strong enough to attend her funeral. Instead, I lit a candle and prayed fervently that both she and her little boy had found peace together. I cried on reading that Keith's broken NHS glasses, patched up with blue tape, were buried with her in her coffin – it was all she had of him.

Reading some of her quotes in the newspaper obituaries was heartbreaking – I could have written them myself.

'I will never give up looking for him,' she told author Bernard O'Mahoney in letters that he published in a book titled *Flowers in God's Garden* before she died. 'I can't let Keith lie in the unmarked, grotesque grave his murderers chose. Can't people understand the pain that causes my family and me?'

Yes, Winnie, I can.

'I just keep hoping Keith is found before I go to my own grave. I want to go knowing my son has been taken from the place his murderers buried him. I want him laid to rest in a grave of my family's choice.

'I need my Keith to be returned from those bleak, cold and windy moors that look down on me from almost everywhere I turn in my home town of Manchester.

'My heart is torn from me … I can't die yet. I have to find my boy.'

* * *

The following year, 2013, marked the twenty-fifth anniversary of Helen's murder – a quarter of a century without my daughter. It didn't seem possible that she'd now been dead longer than she'd been alive. Yet the grief was still so raw, like having an open wound that never heals.

I organised a memorial mass followed by the emotional release of lanterns outside St Mary's Church. I watched them float into the sky. 'We're still looking, Helen,' I assured her. 'Hold on, love.'

Next, we braced ourselves for another oral parole hearing – again at Garth Prison. No sooner had we got over one than we had to prepare for the next, it seemed. It was due to take place in March but it was another six months before a date was set – for 23 September 2013. (Meanwhile, there had been yet another paper hearing in 2011.)

I was told that this time my submission would be via video link.

'I don't think so,' was my steely response. 'I will be there in person to read out my statement.'

I won that battle only to fight another on the day itself when the panel announced that John couldn't come in with me. I stood my ground: 'I need my husband beside me,' I insisted. 'There are a lot of reporters all waiting to speak to me and this will be the first thing I'll be telling them,' I added, pointedly.

After a few minutes' discussion they said he could sit behind me. My eyes flashed angrily. 'My husband will sit *beside me,*' I repeated through gritted teeth.

Finally, I was giving my statement – with John beside me. But how many others were forced to go through that ordeal alone – with no one beside them?

But the worst was yet to come. For a full two weeks, I was on the edge of my seat – unable to eat, sleep, or concentrate on anything.

What will they decide? What will they decide?

Finally, on the fourteenth day, the phone rang.

'Yes?' I replied. Anticipating bad news, my throat was tightening by the second. It was like a boa constrictor was silently, stealthily, wrapping itself around me, then slowly crushing my windpipe and voice box.

'I'm sorry, Mrs McCourt,' the representative said. 'But Simms didn't attend for his part of the hearing so it didn't go ahead.'

My grip on the phone tightened. 'What?' I asked. 'What did you say?' I was shaking so much, my voice wobbled uncontrollably. 'I haven't slept in two weeks, I haven't eaten in two weeks and you're telling me now that his hearing didn't go ahead? This is wrong, this is appalling. How can they do this?'

I was told that Simms' parole hearing would now go ahead in January 2014 – while John and I were building our strength up in India.

Before then I needed to focus on another vital matter. For the last thirteen years, the issue over the grave had been eating away at me. Occasionally, when no one was around,

I'd head up there with my dowsing rods. And I always got a positive reading.

It wasn't just me who felt that this was unfinished business. That summer, Detective Chief Superintendent Tim Keelan, who was now looking after the case, had approached me.

'Marie, we've been looking at the grave situation again,' he said. 'The family don't want to leave this for their children to sort, they'd like to know one way or another.'

I asked my priest for advice. 'I can't understand why they don't allow it,' he said. 'Let me talk to the vicar.'

Not only did the vicar support us but a new Chancellor, known for being compassionate, had been appointed to the diocese – it was worth another go.

This time, things couldn't have been more different. We put all the papers together and sent them off, along with a fee of £250 to cover costs.

Within days, we had our answer. Permission was granted – not just for cameras but for a full exhumation on Wednesday, 16 October 2003. The feeling was unanimous: this needs to be settled once and for all and an exhumation is the only way of doing it.

* * *

The night before the exhumation, I lit my candle and said my novena. Finally, were my prayers about to be answered? I don't think I'd ever felt so hopeful, so positive, of getting a definite result.

I never slept a wink that night. My stomach churned, my hands trembled uncontrollably.

The day of the exhumation dawned wet and windy. I felt so sorry for the forensic teams working in those horrendous conditions. The police explained they would seal the area off with tents and work within them. They were as discreet as they possibly could be, but of course, it didn't stay quiet for long. Someone must have tipped off the papers as, suddenly, reporters and photographers poured into the village. My phone rang off the hook, but I let the answer machine kick in.

Michael and John headed up there but everyone agreed it was best if I stayed at home until there was news.

A friend from the gym volunteered to come and sit with me. (I'd taken up yoga then Pilates in my quest to stay fit, well and healthy for Helen.) Outside the rain had become torrential. I followed the sound of ominous drips to find the porch was leaking.

Hours crawled by. John promised he'd come back as soon as he could with news. It was dark when he finally pulled onto the drive.

Choked by hope, I ran to the door. Was this it? Was our nightmare finally over? Was our girl coming home?

It took a few moments for me to register that his head was shaking, that an expression of sheer, abject misery had settled across his features.

Gently, he took my arm. Dazed, I allowed myself to be steered to the settee. My friend slipped away. A deep sigh emanated from every fibre of his being.

'She's not there, Marie,' he said.

My brain was whirling with questions – *what? WHAT? Are they sure? Definitely sure?*

I let out a long, shaky exhalation of breath. Beyond shocked, I was stunned. Devastated. Crushed.

How? How could we have all got it so wrong?

We sat in miserable silence, listening to the sound of the rain thundering onto the roof of the conservatory. Then I stood up.

'I want to go down there,' I said.

Uncertainty clouded John's face. 'Marie, I'm not sure it's a good idea,' he began. But I interrupted him.

'I need to go down there and thank every one of the officers who have worked on this,' I told him.

The wind was brutal as we struggled along the footpath into the churchyard. It was just like that night twenty-five years ago when this nightmare first started. I pulled the hood up on my purple raincoat to shield my face from cameras and rain and clung to John.

Michael steered me into a tent out of the biting wind and someone put a hot chocolate into my shaking hands. Around us, the canvas tent frame was being whipped relentlessly by the wind. 'This is going to go,' someone shouted above the noise of the poles rattling.

We'd just moved into a police caravan when the tent collapsed. DCS Keelan came up the steps, dripping with rainwater. He looked bereft – they all did. 'Mrs McCourt,' he began. 'As you know, we've completed the exhumation. The grave matches official burial records. Only two skeletal remains have been found – Helen's not there.'

My heart went out to him. I nodded to show I'd understood.

'Thank you,' I told them. 'Thank you … for everything. I'm so grateful.'

The windscreen wipers thrashed back and forth as John drove us home. Neither of us spoke. Occasionally, I shook my head as the disbelief hit me all over again. Three mediums had led me there, for heaven's sake – not to mention the young man who dreamed Helen was there.

But she wasn't, she never had been.

It was over.

Plodding wearily inside, I fought back an overwhelming urge to violently kick the porch buckets into next week. Rage and spite rose within me as my eyes fell on the statue of St Martha. 'Well, St Martha,' I hissed. 'You're sacked! I will never light a candle to you again. And I will never ever pray to you again.' Blinded by tears, I stormed from the room.

After the trial, the local paper had printed the novena that had kept me going, in full, in response to requests from readers. But where had it got me?

I spent the next two days swallowing my heartache and answering the phone to reporters.

'Yes, it was horrific to think she could have been in someone else's grave, but this disappointment is even harder. Sadly, our torment goes on. We're right back where we started – at the bottom of the barrel.'

I also expressed my thanks and gratitude to the family for allowing us to check. I felt so sorry that they'd been put through this, but at least we now knew for definite: there was no more doubt.

That weekend, we'd been due to stay with friends, Katrine and Ian, in Garstang. 'We can cancel if you want, love,' John said. 'I'm sure they'd understand.'

But I shook my head. 'I have to get away from this house – and that phone,' I said firmly, as it rang yet again.

It was a relief to slip away from Billinge. On Saturday night, Katrine asked if John and I would mind slipping out quietly for mass next morning.

'I'll have a nice breakfast when you're back,' she said.

I stiffened in my chair. 'Don't worry,' I said bitterly. 'We won't be going tomorrow.'

She looked from me to John, bewildered.

'But, Marie,' she said, 'you always go to mass.'

'Used to,' I corrected her through clenched teeth. 'Not anymore.'

I meant every word. I'd had it with God and St Martha and the whole lot of them. For more than a quarter of a century I'd prayed and prayed and it had got me nowhere. They weren't listening. My faith had been the only thing keeping me going all this time, but now I felt abandoned. I'd never felt so let down and alone.

Turning out the bedside lamp, I was still adamant. Tomorrow morning, I'd have my first Sunday lie-in – the first of many. But 4am found me wide awake, staring at the ceiling. My mind was reeling.

How could I deliberately not go to mass? It was a mortal sin.

At 6.30am, John stirred.

'I've changed my mind,' I confessed. 'I'm still angry, but how can I not go to church? How can I not pray to St Martha anymore?'

He smiled as he kissed my cheek – he's become used to my U-turns over the years. As mass started there we were, at the back. I gazed up at the crucifix of Jesus on the cross.

I'm back again, God.

After the readings, then the Gospel, the priest stepped up to the pulpit for his homily.

'Haven't we all prayed for something we have dearly, dearly wanted?' he began.

My ears pricked up immediately.

'We've all done it, haven't we?' he asked, looking around earnestly at the congregation. He seemed to be looking straight at me.

'Sometimes our prayers are answered. But sometimes they are not,' he continued, softly.

I listened, transfixed. His words wrapped themselves around me, comforting me, soothing me, like a soft blanket.

'It can be so painful when that happens. When you've prayed so hard for something and don't get it.'

His words were reaching into my very soul. By now, hot tears were spilling down my face and neck. I fumbled in my bag for a tissue for my streaming nose. Of course, there wasn't one.

'But there is always a reason,' he said. 'Maybe it's just not the right time? Maybe what we want so badly could be harmful for us.'

Helplessly, I dabbed at my eyes and nose with my sodden sleeve. My shoulders shook helplessly as silent sobs convulsed me.

He was right, he was right.

'Don't give up and don't lose faith,' the priest urged. 'Keep praying. God will always listen to you. One day, your prayers will be answered ...'

I was so glad we were tucked away at the back of the church so no one could see or hear my emotional outburst. As the tears ebbed away, a feeling of calm settled over me. I was meant to come to mass today to hear that message. God hadn't abandoned me at all, He was right here. Beside me. Holding me up. It was like the sun finally emerging from behind dark, heavy clouds.

Outside, after mass, the priest held out his hands to me.

'Hello, there,' he said, warmly. 'I haven't seen you here before.'

I explained we were visiting friends.

'Father,' I said, falteringly. 'I want you to know your sermon has helped me so much this morning.'

Then I poured it all out. How our hopes of finding Helen had been so cruelly dashed. How my faith had been tested like never before.

The priest listened, nodding. He remembered the case, he extended his condolences. 'Please don't give up,' he urged. 'Your prayers will be answered. It may not be in the way you want, but it will always be done in the best way possible for everyone.'

Over the years, those words have come to make so much sense. I've accepted now that, in some strange way, Helen had to go missing in order to highlight a terrible injustice. I was meant to fight this battle for her. And I am still convinced she will be found even if it's not in my lifetime. But my daughter *will* be found and *will* be laid to rest.

The following Tuesday, I gathered my candles and lit them one by one in front of St Martha's statue. There was something important I needed to do – and I needed her now more than ever.

Chapter 15

The fight begins

What now? Those two words swirled round and round my head like annoying, buzzing insects. If I tried to ignore them, they just got louder.

'At least we, and this other family, know now that Helen is not there,' John kept saying. 'We can cross it off and move on.'

But to what?

After all these years we were back to square one. It was like a sick game of snakes and ladders; we'd been doing so well only to find ourselves slithering helplessly down the longest snake on the board. We were right back at the start. Would I even have the strength to throw the dice, let alone haul myself up the next ladder?

I gazed up at Helen's portrait, hoping for inspiration. I'd told reporters I'd carry on fighting, continue to try and put pressure on Simms to tell me, once and for all, to end this misery and say where she was.

I was talking the talk, but deep down, I was broken – I didn't know what to do. I was seventy and had recently been diagnosed with osteoporosis. How could I go back to scrabbling around fields and sewage pipes and risk breaking a hip if I stumbled?

We also had Simms' adjourned parole hearing to prepare for. I'd been adamant that the Parole Board should know all about the exhumation – the lengths we were still being forced to go to because of Simms' cruel actions. Afterwards, I contacted my victim liaison officer: 'I would like to amend my Victim Impact Statement,' I told her.

The statement itself couldn't be changed but it was agreed that I could attach an addendum. Writing about this crushing disappointment tore me apart all over again. Finally, it was sent. The adjourned parole hearing, involving Simms, took place while John and I were in India. (I'd presented my submissions back in September, remember, when Simms hadn't shown up for his hearing.) Thankfully, Simms was turned down.

But we couldn't get too complacent. Another Parole Board hearing was looming just around the corner in 2015. Once again, I was determined to give my statement in person.

At least if you're in the room you can make an impact: walk in with dignity, place a photo of your loved one on the table, make sure judges hear every single painful word. On a video screen, it's all too easy for them to switch you off afterwards.

Out of sight, out of mind.

* * *

In April 2015, the representative for the Secretary of State met us in the car park of Garth Prison, where the previous parole hearing had been held. But rather than heading for Category B Garth, we were steered towards Wymott, the Category C prison next door.

I stopped walking. 'Hang on, where are we going?' I asked.

She looked uncomfortable. 'I'm sorry, Marie, but this is the prison he's now at,' she said.

I stared at her in utter disbelief. Simms had been downgraded to a less secure prison and I hadn't even been told. He was clearly moving through the system – being prepared for open prison and eventual release.

I shook with both grief and fury while giving my statement. It was just a matter of time now before he was granted parole. I had to stop him. But how?

Back at home, I rang Fiona Duffy to fill her in: 'I've shouted until I'm hoarse about how unfair this all is,' I said. 'Everyone agrees this is awful, this is wrong. But nothing happens. All they care about is human rights for these prisoners. But what about my Helen's right to life – and my right to bury her? Aren't they the most basic human rights of all? Shouldn't we all be shouting for this?'

(Even more frustratingly, once again – there was a delay on Simms' side. It was delayed until the summer, then the autumn, then January 2016. Once again, our one and only holiday, a chance to recharge our batteries for the rest of the year, would be overshadowed by the worry of yet another parole hearing.)

I was on a roll now. 'Surely, if prisoners knew they would never be released unless they revealed where their victims were, they'd start to co-operate.'

Suddenly, I had an epiphany. I sat bolt upright. 'Wait!' I cried. 'What if I start a petition asking people to back me? If enough people signed, the Government would have to do something, surely?'

Fiona agreed. 'It's a great idea, but this is a huge area of legislation. We have just one chance to do this so we need to get it right first time. We need to know everything there is to know about old burial laws, life tariffs and parole requirements. Let me go away and do some research and come back to you.'

Fired up now, I asked John to order more ink and paper. I genuinely believed I'd be walking the streets with old-fashioned forms on a clipboard asking people to physically sign their name. It was a revelation to learn that a petition could now be hosted online with signatures added digitally within seconds. But we'd need to get the message out to thousands of people and that meant getting to grips with social media.

Just setting up a Facebook account took days – there was so much to get my head around.

What's a wall? I wondered. *And why are people showing photos of their dinners?*

Persevering, I learned how to request friends, like and share posts, pick out emojis, spot scams and ignore tripe. But some aspects still baffle me now!

Through poring over research, Fiona discovered Graham McBain, a retired lawyer and expert in English legal history who, by chance, had written a paper on the need for reforming burial laws. He was an absolute godsend in explaining the current laws, referring us to heavy law books in big libraries to find details of significant cases where these laws had been applied (for instance, Regina v Hunter – a relevant case from 1974) and suggesting where we needed to ask for change.

Graham explained that unlawfully preventing a coroner from inspecting a corpse was a very serious offence back in the twelfth century when coroners – officers of the Crown – investigated violent deaths to establish a cause of death. If someone hid a body, thereby obstructing the coroner, the entire town would be fined, often ruinously. As a result, villagers would do everything in their power to apprehend a killer and produce the corpse. This then led to a further common-law offence of unlawfully preventing the burial of a corpse.

'So, by failing to disclose the whereabouts of his victim a killer commits other offences – in addition to the murder,' he explained.

I was stunned.

So, centuries ago these were seen as heinous crimes with

hefty punishments yet today they're rarely used. Why? Aren't we supposed to have advanced as a race, become more civilised? We've sent men to the moon yet we are letting these appalling crimes go unpunished?

'These are serious crimes and they should be applied whenever a murder is suspected and the body remains missing,' I argued. 'And surely, the more charges a person is convicted of, the more severe the sentence should be?'

In my petition I also wanted to demand automatic life tariffs in cases of missing murder victims – and a denial of parole when the killer refuses to reveal the whereabouts of their victim's body.

My head was aching trying to absorb so much information all at once.

'We also need a short, dramatic statement, explaining why not being able to lay a loved one to rest exacerbates your grief,' said Fiona. 'Something that will really bring home the horror of what you and these other families are going through.'

I sighed. It was so hard to put into words but I had to try. 'Losing a loved one is devastating,' I began, 'but to lose a loved one to murder is awful, shocking, horrific. And to be denied their funeral, on top of all of that, well, it's just unimaginable ...'

There was a silence on the phone. I heard the sound of scribbling.

'That's it,' Fiona said. 'Perfect.'

Eventually we'd condensed the whole campaign onto one sheet of A4. Under the heading, Please Support Helen's Law, and my daughter's familiar portrait, were the words:

> To lose a loved one is devastating
> To lose a loved one to murder is horrific
> To be denied their funeral causes unimaginable suffering ...

Next, we explained the reason for the campaign:

Ian Simms is serving a life sentence (on overwhelming forensic evidence) for the murder of my daughter, Helen McCourt, aged twenty-two, on 9 February 1988, in Billinge, Lancs. For almost three decades Simms has refused to reveal the whereabouts of Helen's body – denying us the chance to grant her the dignity of a funeral and resting place.

The case made legal history as only the third ever UK murder trial without a body. Sadly, as killers go to ever-desperate lengths to hide evidence and evade justice such cases have become more common. Without stiffer penalties, they will continue to rise.

In January 2016, a Parole Board will decide on Simms' application for freedom. As it currently stands, the English legal system does not require a convicted murderer (at the end of their determined tariff) to admit guilt or reveal the location of a victim's remains before being released.

If parole is granted, my hopes of finding my daughter may never be realised. No other family should live this ordeal.

Next, we spelt out the three points of my campaign. To petition the Prime Minister (then David Cameron) and Home Secretary (Theresa May) to acknowledge the pain and distress caused to the families of missing murder victims by:

Denying parole to murderers for as long as they refuse to disclose the whereabouts of their victim's remains.

Passing a full life tariff (denying parole or release) until the murderer discloses the location (and enables the recovery) of their victim's remains.

Automatically applying the following rarely-used

common-law offences in murder trials without a body;★
preventing the burial of a corpse and conspiracy to prevent
the burial of a corpse, disposing of a corpse, obstructing
a coroner.

Now we needed supporters, people who would back us and help
us shout from the rooftops.

We spent months emailing human rights lawyers, barristers
who had prosecuted other missing murder cases, law centres, pro
bono organisations, legal advice clinics. Sadly, some didn't reply.
Others did but said they couldn't help.

Our luck changed when we contacted the campaign group
called Voice4Victims. Its founder, Claire Waxman, (now victims
commissioner for London) had been the victim of a horrendous
stalking campaign for twelve years but had been successful in
changing stalking laws. She advised us to get other families in
the same situation to join us in our campaign: 'Then you need
to get attention, through the media, and get MPs to publicly
support you,' she said. 'The more vocal you are, the better!'

Claire put us in touch with prominent forensic psychologist
Dr Keri Nixon who had, by sheer chance, just written an article
on the devastating impact that denying a funeral can have on
families. She agreed to back me 'one hundred per cent'.

Dr Nixon not only provided us with a brilliant quote to use
on our petition – 'Denying a funeral is the last repugnant act a
murderer can enact on his/her victim's family' – but she also
offered to distribute it far and wide among legal experts she
knew and has continued to support us over the years.

★(as in the case of R v Hunter, 1974 (from Archbold, *Criminal Pleading Evidence and Practice* 2015). Just to clarify, I have since learned that the correct wording of the offences are: 'unlawfully preventing the burial of a corpse, unlawfully disposing of a corpse and 'obstructing a coroner (in the execution of his duty)'. There was also no need to specifically include 'conspiracy to prevent the burial of a corpse' as this would have been automatically covered by the offence of preventing the burial.

Now, I just needed to get our new MP, Conor McGinn, on board. Conor had succeeded Dave Watts (who accepted a peerage in 2015 and took his seat in the House of Lords) at the General Election in May 2015. He was a young Irish-British politician who had been voted in with a massive 12,000 majority. His warm, approachable face frequently smiled out of the local paper.

Right, I'd like a word with you, I thought, picking up the phone.

Conor came out to my house and listened compassionately and attentively as I told him about my story and campaign. (I kept him for so long that he missed his train back to London – something he still teases me about to this day!)

'I will help you in any way I can,' he promised in his strong Armagh accent. He said he would speak with other MPs and ministers and raise it as a debate in Parliament.

A few days later, he sent the loveliest letter, setting out all his promises to speak with other members and ministers – and raise it in Parliament – and signing off 'Yours sincerely and God Bless, Conor'.

What a wonderful man, I thought. I've been fortunate in always having the most supportive, compassionate MPs on my side, but Conor, who I now regard as a good friend, went above and beyond the call of duty and I will never, ever be able to thank him enough.

He too added a strong quote to the campaign and Fiona asked a graphic designer friend to create a bold poster (I'm awed by the generosity of those willing to help out a complete stranger). Pulling the first bundle out of the envelope, I beamed. It was brilliant – bright, eye-catching and dramatic. I peeled off the first one and stuck it proudly to my porch window for all the neighbours to see.

Next, we had to sort the petition. There were various platforms, including a government petition site, but I'd heard good things about change.org. Fiona emailed our poster to the press office and they rang just seconds later.

'This is a brilliant idea – how can we help?' they asked.

I could have kissed them.

They advised us on how to polish my appeal to make it even more emotive and reach out to more people. A few versions pinged back and forth but finally we were good to go.

Two local mums who were also going through the same ordeal agreed to come on board for the campaign launch.

Jean Taylor's daughter, Chantel, twenty-seven, was killed by ex-soldier and childhood friend Stephen Wynne in 2004. Two years later, Wynne (then twenty-eight) pleaded guilty to her murder and was sentenced to life.

Joan Morson's son, Paul, thirty-one, was killed in 2011. Two ex-business partners, John Anthony Burns, thirty-four, and Raymond William Brierley, fifty-nine, were given life sentences in 2012 for his torture and murder.

Like Helen, Paul and Chantel have never been found.

Now, we just needed a newspaper to launch the campaign with. So many newspapers had supported me over the years but as Conor was a Labour MP, it made sense to go with the *Daily Mirror*. Fiona had written for them, as a freelancer, for years and loved the way they highlighted injustices in society and championed changes. She worked with a reporter called Louie Smith, who agreed it was a strong story and arranged a photoshoot at SAMM Merseyside's headquarters. We all held up a framed photograph of our missing murdered loved ones for a dramatic group photo and Fiona interviewed us at length.

A tearful Joan described how she had a plaque in the garden for Paul but longed for a grave she can visit and lay flowers on: 'All we want is closure,' she said wistfully.

Jean recalled the awful moment she had to tell her grandchildren that their mum would never come home: 'They asked, "Where is she, then, Nanny?"' she recalled. 'And we're still asking that. Without a body to bury, that sense of disbelief will always remain.'

Sitting side by side with these women, listening to their stories, convinced me even more that we were doing the right thing. We'd lived this nightmare for too long. And, without a change in the law, more families would be joining us.

On Sunday evening, 13 December 2015, Fiona rang: 'It's running tomorrow,' she said, excitedly. We arranged for the petition to go live on change.org at the exact moment the story hit the *Daily Mirror* website at 11pm. In the early hours, the first signatures from night-owls and shift workers started to trickle through.

I was pouring tea next morning when John returned from the newsagent with a huge smile on his face. 'Ta da!' he cried, unfolding the *Daily Mirror* with a flourish.

'Oh my God, it's the front page!' I cried in disbelief.

Fiona had been told it had a good chance of making the cover but didn't want to raise our hopes. Stories can change right up to the eleventh hour, depending on what else is happening. But there it was – under a giant headline of 'Tell Us Where Our Kids Are Buried'. Two other straplines included 'Mums' Plea for Law Change' and 'Keep Killers in Jail Until They Release Sites of Victims' Bodies'.

Inside, was a double-page spread telling our stories in detail: 'To Be Denied the Chance to Say Our Final Goodbyes is a Torture That Never Ends,' read the headline. All my emotive quotes were included, including details of my friendship with Winnie Johnson and my plea: 'Don't let me die like Winnie, not knowing where my daughter is'.

I revealed my terror that Simms could be released to dance on Helen's secret grave and explained the need to have this closure: 'I know deep down that Helen is never going to walk back into the house. I know that I am never going to see her smile or hear her voice. But, without a funeral, there is always a tiny part of me that can't accept she has gone. I will fight until my last breath.'

Almost immediately, my phone started ringing and never stopped. The story was picked up by papers, TV, radio ... I went from one interview to the next without pausing for breath.

Pressing the 'refresh' button on the petition page of change.org became addictive – seeing the numbers flicker dramatically before reaching an ever-higher total. I was delighted when we reached our first one hundred. One hundred people backed us, believed in us! Then, 100 became 1,000 ... 10,000 ... 20,000.

A few days earlier, on 8 December, during a debate on parole hearings, Conor McGinn had raised my plight in the House of Commons, calling for a review of guidelines in cases such as mine – where the killer refuses to reveal the location of his victim. There and then, Minister for Victims, Mike Penning, responded and said he would like to meet me. Sadly, it couldn't be before Christmas, but a date was set for 4 February 2016.

Afterwards, Conor issued a statement reading: 'I'm glad the Minister has agreed to meet with Marie and I hope that this will lead to a review of the guidelines.

'The impact of a murder to the family and friends of the victim is devastating, even more so when the killer refuses to allow a dignified final resting place.

'Those who are convicted of murder should not be considered for release if they do not provide information about the location of their victim's remains, which compounds the loss and devastation of the victims' families.'

Meanwhile, the signatures poured in. Some of the comments from supporters had me in tears. Many expressed shock that this wasn't law already. Others remembered Helen from their schooldays. More vowed to take the matter up with their own MPs. And one woman simply wrote: 'I don't think I have ever been so moved by a petition'.

Yet more families came forward. They included Anita Giles, whose mother Sandie Bowen, fifty-four, vanished from her home in Llandogo, Monmouthshire in August 1997. Sandie's second husband, Michael Bowen, was convicted of her murder the following year, and sentenced to a minimum of eighteen years.

In 2002 he finally admitted the killing, saying they had argued on his fishing boat and, after hitting her, she had fallen overboard – but still refused to say where she could be recovered from.

In February 2015, ten months before the launch of my campaign, Bowen had been released on life licence. 'I can't believe they let him out,' I told Anita, genuinely shocked.

'Thank you for campaigning,' she said. 'What you are doing is so important. But I don't think I'm ever going to find my mum now,' she'd added sadly.

'Don't lose hope,' I urged. 'There is always hope. It only takes someone walking their dog and coming across something.'

But I felt her pain, her despair, only too well.

'Sign and share' became my mantra. I distributed posters at the gym, at the local shops: 'Please encourage everyone to sign,' I urged.

Within days, I watched – flabbergasted – as, with one brief click, 99,999 became 100,000. I punched the air with delight.

I was encouraged by Ann Ming, mum of Julie Hogg who was murdered just twenty-one months after Helen. We had met at various victims' conferences over the years and became good friends. Ann had successfully and single-handedly fought for seventeen years for an age-old double jeopardy law to be abolished so that her daughter's killer could be brought to justice.

Billy Dunlop was tried twice but each time the jury failed to reach a verdict. (Ann said police errors meant crucial evidence, which could have nailed him, either wasn't gathered or wasn't allowed.) After the second trial, Dunlop was formally acquitted.. When mum-of-one Julie first went missing, in November 1989, police searched her empty home extensively but reported no sign of her.

Three months later, when the house was finally opened up again, Ann went inside. As a nurse, she immediately recognised a distinctive smell. The horrific moment when she discovered her daughter's body hidden behind a bath panel still haunts her to this day.

You see, it's not just families of missing murder victims who suffer torment but those of 'discovered' murder victims, too. When killers go to extreme lengths to hide the evidence of their crime – including hiding and dismembering bodies – it tears their loved ones apart. Surely those common-law offences of obstructing a coroner, hiding a corpse and preventing a burial should have applied in this case, too?

First, there are legal implications. In Ann's case, her daughter's body was so decomposed, it hampered the recovery of crucial evidence such as cause of, and time of, death – information that would have convicted Dunlop when he first went to court.

Second, these cruel acts have an appalling impact on the victim's family. I always advise grieving families to ask the undertaker if they can have a lock of hair of their murdered loved one. It's something tangible that they can put in a locket and always hold close to their heart.

I will never forget the awful moment I suggested a grieving mum do the same for her murdered daughter.

'Marie, I can't,' she explained, her voice breaking. 'He tried to burn my daughter's body, there is no hair.'

My heart broke for her – and all those in her situation. To not have a body to bury is awful, to have that body desecrated is horrific.

These deaths are not the result of spontaneous crimes of passion or temper. These are planned killings. And planned disposals.

On two horrendous occasions, Ann could only watch, helpless, as Dunlop walked free from court. But on hearing that he was boasting openly about getting away with murder she was spurred into action.

Writing letters by hand at her kitchen table, Ann went to MPs, the Home Office and the Lords, and was successful in having the 800-year-old double jeopardy rule – which prevented people being charged twice with the same crime – overturned.

As a result, Dunlop was brought back to court in 2006, where he finally pleaded guilty to murder. He is currently serving a life sentence.

'Never give up,' she told me. 'Loads of people told me it couldn't be done. My solicitor told me I was wasting my time. But I did it – and so will you.

'Our conviction came seventeen years after Julie's murder but it finally gave us closure and it made such a difference.'

When starting my campaign years earlier, I'd warned that improved forensic science techniques would see killers resort to increasingly desperate – and horrific – measures to get away with murder. Sadly, I was right.

Who can forget little April Jones, just five years old, who was abducted while playing outside her home in Machynlleth, Wales, in October 2012?

Mark Bridger, forty-six, was convicted of abduction, murder and attempting to pervert the course of justice (a charge referring to the unlawful disposal and concealment of a body). Only the tiniest fragments of bone were recovered from Bridger's fireplace.

In March 2016, I wept when I heard that police searching for missing teenager Becky Watts in Bristol had found body parts. In November that year, her step-brother Nathan Matthews, twenty-nine, was sentenced to life with a minimum of thirty-three years for murder. His girlfriend Shauna Hoare, twenty-one, was jailed for seventeen years for manslaughter. Both were also convicted of conspiracy to kidnap Becky, perverting the course of justice and preventing a lawful burial.

A month after Becky disappeared, children's author Helen Bailey, fifty-one, vanished from her home in Royston, Hertfordshire – along with the dashchund dog she doted on. Her fiancé, Ian Stewart, said he'd found a note that said she needed space.

For three months her location was a mystery. A police search of the couple's house and garden revealed nothing.

Then a neighbour alerted officers to a secret cesspit underneath the garage. (Stewart had parked his vehicle over the top to hide it). Inside, police discovered the bodies of Helen and her dog.

Tests revealed she had been drugged over a period of time before being suffocated. Helen's brother recalled her joking, within earshot of Stewart, about how the cesspit would be the perfect place to hide a body.

In 2017, Stewart, then fifty-six, was found guilty of murder, fraud, preventing a burial and perverting the course of justice. Poor Helen – widowed in 2011 when her husband drowned on holiday – thought she'd found happiness again when approached by Stewart on an internet bereavement group – only to be brutally murdered.

(Stewart has since been charged with the murder of his first wife, Diane, in 2010 and will stand trial in 2022.)

Every single awful case broke my heart. The details were so appalling, so disturbing, I imagined others grimacing as they turned the page or switched channels. But I couldn't. I felt compelled to take in every single word then add the case to my now bulging files. 'This is why I'm fighting,' I reminded myself.

I gave interview after interview spelling out why legislation was so badly needed. 'Without new laws to reflect the heinous nature of these crimes, these cases are going to rise,' I warned grimly.

The pain inflicted on the family is only one reason, I argued. What about the impact of a missing murder victim on the local community? The huge cost of a file remaining open? Of new searches being carried out when new information arises? Surely that's in the public interest? These offences are there. They need to be used – in all cases.

I understand that when a body remains missing all efforts, naturally, are focused on a) proving the person is no longer alive and b) that their death has been caused by the accused and c) getting a conviction.

A successful result in court is, of course, a huge relief. But while the police and prosecutors move onto their next case, the victim's family continues to suffer the most horrendous torture.

That door exposing their grief, their pain, their nightmares, will always be wedged wide open. Without a funeral it will never, ever close.

* * *

We flew off to India for New Year feeling more hopeful than we had done in some time. Yes, Simms' parole hearing would take place while we were away – and we'd return to the twenty-eighth anniversary of Helen's murder. But a campaign in her name was up and running.

Locking up the house, as John loaded our suitcases – containing my novena candles – into the car, I kissed Helen's portrait and told her we'd be back before she knew it.

She'd have been astonished to think that her lovely face was gazing out of newspapers and computer screens all over the country. That her name had been mentioned in the House of Commons.

'We're on our way, love,' I told her. 'Things are finally happening.'

Chapter 16

To Downing Street and Parliament

E ven on holiday, I didn't let up on my campaigning. Struggling through painful sciatica, I told everyone we met about Helen's Law and distributed dozens of posters. Fiona Duffy texted us continually with spiralling figures. We were up to 200k, then 250k.

'A quarter of a million!' I gasped.

These were figures I'd never even dreamed of.

Simms' parole hearing, adjourned from the spring, then summer, then autumn, took place while we were away but I was heartened by a story in the *Liverpool Echo*, in which a Ministry of Justice spokesman said that the independent Parole Board would 'take into account' the killer's co-operation in finding her body.

They wouldn't release him to open prison after all this, surely to God?

Our meeting with the Minister, and presentation of my petition to Downing Street, was scheduled for Thursday, 4 February 2016.

On the Wednesday afternoon, I was driving home from the chemist, with prescribed painkillers for my back, when my mobile rang: it was my victim liaison officer.

Two weeks had passed since Simms' parole hearing. This was it, the verdict.

With trembling, sweaty hands, I pulled over. My heart was racing.

'Are you at home, Marie?' she asked.

And there it was: the hint that bad news was about to be broken.

'Please,' I sighed. 'Just tell me.'

The indicator ticked away the seconds; I braced myself.

'I'm sorry, Marie,' she began. With those three words, I crumpled. I didn't hear her next sentence – I didn't need to. The Parole Board had recommended his move to an open prison.

Grimacing, I leaned my head on the steering wheel in disbelief and despair.

How could they do this? What about my campaign?

I didn't want to ring Michael at work with upsetting news. I decided to wait until he was home. I was about to pull back out onto the road when my phone rang again.

'Would you like to comment?' a journalist asked.

'On what?' I asked, cautiously.

'Simms being moved to an open prison.'

I gripped the phone in disbelief. 'How do you know about that?' I asked. 'I've only just been told myself!'

The Parole Board had issued a press release, apparently. Before I'd even had a chance to tell Helen's nearest and dearest, the story was pinging onto news desk screens across the country. And this is yet another way that victims and families are let down. For some inexplicable reason, usually to benefit the prisoner, no doubt, the powers-that-be fall over themselves to release news of decisions.

Would a few hours' advance notice for families of victims really hurt? I couldn't have Michael hearing this on the next news bulletin. Reluctantly, I rang him at work. He could hardly speak. I could feel his pain emanating down the telephone line.

'I am going to do everything in my power to keep him inside,' I promised.

* * *

Early next morning, I popped painkillers as we headed for the train to London. It was going to be a long day.

Conor McGinn greeted us like long-lost friends in the chilly Westminster hall before leading us down a warren of carpeted corridors. Minister for Victims Mike Penning was outside his office and led us in.

I introduced us all. 'And this,' I said, reaching into my handbag and pulling out my precious framed photograph, 'is my daughter, Helen.'

Mike Penning gazed closely at the image. 'I've seen that photo before but it's different seeing it in colour, isn't it?' he said. 'I've got two daughters myself of a similar age. I can't imagine what you're going through.'

He told me how pleased he was that I was campaigning: 'We need more people like you,' he said, inviting me to work with him on the Victims' Law.

He listened attentively and sympathetically and said he would ensure that the Secretary of State, Michael Gove, who could veto or approve the Parole Board's recommendation, had all the facts.

'Now, I have something here that you might like,' he added, handing over an official-looking document.

I skimmed it, my eyes widening like saucers.

It was a letter from the Prisons Minister Andrew Selous to the Parole Board Chief Executive, Sir David Calvert-Smith. In it, Mr Selous requested that the board review its guidelines on parole for convicted murderers who refuse to reveal the location of their victim's remains, asking if 'the deliberate or wilful failure to disclose the whereabouts of the victim's body indicates a failure to recognise the full depravity of the crime committed and a significant lack of victim empathy, or remorse'.

I looked up, speechless – this was exactly what we needed.

'You can take that away with you,' he said.

After warm handshakes I left with high hopes, clutching my precious letter. The meeting had gone better than I'd ever imagined.

Next, we headed to Downing Street. It felt surreal, striding towards the famous black door, with my petition box, emblazed with that now-familiar image of my daughter and our Helen's Law logo, containing 320,000 signatures.

After the bustle of Westminster, the heavily secured street was deserted and hushed. The sound of traffic was distant and muffled. It was like being on a film set.

Cameras flashed as we gathered on the doorstep. Then, taking a deep breath, I turned to face the door: this was it. Michael rapped the iconic brass lion door knocker. Almost immediately, the door opened and carefully, officiously, I handed over my precious cargo.

As I was ushered towards the reporters gathered in a pen across the street, I suddenly froze in terror. In an instant, I'd gone from feisty campaigner ready to take on the Government to overwhelmed, petrified grandmother. I felt every one of my seventy-two years. Not only was my back killing me, my mind had gone blank – absolutely blank – and my mouth felt full of cotton wool. I turned to Fiona Duffy: 'What do I say?' I whispered, helplessly.

She scribbled onto a page of her notebook then thrust it in my hand.

Huge step forward … review of guidelines … legacy for Helen.

I read the words, nodding. My mind calmed.

'Speak from the heart, Marie,' Fiona urged. 'You can do this.'

I imagined Helen beside me, smiling encouragingly.

Go on, Mum.

I didn't even need to look at the notes. 'Today, we took a huge step forward with my campaign for Helen's Law,' I began. 'Minister for Victims Mike Penning has assured me that there will be a review of parole guidelines for these cases. The Minister listened carefully and compassionately and I believe him when he says he will do everything he can to help.'

My nerves evaporated as I got into my stride. 'If I can make changes in Helen's name, some good will have come out of her death.

'In light of the Parole Board's recommendation yesterday, to move my daughter's killer to an open prison, I am more determined than ever to fight – not just for me but every other family out there in this situation. We should not be put through this.'

More questions came and I answered them confidently. I was back in control. Cars whisked me to studio interviews for Granada News and Sky. Finally, we arrived home, exhausted but triumphant.

The next morning, I sent a thank-you card to Mike Penning. I also wrote imploring letters to both himself and Mr Gove urging them to postpone any decision on my case and any others until the review had been completed. I thought it was a reasonable request.

The letters were sent by guaranteed delivery. Neither office replied nor acknowledged receipt.

I assured myself that no news is good news and they'd be giving this great thought behind the scenes. Meanwhile – boosted by media coverage – signatures on the petition continued to soar. Plus, Conor was hoping to be granted a ten-minute rule bill – a type of private member's bill – in which he would present the case for Helen's Law in a speech lasting up to ten minutes.

A few mornings later, John woke me with a cuppa.

'Guess when Conor's Bill is being presented?' he asked.

I sat bolt upright.

'Next week?' I asked eagerly.

He shook his head.

'Next month?'

Again, he shook his head.

'For heaven's sake, just tell me!' I snapped.

'Eleventh of October,' he declared.

My mouth fell open, hopes and dreams crashed around me.

'That's six months away,' I cried. 'The year will be almost over.'

It was my first inkling into how frustratingly, creakingly, slowly the wheels of Parliament turn.

'Ah, but guess what day of the week it is?' John added cheerfully.

Sure enough, like all important days relating to Helen, the Bill was being presented on a Tuesday.

'That's something,' I agreed, sipping my tea.

* * *

Through my many years of campaigning, I've met some wonderful people all over the world. A week after our visit to London, change.org forwarded a message from a mum in Australia who was, by chance, fighting for an identical change in the law over there. She, too, had set up a petition on change.org – she wanted to speak with me.

Ten thousand miles melted away as Margaret Dodd and I chatted to each other on FaceTime (I was getting better at this technology lark!) until the early hours. The similarities between us were astounding. She had emigrated from Lancashire (just forty miles away from me) to Western Australia with her family when she was just nine. Her daughter, Hayley, seventeen, had gone missing on Helen's birthday – 29 July 1999 – on her way *to* work. Helen had vanished on her way home *from* work.

In both cases, witnesses reported hearing a female scream

seconds after the girls were last seen – and a solitary earring belonging to the victim was found in the suspect's car.

We both had memorials to our girls – who shared the same initials HM (Helen Martha and Hayley Marie) – but no graves to lay flowers on.

But the biggest shock came when we proudly held up photos to the camera.

'Oh my God,' I gasped, incredulously, 'they look like sisters!'

Both Helen and Hayley had the same long, glossy dark hair, sparkling eyes and thoughtful expressions. In toddler photos, you'd swear it was the same child.

Poor Margaret's pain was exacerbated by not even having a conviction for Hayley's murder.

It was only during a cold case review in 2013 that police had recovered crucial evidence and arranged to extradite a suspect from Queensland (where Francis John Wark was serving a prison sentence for raping a hitchhiker).

(I supported Margaret during the 2018 trial and was so relieved when her daughter's killer was convicted. Early in 2020, however, he won an appeal and the conviction was quashed. At the time of printing, his retrial has been provisionally scheduled for early 2021.)

Margaret wasn't alone. Another family in Cairns had launched a No Body No Parole campaign in October 2015 – just as I was finalising my petition. What were the chances? Not only were similar campaigns springing up all over the continent, Southern Australia had actually passed a No Body No Parole Law in July 2015.

Fiona Duffy arranged for us to have a Skype meeting with Tony Piccolo, the MP who had introduced the law in that state. He told us: 'Being able to provide the families of victims of crime with an opportunity to grieve and obtain closure is very important to any justice system.

'What these laws do is provide an incentive for the person convicted of murder to provide the information required for that to occur. Also, it provides enough sufficient checks and balances to create no new injustices.'

The idea was simple, he explained. Parole is only granted if the Chief of Police can produce a certificate confirming that the prisoner has 'co-operated' in investigations: no certificate equals no parole.

'That's a brilliant idea,' I told him. 'They're the ones who have investigated the case and seen all the evidence – and know far more than any Parole Board.

'The police have gone in to see Simms numerous times and he refuses to speak with them. That's not co-operation.

'We don't want to see these killers locked up forever,' I added. 'All they have to do is co-operate. Just give us back our loved ones, that's all we want.'

That meeting gave me such hope: 'If they can do it, so can we,' I said.

As I was to discover, however, it wasn't going to be so straightforward.

* * *

Margaret Dodd and I continued to chat, encourage and support each other. We were both familiar with those days so awful that despair and misery weighs you down like a heavy, rough blanket.

In April 2016, my victim liaison officer phoned with an update: the Home Office had approved the recommendation for Simms' move to an open prison.

Too stunned to even speak, I sank into a chair. All those assurances, all those promises, counted for nothing. In desperation, I rang Conor McGinn. He said he would ask for an urgent review of the decision and raise it in the Commons when it returned after the Easter recess. But it had no effect.

In one final, last-ditch attempt for intervention, I wrote to Mike Penning, imploring him 'as a father, MP and Victims Minister – to seek a postponement on any decision until after MP Conor McGinn has raised the issue in a private member's bill in October. It is not much to ask.

'Surely, if a Minister of her Majesty's Government, with responsibility for prisons, has asked the Parole Board for a review of guidance, any cases that may be affected by such a review must be put on hold until a decision has been reached?'

I mentioned that I had waited almost three decades to bring my daughter home – and devoted my life to helping and supporting families of victims. All I was asking now was six months.

Again, there was a resounding silence.

I had to face facts: Simms was on his way from a Category C to an open prison and there was nothing I could do to stop it. I have no idea what an open prison looks like but it sickened me to imagine lots of free, open fields and rose-filled gardens with skipping inmates free to come and go as they pleased.

Next would be escorted and unescorted visits. Then release. Blocking it became my reason for living, for getting up in the morning. Determination would surge through my veins, pushing me on.

* * *

Over the summer, as Brexit chaos reigned, we pushed for more signatures. David Cameron had stepped down after the referendum in June so we now had a new prime minister, Theresa May, and Home Secretary, Liz Truss.

Meanwhile, in Australia, I was heartened at the news that No Body No Parole laws had now been passed in Northern Territory.

As advised by Conor McGinn, John put together a detailed

booklet for MPs, telling the story behind our fight and the need for Helen's Law. Inside, we explained that, by now, we knew of fifty-four cases where a murder conviction had been secured either without a body or recovered after a considerable time – contributing to the distress of families.

I also stressed that advances in forensic science meant that killers were now resorting to increasingly desperate measures to hide or destroy evidence of their crimes, i.e. their victims. This situation was only going to get worse.

And talking of advances in forensic science … I'd been yearning to get the DNA evidence that had convicted Simms tested again to see if it had grown even stronger over time. I'd been all set to pay to have this done in a private laboratory but, in 2016, I got chatting to the new Merseyside Chief Constable at a SAMM Merseyside meeting, and he arranged to have it done for me. The result was astounding: the likelihood of the blood on Simms' clothing not belonging to a child parented by Helen's parents was now a billion to one. Triumphantly, I stored it in my bulging dossier for why Simms should never be released without revealing where my daughter's body was.

Finally, I added the significance of funerals in the grieving process: 'Laying the body of a loved one to rest is a fundamental but basic human right, regardless of creed, race, religion or society,' I wrote.

'Since time began, the human race has revered the bodies of their loved ones – either by preserving them or carrying out funeral rights. Being denied this basic right causes untold suffering to the families left behind.'

We printed, stapled and posted 650 colour copies – one for every single MP.

My campaign was also catching the attention of students. One group of young journalists made an impressive documentary; another, Jessica Perrin, who was studying policing and criminal investigation, wrote her Master's thesis on missing murder victims after hearing a talk I gave at John Moore University in Liverpool. She has now come on board to help us with the campaign and is an incredible support.

While researching other cases of missing murder victims over the years, Fiona Duffy and I were staggered at just how many cases there are – and how they have grown. If you remember, back in 1989, Simms was said to be only the third person to be convicted of murder without a body since the Second World War. That figure has been widely reported ever since. However, by delving through research for the purposes of this book, we have come across five further cases that happened between 1945 and 1988. This would make Helen's the eighth case, not the third.

We try to follow and record cases, but not all trials and convictions are covered or get the attention they deserve. Even now, we still come across missing homicide cases we have never heard of before.

We estimate, from our own research, that there are now between five and seven cases a year and they are only the ones we know of. Remembering Voice4Victims founder Claire Waxman's advice, we began to make tentative approaches to other families – inviting them to get involved as little or as much as they wished, if and when they felt in a position to do so.

For some, it was obviously too much. We never heard back. Others wished us well but explained they had put this painful part of their lives behind them and felt unable to revisit it. Others backed us privately, but for a variety of reasons (from ill-health to protecting younger members of the family who were unaware of all the details) were unable to take part in any publicity. Some came on board initially, but decided to fight for justice independently. Others joined us, played a huge part in promoting the campaign, and continue to do so.

I have nothing but respect, compassion and thanks for each and every one of these families in this position.

We encouraged all of them to reach out to their own MPs and share the petition far and wide – and also invited them to the House of Commons to hear Conor McGinn present his Bill.

As the big day approached, in October 2016, I cranked up my appeals on Facebook and Twitter – asking supporters to urge their MPs to attend the Bill reading and vote. I also gave countless media interviews – I was so grateful for their interest.

Fiona arrived at my London hotel on the Monday evening to find me on the phone with steam coming out of my ears.

'Absolutely not!' I fumed.

'They're trying to push back the Bill until later in the afternoon because of an emergency debate on Syria,' John whispered.

I gripped the handset even tighter. 'Grieving families have travelled a long way especially to hear this Bill presented tomorrow morning,' I said tightly. 'Now, please go back and tell whoever is organising the schedule that I will be appearing on *Good Morning Britain* with Piers Morgan tomorrow morning – early. If this Bill is pushed back, it's the first thing I'll be talking about – how we've been messed around and disappointed.

'This reading has to go ahead at the arranged time.'

A few minutes later, the phone rang again: the Bill was staying where it was.

'Thank you,' I said, graciously.

I should think so, too!

* * *

Early next morning saw me join Piers Morgan and Susanna Reid in the GMB studio. It was a prime slot and a strong interview – a chance to really let viewers know all about Helen's Law. They were both so warm and supportive. Afterwards, they asked for copies of our petition booklet and Piers also said he would post about me on his Twitter feed where he has a huge number of followers. Then it was back to the hotel to pick up Michael and Fiona before heading to Westminster.

Among the other families were Linda and Tony Jones (parents of fifteen-year-old Danielle Jones, who was murdered in June 2001 by her uncle, Stuart Campbell); Tracy Richardson (daughter of Michelle Gunshon – murdered in 2004 by pub glass collector, Martin Stafford, at the Birmingham pub where she was lodging); Sam and Neil Gillingham (daughter and grandson of Carole Packman – murdered by her husband, Russell Causley, in 1985); Claire and Maxine Harrison (sisters of Jane Harrison, killed by her partner, Kevin Doherty, in 1995); Sheila and Nina Dolton (mum and sister of Jonathan Dolton, twenty, who was killed by a colleague in 2002); plus the son and daughter of Joan Morson – who had been with me at the original launch of the campaign.

It was the first time most of us had met and we embraced warmly and emotionally. Many felt a huge a sense of relief and belonging that they were finally among others who understood what they were going through. We had all brought a framed photo of our loved one, which we clutched tightly and proudly. We'd also received an eleventh-hour message from yet another family. It was too late for them to attend Parliament but Ann and Brian Nicholl, parents of Jenny Nicholl, nineteen, who was murdered in 2005, also pledged their support.

Tragically, for the families of both Michelle Gunshon and Jonathan Dolton, the unthinkable had happened: the killers had died, taking their macabre secrets with them. They were now lying in their own cosy, respectable, comfortable graves while condemning their victims to remain forever lost and their families forever grieving.

'Your loved ones can still be found,' I urged. 'We'll keep working together.'

Conor McGinn had arranged for me to sit in a special viewing area in the chamber itself, while John, Michael, Fiona and the other families headed upstairs to the public gallery. As I was led to my seat, I gazed around, incredulously, at this famous setting. The familiar green leather benches, the dark panelling, the microphone wires which picked up every word uttered. I couldn't believe I was here – in Parliament. I took a deep shaky breath. There had been so many important debates and votes cast here over the centuries. The next one would leave me either overjoyed or crushed.

The Commons was packed to the rafters – I'd never seen it so full. A full-scale debate on the NHS was underway and an MP was trying to read out an extract from a report when she was interrupted by the Speaker, John Bercow.

'Perhaps we can leave it there, because we are short of time and I want to proceed. Unless there are further points of order then we will come on to the ten-minute rule motion. I call Conor McGinn.'

This was it.

To my left, on the back row of the Labour benches, Conor rose to his feet, clutching his papers. He glanced across at me, smiled nervously, then began. It was his first private member's bill, or backbencher's bill, to a packed house – a huge occasion for a new MP.

'I beg to move …' he began. 'For a parent to suffer the anguish of losing a child is beyond words, but the horror of having such a loved one murdered is surely too awful even to contemplate so it is harder still, if even possible, to imagine the pain of being denied the chance to hold a proper funeral and lay that loved one to rest.

'My constituent Marie McCourt does not need to imagine it, because for twenty-eight years she has been forced to endure what she describes as the special kind of torture of knowing she could die without ever discovering where her daughter's body is or being able to lay her daughter to rest with the dignity she deserves.'

As he glanced in my direction, other MPs followed his cue. I clasped my hands tightly to stop them shaking. John, Fiona and the other families were directly above me – I hoped they were OK.

'She had Helen taken from her in the cruellest circumstances, only to be denied the sacred right to bury her daughter. Few could have found the strength to carry on, let alone mount such a formidable campaign to have the law changed so that others do not suffer in the way she has suffered. Her quiet dignity and powerful determination are an example to us all.

'New Home Office figures revealed that, since 2007 alone, there had been thirty murders in England and Wales where no body had been recovered,' he added. 'But as it currently stands, the English legal system does not require a convicted murderer, at the end of their determined tariff, to admit guilt or reveal the location of a victim's remains before being released. Marie believes that if parole is granted to Helen's killer, her hopes of finding her daughter will never be realised.'

I nodded sadly.

Conor had included all three elements of my petition in his Bill. 'In essence, the proposals are simple: if a convicted killer refuses to give information to reveal the location of a victim's body, they should not be considered eligible for parole and they should stay in prison. The proposals would effectively mean a whole-life tariff for murderers who refuse to disclose the location of their victims and enable their remains to be recovered to give families a chance to pay their last respects.'

He also stressed that the Bill would not affect any prisoner's right to maintain their innocence and went on to mention, by name, some of the other victims we were fighting for.

Upstairs, poor Tracy Richardson fled the gallery, sobbing, when her mother's name was mentioned. She had been just twenty-one when Michelle had vanished while working in Birmingham. Tracy was a mum herself now to two gorgeous boys but that pain, that grief, was still so raw. Without a funeral, some sense of closure, it never goes.

'For those who have had to face the loss of a loved one at the hands of a callous murderer, there is nothing we can do to make up for their loss, but if there is a way to help them receive the justice they deserve, we must take it,' said Conor, passionately. 'If there is a way to compel those who have committed the most awful crimes to assist in this task, we must do it. Most importantly of all, if there is a way to ensure that no family has to endure the suffering that Marie McCourt and so many others have, we – in this of all places – have a duty to act.'

As his final words died away, he sat back down.

I waited, nervously.

The Speaker's voice rang out: 'All those in favour?' The chorused 'aye' from all sides of the House, in all tones, was loud, dramatic and melodious.

'All those not in favour?'

I held my breath, braced myself.

Silence.

'The ayes have it,' said John Bercow. 'The ayes have it.'

It was unanimous, not a single MP objected. We had cross-party support.

I closed my eyes and whispered a prayer of thanks. Upstairs, there were hushed tears and hugs among the families.

Rising to his feet, Conor approached the floor of the House. Then, followed by a team of MPs who would work with him on the Bill, he proceeded to the long oak table on which stood the famous Mace.

Handing the Bill to a clerk, he nodded once – then retreated.

The Speaker announced the Bill would have its second reading on 3 February 2017.

Yes! He'd done it, he'd presented the Bill to the House. We were on our way!

* * *

As more business got underway, I slipped outside to where Conor was waiting. I was tempted to perform a jig up and down the hallowed halls of Westminster but settled for hurrying towards him, my arms outstretched. I was so emotional, I could hardly speak.

'You were brilliant,' I whispered, hugging him tightly. 'Thank you.'

Fiona, John and the families joined us, red-eyed and flushed, but beaming with relieved delight. We all embraced and congratulated Conor.

'I was really overwhelmed by how many MPs were there,' Conor told Fiona, who was busily taking notes. 'That's really unusual for a private member's bill. It shows that there is widespread support for this in Parliament. Which is why the Government should take this up and make it the law.

'Although the next reading has been scheduled I hope, before then, that the Government takes this up and brings it to fruition.'

Outside, we approached the waiting TV cameras – each family holding the photo of their loved one.

My voice wavered with emotion. 'I am so grateful for all the support we have been given,' I said. 'Today was the day I thought would never happen. And to hear Helen's name mentioned in Parliament was one of the proudest moments of my life.

'The first reading was very well received. We are hopeful the second reading, in February, will have a successful conclusion. It's been a long time coming but we are hopeful that, before too long, we might see Helen's Law become real.'

Writing these words now, I can't believe how naive I was to think things would happen so quickly. Unbeknown to us, we were about to face a heady mix of hiccups and hurdles – from ministerial resignations to snap General Elections, from Brexit stalemates to a global pandemic. And with every day that passed, Simms was moving ever closer to release.

Chapter 17

Stalemate

We were on such a high following the successful first reading of the Bill. Messages of congratulations and support flooded in and petition signatures soared to 400,000.

In November 2016, I was stunned to win the Pride of St Helens Award for my work on the campaign. 'I wouldn't be here without your support so this award is for all of you,' I told the delegation, applauding the entire room. Two further awards from the *Liverpool Echo* also followed. At another awards presentation, in Liverpool, I was introduced to local artist Anthony Brown who was so moved by my story he said he'd like to create a piece of artwork of Helen for me. The resulting portrait – made up of all the newspaper cuttings and magazine stories that have been written about her – was breath-taking and brilliant. I will always treasure it.

Keen for the Government to now take up Helen's Law, without having to wait for the Bill to proceed, Conor McGinn urged action in Parliament and requested meetings with the Ministry of Justice. Meanwhile, I continued to give countless interviews stressing how this proposed change in the law was our last and only chance of ever finding our missing murdered loved ones.

'People think it gets easier but it's more painful now than it ever was,' I explained. 'In those early days, there was always hope … Hope that she had been kidnapped, someone would come forward with information or Simms would finally confess.

'But all hope has long gone. A change in the law is all we have left to end this sheer and utter hell.'

In December 2016, I was delighted to hear that a third Australian state, Victoria, had introduced No Body No Parole laws. Maybe the UK would be next?

For New Year, John and I returned to India. We'd made good friends there and they rejoiced that we were finally getting somewhere.

Logging onto the change.org petition page to see the numbers continue to rise and read the comments below became addictive. One girl, now living in Spain, wrote: 'That picture is just how I remember Helen. I often travelled on the same bus. She was such a lovely girl. I wish I could sign this petition a million times for you both.'

Bless you, love, I thought.

* * *

On 3 February 2017, just six days before the twenty-ninth anniversary of Helen's murder, we set off for London for the second reading.

I appeared on BBC *Breakfast News* and the *Victoria Derbyshire* show on BBC2, before meeting with our families once again and filing into the hushed public gallery.

At 2.30pm, Conor McGinn rose to his feet: 'My Bill to introduce Helen's Law was due to be read a second time today. Unfortunately, but not unexpectedly, that has not happened.

'I thank the 400,000 members of the public who signed the

petition, and I particularly want to recognise the families of victims who have travelled to be in Parliament today.'

He pointed out there was 'lots of support for it on both sides of the House and I am working with the Government. Today is not the day, but there will be a day for Helen's Law.'

Madam Deputy Speaker, Eleanor Laing, said she appreciated 'that it is sometimes difficult for those who do not have a full grasp of parliamentary procedures'.

You don't say! I thought. What was there to grasp? It was due to be read today, so why the hold-up?

She continued: 'The fact that this Bill has not been read today is not an indication that it is not held in high esteem. The points he [Conor McGinn] would have made would, I am sure, have had a lot of support in this house. What he is trying to achieve is very, very worthy. But as he said, there will be another day …'

And that was that. For some reason I'm still struggling to fathom the Bill was objected to and adjourned to 24 February. We left, deflated.

Over time, I learned that only a handful of bills ever actually had a second reading; each was scheduled in the hope that the Government would take it up independently – at which point the MP would take the Bill off the table. That is why, behind the scenes, Conor McGinn was urging the Ministry of Justice (MOJ) to act.

On 24 February, the reading was adjourned yet again for another month. However, this time, the MOJ confirmed that it had asked the Parole Board for a review of guidelines and assured MPs that the Government was taking the issue seriously.

For the next scheduled reading, I saved time and money on wasted train fares by watching proceedings on *Parliament Live*. Once again, the reading was adjourned, this time to Friday, 12 May.

I shook my head, exasperated.

How on earth does anything get done in that place? I wondered.

In April, Conor told me there was talk of making Helen's Law an amendment to the Justice Bill. He had been working behind the scenes and there were about fifty Conservative MPs all willing to support it.

Please God, I thought, crossing my fingers.

Then, just after Easter, disaster struck. The television was on in the background when a newsflash filled the screen: Theresa May had called a snap General Election.

A prickle of unease crept up my spine as a political expert explained some of the impacts. 'Parliament will be dissolved and, of course, all unresolved Bills will now "fall",' he said. Snatching my iPad, I hurriedly googled 'what happens when a Bill falls?'

The answer left me slumped in my chair. It's abandoned. Let go. Dropped from a height. In despair, I rang Conor McGinn.

'Can't they just put it on hold?' I pleaded.

Apparently not. Once a Bill falls, that's it. It has to be restarted from scratch in a new Parliament. Helen's Law, along with all the other outstanding Bills, would be kicked into oblivion.

An amendment to the Justice Bill also looked unlikely. Who knew which MPs would get voted back in? And there'd be a mass shuffle of Ministers afterwards – there always was.

I could have wept.

'All that work and effort. For what?' I fumed.

Conor assured me all was not lost. Once the dust had settled and a new Government was in place, we would continue to lobby the MOJ. But with every day that passed, Simms was coming that bit closer to release.

Thank heavens, then, for a miraculous result for one of our families. For all these years so many of us had dreamed of receiving news that our loved one had been found.

And for one grieving daughter it had finally happened.

I was just leaving my Pilates class in February 2017 when Anita Giles rang out of the blue. 'Marie,' she said breathlessly. 'The police in South Wales have found a body. It's a woman. They think it could be Mum.'

By complete chance, Wentwood Reservoir in South Wales, seventeen miles away from her murdered mother's home, was being drained for the first time in nearly a century for maintenance works. As the water level dropped, a passing dog walker spotted a body at the bottom of the lake and raised the alarm.

It took five weeks for DNA tests to be carried out and dental records checked. Then Anita rang me again. 'Marie, it's Mum,' she said emotionally.

My heart lurched sideways. 'Oh Anita,' I breathed. 'I am so, so, pleased that she's been found for you.'

I could sense the maelstrom of emotions surging down the telephone line; both her relief and renewed grief, but also heartache, anguish and guilt that, while her nightmare was now over, mine was still ongoing.

'I just hope Helen is found for you, Marie,' she said. 'I really do.'

Sandie's body had been weighed down with a heavy ceramic sink. (So much for Bowen's claim that she had fallen overboard). An inquest ruled she had been killed unlawfully. I gather local police discussed the case with the CPS but no further charges resulted. Surely, if there was a case crying out for additional charges of preventing a burial and obstructing a coroner it was this?

In April 2017, Anita was finally able to give her mother a proper, dignified goodbye. Four months later, on the twentieth anniversary of Sandie's murder, she scattered her mum's ashes at a favourite beach they'd both loved when Anita was growing up.

Having that closure has made the world of difference to Anita and we couldn't be happier for her. The discovery of her mum's body has given us all renewed hope that, one day, we'll be getting that same knock on the door. For it finally to be over.

One day.

* * *

The General Election, on 8 June 2017, was a disaster for Theresa May – leaving her with a hung Parliament.

Conor McGinn, along with Linda Jones' MP, Stephen Metcalfe, were, thankfully, voted back in and tried to secure us a meeting with the new Minister for Justice, but with just a few weeks before the summer recess and Brexit dominating everything, we were back to square one on that Snakes and Ladders board.

In August, Queensland became the fourth state to pass No Body No Parole laws.

'So, what's happening in the UK?' Margaret Dodd enquired.

'Don't ask,' I sighed.

Throughout the autumn, John and I continued to work with SAMM Merseyside in supporting families. Our geographical area now included most of the North, plus North Wales and the Isle of Man. We'd grown incredibly close to one elderly lady, in Wales, who had lost her only son to murder. When she became terminally ill, we stepped up our visits and were comforted when she slipped from this world peacefully, and with dignity – a right denied to so many of our loved ones.

With the thirtieth anniversary of Helen's murder approaching it was more important than ever to keep fighting. We'd endured three long lonely decades without her in our lives. No other family should have their lives destroyed like this, I vowed.

Anyone who had ever known Helen was invited to a commemorative mass at our local church. Her marble seat was decorated with lanterns and yellow ribbons. Not only was a yellow ribbon the international symbol for a missing person but it was also Helen's favourite colour and represented her lovely sunny nature. It became our symbol for Helen's Law.

That night, 400 relatives, schoolfriends, colleagues, retired police officers who had worked on the case and supporters streamed into the church. Fresh yellow blooms filled every windowsill. A local florist had made a beautiful display of golden daffodils especially for the altar.

The words in the Gospel reading 'Blessed are those who hunger and thirst for justice. They will be satisfied,' and 'Blessed are those who mourn. For they shall be comforted' had never felt more apt.

Afterwards, we all gathered in the church hall, where Helen's familiar portrait took pride of place on an easel on the stage. Throughout the evening, I'd catch guests gazing, transfixed, at the showreel of photos being played on a giant screen – there was Helen as a baby, having her first drink at eighteen, laughing with her brother, always laughing.

Nervously taking the microphone, I thanked everyone for coming. 'Tonight, I can smile,' I said. 'I'm normally crying when it's Helen's anniversary – but not tonight.

'I really am humbled that thirty years on, you all have put things aside in your busy lives and come out on a really, really cold night to be here for Helen.'

My voice wavered as I added, 'She may not be here in body but she's certainly here in spirit, I know that.'

Then I urged them to keep supporting the campaign: 'Every one of us in this room has lost someone we love. Knowing that they have had that last service and that last goodbye helps you to deal with your grief and go forwards. Sadly, all of our families don't.

'Please keep signing and sharing the petition. To have half a million people saying this law needs to be changed would make such a difference. Your support will help so many other families in the future.'

Then Conor McGinn took up the mic and gave the loveliest speech recalling how I had impressed him with 'my dignity, integrity, strength, warmth, selflessness and caring for others' the first time we met, and how he felt proud and humbled to represent such a loyal, caring community.

'We will keep fighting for Helen's Law,' he vowed. 'I think we are making progress. It's been slow and it's been frustrating, but I'm confident we're going to get there and if the spirit involved tonight helps us get there then that will be all the better.'

Then, turning to me, he added: 'Marie, you've taught me a great lesson in valuing, caring about and treasuring every moment with the people you love and I'm very grateful to you for doing that. As I left home tonight, I hugged and kissed my children. I feel very lucky and very glad to have them, and you, in my life, so thank you.'

Applause rang out as we hugged.

'Thank you – for everything,' I told him.

Two months later, in April 2018, Conor organised a Day of Action for Helen's Law at Westminster. By then, yet another state – Western Australia – where Margaret Dodd lived had passed No Body No Parole.

It was an unseasonably scorching day as we gathered in a room for MPs to pledge their support. I lost count of just how many politicians I was introduced to and photographed with.

Later, we marched to Downing Street to present signatures now totalling 440,000, including 8,000 letters from readers of *Take a Break* magazine, which had come on board.

Finally, came the most nerve-racking part of the day: a meeting with David Gauke – the Justice Minister himself.

Fiona and John had worked around the clock putting together a folder of information for me to hand over, including articles, supportive statements from families, bereavement experts and even police officers who had worked on the case at the time who could vouch for Simms' refusal to co-operate in locating Helen's body.

We also provided more information on the No Body No Parole situation in Australia. Fiona had recently been working in Queensland, Australia, on a separate story and, by chance, (again I thank St Martha) heard of a local case involving a newly convicted killer who led police to the location of his victim. His actions were thought to be a direct result of the new legislation. 'The laws are working, David,' I told him. 'We know of two bodies recovered, one parole denied and one prisoner begging to co-operate so that he would be considered for release.

'We are not malicious people,' I added. 'We don't want to see killers locked up forever. All we want is our loved one home so we can lay them to rest. We need the same carrot and stick approach, David, a reason for these killers to cooperate,' I insisted.

Mr Gauke listened attentively. 'There are some obstacles which we have to try and work around,' he said.

Ah, now we come to the crux of the matter.

'Can I take it these small obstacles are connected to the Court of Human Rights?' I ventured.

He nodded.

I shook my head. Once again, the rights of prisoners were being put ahead those of innocent victims and their families.

Surely, once you take the life of another person, you forfeit all claim to human rights? And while we're on the subject of human rights, what about the right to life? And the right not to be tortured or treated in an inhumane way?

Mr Gauke promised he would come back to us.

'We think he is a fair man and pray he will give us this long overdue justice,' I told reporters later.

Afterwards, in the late afternoon sunshine, Linda Jones and I shared confidences. We had both lost our only daughters. 'It's like being tortured continually,' I said, and she nodded knowingly. 'It's as if there is a constantly running tap over your head. The killer is responsible for the "drip, drip, drip" – there's no escape from it.

'We are subjected to this morning, noon and night. There is no respite – even when we sleep, we suffer the most appalling nightmares about our loved ones' final moments and where they could be.'

Linda agreed. 'It's as if I have a "smiling" mask hanging by the front door,' she sighed. 'I put it on when I leave the house and take it off when I come in. The real me hides behind it.

'It's like being trapped in the middle of a carousel. The rest of the world goes on turning without you. Everywhere you look, people are living their lives, enjoying themselves and laughing. But where we are there is nothing.'

We also talked about another sad impact for families in our situation.

'My sons never wanted to celebrate achievements in life like passing exams or driving tests – simply because their sister never got to do those things,' said Linda. 'Until we can lay her to rest, it will always be there.'

Such intense and all-consuming pain and anger can tear families apart, we agreed. Needing to find our loved one can become an obsession that takes over everything else.

'I am starting to accept now that Simms is not going to tell me where my daughter's body is,' I admitted. 'I can deal with that now. But I will continue to fight to prevent other people going through what we are going through. This cannot happen to other families, we have to keep fighting.'

Three weeks later, in the run-up to Prince Harry marrying Meghan Markle, my victim liaison officer called. I braced myself for the inevitable bad news.

'Simms is being prepared for escorted release on temporary licence,' she said.

The blood ran cold in my veins. The thought of that man being let loose on the streets, escorted or not, both sickened and terrified me.

His cruel words – his vow to get justice – were still emblazoned on my mind.

Because of all the interviews I'd given over the years to find my daughter he knew what I looked like.

What was to stop him coming to find me at the first opportunity?

'Marie?' she said. 'Are you still there?'

I realised I'd been trying to speak but the words were trapped in my constricted voice box.

'You do know he's a psychopath, don't you?' I eventually gasped. 'This can't happen.'

The *Daily Mirror* ran an exclusive story and Conor McGinn raised it in Parliament that very day – urging the Justice Secretary to intervene and for the Government to introduce Helen's Law legislation. Sadly, it changed nothing. By the end of May 2018, I was informed that Simms' two escorted releases from prison had gone so well that the authorities were now planning unescorted release.

Once again, the media covered the story. I was no longer just afraid at this point – I was livid.

'Right,' I stormed to reporters, getting into my stride. 'If this is going ahead, I want restorative justice. I want to meet him and ask him where Helen is.

'He wouldn't do it, though. He'd refuse, like the coward he is. He won't even attend parole hearings. Is it because he knows he'd lose his rag?

'Well, what happens if he bumps into me in the street? Will he attack me?

'It's all very well for these pen-pushers rubber stamping their decisions. They are not sitting in the house wondering who's going to appear at the front door. How can they possibly keep an eye on them twenty-four hours a day to ensure they don't go into exclusion zones?

'They can't! If I or my family are attacked, I will sue the Parole Board and the Government,' I vowed.

I was heartened when the issue was raised in the Commons, in early June 2018. Prisons Minister Rory Stewart said the MOJ was working on a solution to, and consequences for, the 'absolutely disgusting practice' of killers hiding bodies.

'There is something peculiarly disgusting about the sadism involved in an individual murdering somebody and then refusing to reveal the location of the victim's body,' he said.

Officials had drawn up two options which he would discuss with Justice Secretary David Gauke within days to come up with a 'solution'.

'There have been delays in terms of framing the right kind of legal response but I am absolutely confident we can overcome that and officials are now bringing forward advice which I hope will achieve exactly what people have been campaigning for.

'But we are absolutely clear this is an absolutely disgusting practice and we ought to be able to use legal methods to impose consequences on individuals who refuse to reveal the location of a body.'

I was so bolstered by his words. *That should nip his unescorted prison release in the bud*, I thought.

Did it heck! Probation told me that the Prison Governor was 'standing by the decision' to allow Simms 'unescorted release'.

'Who on earth do these governors think they are?' I ranted. 'Their job is to run prisons – not release dangerous inmates.'

I gave countless interviews to papers, radio and TV news programmes – urging the Ministry to freeze any release plans until a decision had been made on Helen's Law. Meanwhile,

Conor McGinn sought urgent meetings with Ministers to block Simms' release.

I was heartened by the John Worboys' case – if you remember, he was the Black Cab rapist recommended for release by the Parole Board in January 2018. However, furious victims launched a High Court challenge which resulted in the Court quashing the release decision. Worboys was recalled to prison and a new Parole Board hearing led to him being turned down for release in January 2019.

The more I spoke out, the more messages of support and encouragement continued to flood in. Signatures continued to soar on the petition – it seemed every single person in the country was behind me.

But we may as well have been whistling in the wind for all the good it did. By July, I wept as my probation officer confirmed Simms had, indeed, enjoyed 'two or three days' out from his open prison and would now be progressing to weekend release in a hostel.

'I couldn't take in what the officer was saying as I kept breaking down and crying,' I told Fiona Duffy afterwards. 'I asked her: "Do they know it's my murdered daughter's birthday at the end of this month?"

'It's bad enough that I am enduring the thirtieth birthday, since her murder, without a grave to lay flowers on. But I can't even mark the day quietly, in peace, knowing that he is already out enjoying himself, living his new life, in a hostel. He is there, in my head, all the time,' I said, jabbing my forehead with my finger.

I gave interview after interview until I could barely think. 'I'm sickened, in torment, at the thought of him enjoying freedom while, thanks to his cruel actions, I still don't even have a grave to visit and remember her by,' I told reporters.

Then, I vocalised the thought which really distressed me – which had me lying wide awake in the early hours: 'I'm not getting any younger,' I said, in a breaking voice. 'I'm seventy-five – just three years younger than Winnie Johnson was when she died not knowing where her son was.

'The thought of leaving this earth while Helen is still out there, lost and alone, breaks my heart. This law is my only chance of getting him to reveal where she is, that is all I want.

'This Government has led me to believe that the Parole Board would not release prisoners until a decision is made on Helen's Law. So why is this appalling injustice being allowed to happen?

'He is a danger to the public. I am begging, imploring the Ministry of Justice – please do not let this man free.'

We had 450,000 signatures. If we could get to half a million, surely the authorities would have to act? Throughout the summer, we ramped up the campaign. A local printing company offered to make Helen's Law T-shirts and tote bags, at cost price, and we sold dozens.

I was so touched when I turned up to Pilates to find the entire class wearing vibrant Helen's Law tops in solidarity.

We also got a Helen's Law roadshow underway – setting up a stall in town centres so we could distribute leaflets and yellow ribbons.

'Every signature counts,' John and I would agree at the end of another exhausting day.

Some offers of help moved me to tears. St Helens Council said we could host a stand outside the Town Hall on the day of Helen's birthday. We turned up to find one of our campaigners, Tracy Richardson, there – with a huge arch of yellow balloons. She worked with us all day.

That evening, we all headed down to the Steve Prescott Bridge to see it lit up with soft yellow floodlights – another lovely gesture of support from the council. 'It represents the sunshine of her smile – plus it's the international colour for missing people,' I told reporters.

Tracy Richardson also designed a new, heart-tugging poster featuring our missing loved ones. New families allowed us to include images of their missing murdered loved ones while Keith Bennett's family gave us permission to include his black and white photograph. Even families who felt unable to take part in publicity shared these posters on social media, encouraging people to sign.

It worked. Once again, the signatures were rising.

In autumn 2018, the MOJ contacted Conor McGinn with a proposal for proceeding with Helen's Law. 'But I don't think it goes as far as you would like, Marie,' he said. 'I think we should push for another meeting.'

I couldn't hide my disappointment. It had been three years since we launched this fight and we were no further forward. In the meantime, every day brought us a step closer to Simms' next parole hearing. He was in an open prison with unescorted release. Next step was full release on licence.

It didn't bear thinking about.

* * *

As 2019 got underway we were boosted by two high-profile programmes. We were in India when Judge Rinder's *Crime Stories* featured Helen's case and my fight for justice – but we watched it on John's iPad in our hotel room. It was done brilliantly and I was so thrilled when Judge Rinder himself tweeted: 'Helen's Law is essential. Families of victims must be heard.'

Then in February, the Crime + Investigation channel chose Helen's story to launch its new series of *When Missing Turns to Murder*. Producers from both programmes had spent hours with both us and loved ones.

My sister, Pat, told the interviewer: 'It prevented our children from having a normal life. You couldn't take the dogs for a walk without looking at fields, thinking: "Is she here?"'

And my eyes welled as John spoke: 'I am sure she would have been a mother – probably even a grandmother – by now. It's a big hole.

'She'll always be around us. As long as we breathe, she'll be with us.'

I reached out silently to squeeze his hand.

Where would I be without you? I thought.

My last words on screen were: 'No one ever wants to bury a child. But she deserves a proper, peaceful rest.'

Diana Carter, commissioning editor at A & E Networks which produces Crime + Investigation, had told Fiona Duffy the programme would have a powerful impact.

'It was an education to learn about Marie McCourt's campaign,' she said. 'She is an incredibly powerful speaker; the way she tells her story draws you in and makes you understand the horror of the world she has been put in by the loss of her daughter.

'She does this both by her calmness, poise and grace but also, unfortunately, by the complete and utter injustice of the situation. It just hits home so well that as soon as I finished watching the "rough cut" of the film, which tells the backbone of the story, I went online, searched for Helen's Law and signed the petition.

'The programme will make the hairs on the back of your neck stand up. Marie does her daughter so much justice and I imagine there will be a huge response to the episode.'

And there was. Linda Jones and I were asked to appear together on *Good Morning Britain*, with Susanna Reid and Ben Shephard, while Fiona recruited Professor Elizabeth Yardley of the Centre for Applied Criminology at Birmingham City University to the campaign.

Delighted, John and I travelled to Birmingham to meet her and a story in which she pledged her support appeared in the *Daily Mirror*: 'Justice has only been partially done in this case,' she declared. 'No convicted murderer should even have the possibility of parole whilst still withholding information as to the whereabouts of their victim's body.'

By now, we'd surpassed half a million signatures and were approaching 600,000. Conor McGinn had approached the MOJ three times now to ask for a meeting but heard nothing back. Frustration was consuming me.

A few days after our trip to Birmingham, I answered the front door to a supportive reporter from the *Daily Mail*.

'There's something you need to see,' she said, handing me a stiff-backed envelope.

I pulled out a colour photograph of a man in his sixties, wearing a woolly hat, scruffy too-long jeans and glasses. He had a salt and pepper beard and a definite paunch under his sweatshirt as he stood with his hands in his jeans. Over his left shoulder, he was carrying a holdall.

Confusion jostled with strange sparks of recognition in my brain. There was something familiar about the set of his jaw, that blank expression, but I couldn't quite—

Suddenly, my stomach lurched.

'Is this …?' I asked.

She nodded.

Simms.

For years I'd been asking for a recent photograph of him but the authorities had always refused. Now here he was in all his glory.

Someone must have tipped off the paper as to where he would be on that day. The years hadn't been kind to him: still only in his early sixties, but he looked much older.

'He was waiting for a bus,' the journalist volunteered. 'In Birmingham.'

I nearly fainted. 'Birmingham? *Birmingham?*' I cried. 'I was there on Monday. I could have brushed past him in the street, sat next to him on the train. He could have been following me without me even knowing.' I shook my head.

This was wrong, so wrong.

When a reporter, with the photographer, asked him where Helen was, he'd replied: 'If I knew where the body was I would never have done sixteen years extra in prison, would I?'

Again, such arrogance and flippancy. There was no hint of remorse or regret. Surely, if you were truly innocent, you'd grab that reporter and beg, plead, implore for help in proving the wrong man had been convicted. (Let's not forget, after kicking up a stink Simms had won the right – funded by legal aid – back in the nineties to speak with journalists.) Instead, he was petulant. Sullen. Sulky.

'He should not be afforded any days out,' I told the newspaper. 'This evil man is walking around, enjoying the sunshine, while my daughter is hidden somewhere, discarded, as the judge said at the trial, with the rats.'

For my next novena, I uttered a heartfelt plea to St Martha and all the saints in heaven to answer my prayers.

With a sigh, I watched the candle burn down and fade – like my hopes.

It had been a long thirty-one years and I wasn't sure how much longer I could keep fighting.

Chapter 18

Elation ... followed by 'the unthinkable'

'What are we doing?' I sighed, as the train pulled out of Wigan North Western station. It was Wednesday, 15 May 2019. We were on yet another trip to London.

Justice Minister David Gauke had finally asked to meet with us. But, unlike last time, my hopes were in my boots. It had been more than twelve months since our last meeting and I'd heard little since. Mr Gauke would no doubt tell me that although he sympathised, his hands were tied by human rights laws.

'Let's see what he has to say,' John said, encouragingly. But I visualised myself, in a few hours, making the return journey forlorn, bereft and consumed by red-hot anger.

I'd have to cancel Pilates tomorrow, I wouldn't be able to face anyone.

Last night, I'd lit my candle and knelt before my statue of St Martha – just as I'd done every Tuesday for thirty-one years – praying for my daughter's return. Halfway through my novena, my voice faltered. The words failed me, my mind was empty.

'Come on, St Martha,' I implored. 'I've been saying this prayer for more than thirty years. Give me the words!'

Eventually, I had to look up the prayer just to be able to recite it.

'St Martha,' I beseeched. 'I really need you and all of them up there to pull your thumbs out and turn this around for me. Because right now, things aren't looking good.'

She gazed back at me solemnly, giving nothing away.

Just before leaving the house, Conor McGinn had called to prewarn me that even though changes had been proposed, release decisions would still be left to the Parole Board.

'But that's what happens now!' I spluttered. 'Nothing has changed.

'If I don't like what I hear in there, I'm going to speak out,' I warned.

But I was tired of speaking out. Tired of fighting. We'd had so many knockbacks over the years and this looked set to be the biggest one of all.

I played through scenarios in my mind. I'd be dignified and polite – but honest. 'You have children, Mr Gauke,' I'd say. 'How would you feel if it was your child still missing after being murdered? The whole country wants this. Why can't you grant it? In denying us this, you are assisting sadistic killers and aiding and abetting the torturing of innocent people.'

I nodded in satisfaction at the phrase – *that sounded good*.

By the time we arrived, I had worked myself into a pretty formidable mood. I had, what my mum used to call, a 'tippy lip' (when a bottom lip juts out defiantly).

I would listen politely before telling Mr Gauke exactly what I thought of him and our country's ridiculous prisoner-pandering policies and how he'd let us all down.

Hell hath no fury like a woman scorned? Rubbish! Hell hath no fury like a bereaved mum desperate to lay her child to rest.

I expected Mr Gauke to look a bit sheepish but he smiled

broadly as he shook my hand: 'How lovely to see you, Marie,' he said warmly.

I'd practised a stiff 'Mr Gauke' acknowledgement, but his greeting had sucked the wind right out of my sails. I couldn't embarrass him in front of his staff, so I smiled back, responding: 'Nice to see you as well, David,' before adding pointedly, 'It's been over twelve months, hasn't it?'

Mr Gauke was flanked by half a dozen members of staff, who all looked pleased to be there. The atmosphere in the room felt warm and sunny rather than chilly and forbidding.

'So,' he began, 'Conor has explained things to you. How do you feel, Marie? Do you have any questions?'

I clasped my hands in my lap. 'I'd like to hear it from you, please, David,' I replied.

Here we go, I thought, bracing myself for the inevitable human rights flannel.

Except he didn't say that at all. Well, not entirely. David Gauke, a qualified solicitor, spoke honestly and openly about the limitations that he faced in drawing up this kind of legislation because the UK was still committed to the European Convention of Human Rights.

A blanket No Body No Parole law, as they had in Australia, was impossible. A determined prisoner and a good barrister would take it to the High Court and have it overturned on human rights grounds, it was as simple as that. We'd have lost at a stroke.

I shuddered. It was a prospect that didn't bear thinking about. Instead, he was proposing a new law whereby the Parole Board would be legally bound to take into account non-disclosure of information by a prisoner when considering release.

There were currently guidelines in place for the Parole Board to consider such withholding of information by the prisoner. But that's all they were – guidelines.

The Bill, he said, would have an official title. 'But it would always be known as Helen's Law,' he added. 'It will be a completely new piece of legislation, not an amendment to an existing bill. These people here [he gestured to his team] are ready to start the wording straight away.'

Like sunlight gently warming early dew, that anger, that despair from earlier, was slowly evaporating. Instead, an emotion I hadn't felt in years, and barely recognised, was beginning to flow through my veins.

Hope.

Yes, it was tinged with disappointment, granted. It didn't go as far as I'd have liked it to. But David Gauke had clearly explained why, for now at least, that couldn't happen. I could rant and rave and stamp my feet about human rights until I was blue in the face, but it wouldn't change a thing.

I had two choices – I could upend the table and storm out with nowhere to go, or I could accept that this was a start.

A beginning.

David sat forward. 'This really is the best way forward,' he said.

With this law in place, the Parole Board would have to consider non-disclosure very carefully in order to qualify their decision. And they'd also have to take into account the impact statement from the victim's family – how being denied a funeral had affected them.

'Obviously, things could change in the future,' he added. There would always be the possibility of amending or strengthening the law over time. And with cross-party support, it should pass through Parliament quickly.

I sat back.

Wow, this was really happening! The MOJ really was bringing in a new law ... Helen's Law.

At this point, Conor spoke: 'I don't know how Marie does it,' he said. 'She works so hard and helps so many other people who are hurting, but all the time, she is dealing with her own pain.'

I smiled at him gratefully – we were finally being listened to, the tide was slowly turning in our favour.

Sensing the meeting drawing to a close, I reached into my handbag and pulled out a page torn from the previous day's *Daily Mirror*. 'I would like to read this to you,' I said, holding it up to them. 'It sums up what our families go through when they can't bury their loved ones.'

It was a heart-rending story written by Fiona Duffy and Louie Smith about one of our families.

I pointed out photos on the page. 'This is Sheila Dolton,' I said. 'She is a mother who, like myself, goes out searching for the body of her murdered child.

'Jonathan, twenty, was killed by his business partner, Stewart Martin, in 2002. Martin has since died, taking his secret to the grave.

'"I've spent seventeen years hunting for where the killer hid my dead son's body,"' I read.

'"... I go deep into wooded areas ... At times it's terrifying.

'"Once, I got lost as night fell. I stumbled about in the dark in sheer panic. I sat down and sobbed.

'"I always pack a survival blanket and compass now. We feel it's our duty as Jonathan's parents to find him."'

I looked up. They were all silent, you could have heard a pin drop.

'Now, you can empathise and sympathise,' I said. 'But you will never know just how tortuous this is until you live through it yourself.

'These killers hold onto the bodies like a badge of honour. It's a hold they have over the family and it's evil. Even people who lose loved ones in the most awful ways, in bombings and terrorist attacks, can have that last goodbye. Afterwards, you have a grave ... somewhere to go with your grief and your pain.

'We don't.

'These killers are not ordinary people. These are sociopaths and psychopaths. In hiding the body, they want to get away with murder – literally. We have to take that control away from them.'

No one spoke.

'I'll leave this with you,' I said, handing the page to David. Then I stood up and shook their hands. 'Thank you,' I said. 'Thank you for listening to me.'

My feet didn't touch the ground as Conor steered us towards the Strangers' Bar to raise a glass to Helen. A warm fuzzy feeling flooded through me – and it wasn't just the alcohol. I felt pride and triumph, I didn't want that feeling to ever end.

Arriving home, I headed straight for my St Martha statue. I picked her up and kissed her face.

'Thank you,' I said.

Then, with tears in my eyes, I gazed up at our portrait of Helen. 'And you, love. I know you are there, sweetheart. You have given me the strength to keep going all these years.'

The *Daily Mirror* and *Mail* both ran stories and more interview requests flooded in.

'Seeing a new law unveiled in Helen's name will be a very proud, and poignant, moment. It means that her death – and all this pain – would count for something and make a difference,' I told journalists.

Professor Yardley confessed she had to sit down when she heard the news. 'Things like this just don't happen,' she said, in delighted astonishment. 'This is truly astounding.'

She hailed it as a crucial piece of legislation that will 'enhance the integrity of the criminal justice system in England and Wales' and how it was 'testament to the tenacity and determination of Marie McCourt and the community of campaigners around her'.

'People like Marie are the driving forces behind reform of our system. They expose the ways in which it's not fit for purpose and demand change.

'This is a massive step forwards for everyone affected by homicide – victims' families and offenders alike.

'And it shows that when we do draw attention to gaps and shortfalls, and shout loudly enough, change can happen.'

I'd never felt prouder. I was an ordinary, heartbroken, grieving mum who had shouted loudly and persistently until people finally listened.

Lovely comments flooded my social media accounts, buoying me up.

Sleep came easier to me and there was a lightness in my feet that I hadn't felt since 5.15pm on 9 February 1988.

* * *

On the way home from Pilates, one lunchtime, still wearing my vibrant yellow Helen's Law T-shirt, I stopped off in St Helens.

Outside Boots, a woman placed her hand on my arm. She looked vaguely familiar but I couldn't quite place the face. 'I'm Helen's old Brown Owl,' she said. 'I just want to say well done on your campaign. She was such a lovely girl and would be so proud of you.'

I beamed. 'Thank you,' I said. 'Helen adored being a Brownie.'

There were no tears, no sadness. Just lovely memories.

As we chatted, another woman hovered: 'Are you the one who's been running that campaign?' she asked. 'I think you've done brilliantly.'

I was no longer just 'Poor Mrs McCourt', I was 'Determined Mrs McCourt', 'Campaigning Mrs McCourt', 'Making a Difference Mrs McCourt'.

For the first time in thirty years, I found myself singing along to the radio, even breaking out into a dance in the kitchen.

Meanwhile, the hard work continued. Fiona Duffy obtained new figures from the Home Office that showed a terrifying increase in cases of homicide convictions without a body. There had been fifty for both murder and manslaughter for a ten-year period up to December 2018.

'That's five a year,' I gasped. 'And these are just the cases we know of – how many more missing people have been murdered and hidden?'

Professor Yardley was surprised the figure wasn't higher – referring to a 'dark figure' of homicide … Killings that we simply will never know about.

'There are many homicide victims hidden in the missing persons statistics,' she explained. 'And those are the people who have been reported missing, many are not. Just as law enforcement becomes more skilled and adept at investigating homicide, perpetrators will try to stay one step ahead of them, and some will succeed.

'Killers in the twenty-first century are increasingly forensically aware. In an age of the internet and countless true crime television shows, they have access to a lot of information about the investigation of homicide – they know that every contact leaves a trace and that the most valuable piece of evidence in any homicide investigation is the victim's body.'

Until now, the MOJ hadn't confirmed any details from my meeting with David Gauke. I began to wonder if I'd dreamt the whole thing. So, it was a relief when they issued a press release early in July 2019. 'Helen's Law Victory' screamed the front page of the *Daily Mirror.*

Killers who refuse to disclose the whereabouts of victims remains are set to serve longer behind bars, the Ministry of Justice has confirmed.

Justice Secretary David Gauke has announced that the MOJ is bringing in new legislation which will make it harder for parole to be granted to unco-operative prisoners who prolong the agony for victims' families.

The announcement is a huge victory for Marie McCourt, mother of missing murder victim Helen McCourt, who has fought a tireless battle – backed by the *Daily Mirror* – to see the law changed.

'Knowing that a legacy is being created in my daughter's name, and she will never be forgotten, brings us some comfort,' she said.

Conor McGinn hailed the news as 'a good day for British justice'.

In a strongly worded statement David Gauke said: 'It is a particular cruelty to deny grieving families the opportunity to lay their murdered loved one to rest, and I have immense sympathy with Marie McCourt and others in her situation.

'"Helen's Law" will mean that the Parole Board must consider this cruelty when reviewing an offender's suitability for release – which could see them facing longer behind bars.

'The profound grief inflicted on families and friends of the murdered is incalculable. Those responsible should know that if they choose to compound this further through their behaviour, they will be held accountable.'

Many papers also covered reforms to the parole system which had been announced earlier that year – in response to the John Worboys situation – allowing victims the opportunity to challenge decisions they felt were fundamentally flawed.

It was all coming together nicely. In a flash, I remembered the priest's words from seven years earlier: 'Your prayers will be answered. It may not be in the way you want, but it will always be done in the best way possible for everyone.'

Maybe this was how it was meant to be. Who knows what our purpose is on this earth? Maybe Helen and I were destined to go through this awful ordeal in order to highlight a terrible injustice.

God might not have let me find her body yet, but he had

blessed me with good health so I could keep shouting for change. Apart from a broken heart, arthritis and osteoporosis (I fractured my wrist when I fell, gardening, a few years earlier) and despite the poor health that had plagued my childhood, I have been fighting fit and healthy for years.

I'm rarely ill. All around me I have seen so many others fall ill with cancer, heart disease, stroke, dementia. I am still here. I have to be.

In a strange way, maybe Helen wasn't meant to be found just yet, I reasoned. For as long as she was missing, I'd go on fighting. And when the time was right, she would be found – I was sure of it.

That summer, the sun shone brightly. Sadly, David Gauke resigned over Brexit issues. But his replacement, Robert Buckland, had a promising track record when it came to helping grieving families.

You may remember a shocking case from back in March 2011 when police in Swindon arrested cab driver Christopher Halliwell following the disappearance of twenty-two-year-old Sian O'Callaghan on her way home from a nightclub.

Through brilliant work by Detective Superintendent Steve Fulcher, Halliwell not only confessed to the murder and led officers to the body, he then – out of the blue – volunteered information about 'another one' – leading police to a remote field in Gloucestershire. There they recovered the body of twenty-year-old Becky Godden-Edwards who he'd killed back in 2003.

Yet because DSI Fulcher hadn't followed police guidelines in reading Halliwell his rights and offering him a solicitor (who would, no doubt, have advised him to stay quiet) a judge ruled the confessions were deemed inadmissible and the second murder charge was dropped. DSI Fulcher should have been knighted. Instead his career was ruined.

Although Halliwell pleaded guilty to Sian's murder and was

sentenced to twenty-five years – Becky's determined mum Karen Edwards wanted justice for her daughter, too. Her MP gave her his full backing, encouraged her to launch a petition and raised her plight in the House of Commons.

In 2016, Halliwell was finally convicted of Becky's murder and given a whole life order. That helpful MP was Robert Buckland. So, you can understand why I was so heartened to hear that he was the new Lord Chancellor and Secretary of State for Justice. (Both Karen and Steve Fulcher have backed my campaign – support for which I am so grateful).

Nothing could go wrong, now, surely? There was even talk of Helen's Law being included in the Queen's Speech in October.

More good fortune came our way when Louie Smith at the *Mirror* suggested we ask an expert to cast a fresh eye over our old searches.

Professor John Hunter OBE, forensic archaeologist who specialised in finding the graves of missing people, had looked closely at our search with Fiona, back in 2002, along with a colleague, but had since retired. But Fiona had recently met Peter Faulding of Specialist Group International – one of the country's leading search and recovery experts – while working on a story of yet another missing young woman (Nicola Payne of Coventry, a young mum who vanished in 1991).

He'd worked on other well-known cases including the search for little April Jones in Wales and finding vital evidence for the conviction of Scottish serial killer Peter Tobin. And I was humbled when he said he'd be delighted to help.

I have nothing but gratitude and thanks to Merseyside Police and all the officers who worked on the initial case. In asking Peter Faulding for his invaluable help we meant no criticism of them. The fact is, search techniques have improved dramatically since the late eighties. Indeed, I'm convinced that had people like Peter been around back then, with his state-of-the-art equipment like sonic radar and magnetometers, to detect soil disturbances, Helen would have been found.

First, however, he needed information. And lots of it. We pored over files – from transcripts of the court case and witness statements to Simms' hobbies and interests and vital evidence.

Once Peter had absorbed every detail, he came to visit – along with Fiona and Louie. He agreed with our basic instincts that the area around Rixton – where the spade had been found – was key.

On two separate occasions, we spent days exploring possible burial sites – clambering over rough ground, being savaged by giant mosquitoes and getting drenched in torrential downpours.

The advancing years had caught up with John and I and we found it long, hard, exhausting work. Poor John, still prone to falls, suffered backache for a week after a spectacular tumble down a muddy slope. At times, Peter insisted we rest in the car. Otherwise, we fetched and carried tools, while he worked like a Trojan.

And at times our hopes soared sky-high. I trembled when Peter delicately unearthed a buried length of electric wire. Then I peered eagerly into the soil only to find it was an old-fashioned twisted flex rather than the plastic-coated type Simms had used to strangle Helen.

Another time, Peter's spade revealed a corner of thick, clear plastic. My heart froze in my chest. Had Helen been wrapped in it? But it was garden sacking that had somehow ended up being buried.

Peter is still very involved and preparing for his next visit to try and find Helen – as soon as his busy schedule allows. We will never, ever be able to thank him – and those who so willingly give access to their land. Such consideration really does keep us going.

Meanwhile, the nightmare that was Brexit continued to dominate politics, overshadowing everything else. Leave dates were extended, the new prime minister Boris Johnson took over the helm, Parliament was prorogued, then reinstalled. It was infuriating.

* * *

At the end of September came a phone call which left me reeling. A date had been set for Simms' next parole hearing: 7 November.

My stomach lurched. 'Surely they'll have to wait until Helen's Law has been passed?' I asked desperately.

Apparently not.

I rang Conor McGinn and started to write a letter to Secretary of State for Justice Robert Buckland, imploring him to intervene. To my astonishment, he agreed to see me on Monday, 14 October – the day of the Queen's Speech. I printed off my letter, begging him for his help.

'We can deliver the letter in person,' I told John.

Just as the train was at its noisiest – rattling through tunnel after tunnel – the probation office called. I couldn't hear a thing.

'We'll send an email,' they said, before we lost the connection.

In Robert Buckland's office, I handed over the letter – and threw myself on his mercy. 'When will Helen's Law go through?' I asked.

He turned to his team. Someone said 'Next spring' and I gasped in horror.

'That's too late!' I cried. 'It needs to be now.'

Robert nodded. 'Could we have it for the end of the year?' he asked someone.

I turned to John in despair, then back to Robert. 'That's still too late,' I insisted. 'My daughter's killer might be up for parole in three weeks. Time is something I don't have.

'David Gauke said it could be two to three months when I met him in May. That was five months ago!'

Robert assured me that he had immense sympathy and would introduce the Bill as soon as possible.

'Thank you,' I said.

He was trying his best – and these delays weren't his fault either.

* * *

Back at home, we opened an email from probation. It was official – the parole hearing was scheduled for 7 and 8 November, just over three weeks away.

'Well, that's that,' I sighed.

To cheer me up, John played the Queen's Speech that he'd recorded earlier that day. 'Let's see if a certain Bill has been included,' he said.

I held my breath waiting for her to reach the crucial words in her own inimitable style:

> My Government is committed to addressing violent crime, and to strengthening public confidence in the criminal justice system. [...]
> Laws will be introduced to ensure that the parole system recognises the pain to victims and their families caused by offenders refusing to disclose information relating to their crimes.

And there it was. The Queen herself had mentioned my law.

It had to go through now, surely?

I googled the Bill – now titled the Prisoners (Disclosure of Information About Victims) Bill – and read it out to John, highlighting the strongest words:

> The purpose of the Bill is to ensure that where an offender who has been convicted of murder, manslaughter or taking indecent photographs of children refuses to disclose

certain details about their offences, that is considered by
the Parole Board as part of their assessment as to whether
that offender should be released.

The main benefits of the Bill would be: 'Putting in statute, and
therefore beyond doubt, the Parole Board's established practice
of considering a failure by an offender to disclose specific
information in these cases.'

And 'Making this established Parole Board practice a
legal obligation so families and victims will know that such
issues must be taken into account as part of the Parole Board
release process.

'The main elements of the Bill are: Amending the life sentence
and the extended determinate sentence release test to direct
the Parole Board to take into account circumstances where an
offender, who has been convicted of murder or manslaughter, has
not disclosed the location of a victim's remains.'

'Oh, and listen to this,' I continued. 'Underneath, there's a
section entitled Key Facts which says: "The first measure of this
Bill is a version of 'Helen's Law', which has been the subject
of a campaign by Marie McCourt. Her daughter, Helen,
was murdered by Ian Simms in 1988 and her body has never
been found.

'"The Parole Board already has internal guidance which advises
panel members to consider any failure or refusal by an offender to
disclose the whereabouts of a victim's remains information when
assessing release. The Bill makes this a statutory requirement.'"

I sat back, proudly. Well, it certainly sounded good.

By now, the Bill had been widened to also include cases where
offenders refuse to disclose the identity of children in abusive
images they have taken or made. I had no problem with this.
Helen adored children – she would be proud to think that she
was making a difference in such horrendous cases.

The Bill was presented to Parliament the very next day. That was something at least. Maybe by some miracle, it could whizz through in three weeks?

In the meantime, Fiona suggested we try to secure legal advice. Professor Yardley reached out to 9 Gough Chambers in London and I was choked when top barrister James Thacker agreed to represent me on a pro bono basis.

I can't even begin to tell you how many hours James and his dedicated team spent with me over the next twelve months. They went above and beyond the call of duty and I will never, ever be able to repay them.

Just the day before our first meeting in London, two separate murder convictions without a body were returned by two separate juries on the very same afternoon. One was a recent case, the other was twenty years old. They were Sarah Wellgreen, forty-six, a mum of five who vanished in October 2018, and mum of three Debbie Griggs, thirty-four, who was pregnant when she disappeared in 1999. Both victims were mothers – killed and hidden by the very men who should have loved them. My heart went out to their families. And their children.

Helen's Law had never been so needed.

There was no way of delaying the parole hearing, James explained, but he would support me during the process. We would start by asking the Parole Board to release the 'dossier' on Simms (a folder of information relating to his time in prison) so we could ensure that it was accurate and complete – and relevant to my concerns about risk. We would also ask for a legal representative to accompany me to the hearing. I immediately felt calmer.

On the way back from our meeting in London, a billboard for the *Evening Standard* stopped me in my tracks: 'Oh, dear God!' I said. The Commons had just voted for a General Election on 12 December.

Parliament was falling once again ...

I felt jinxed. Doomed. What else could go wrong? Once again, everything ground to a halt.

The only saving grace this time was that the Bill had been presented to Parliament and included in the Queen's Speech. But there was no way it would pass in time. And what if Conor McGinn or Robert Buckland – my champions – lost their seats? I was a nervous wreck.

On Thursday, 7 November – the day after Parliament had officially been dissolved, John, Michael and I nervously arrived at the Parole Board head office in Canary Wharf.

This was it.

The Parole Board had refused to release the dossier – and only granted permission for my legal representative to attend less than one hour before the hearing. It was a mad rush for them to get there.

Michael, John and I each read our statements. No matter how many times you do this, it's always an ordeal, fracturing your heart into even more tiny pieces as you relive the horror of the murder all over again. But, at the same time, you know that those words only ever reveal a tiny fraction of your true pain.

How can you sum up thirty-two years of torture on a few flimsy pages of A4?

I was thrown when, towards the end of the hearing, the Parole Judge said: 'I would like you to know that I have read Helen's Law.'

I blinked; I had absolutely no idea what to say. I wasn't even sure if this was a test, and a pass or fail for me – or Simms – would depend on my response.

Could asking 'and what do you think?' or 'do you agree?' put me on shaky ground?

I just nodded and said: 'Oh, thank you.'

Downstairs, Fiona led us out to waiting journalists and photographers for interviews. Once again, I held up my precious framed photo of Helen and spoke from the heart: 'I hope and pray the parole judges will listen to my plea and that of my son, Michael, and make the right decision for us.

'And I urge Ian Simms, please, please do the right thing. End this torture and tell us where Helen's remains can be recovered. Then you also can look forward to a day of being released.'

Two weeks later, I was heading into my Pilates class when my mobile rang. My stomach lurched at the number on caller display: victim liaison officer.

'Oh God!' I whispered, as I shakily pressed 'reply'.

Once again, with three familiar words, my world came crashing around my ears.

'I'm sorry, Marie ...'

He was being released.

Chapter 19

A race against
time

The words hit me like a bolt of lightning. I leaned against the gym wall, my stomach churning as if on a fast spin.

It felt as if I was underwater – sounds were distorted and muffled. I desperately wanted to rewind my life to a few moments ago where I was walking into my Pilates class, happily chatting. I'd keep my finger on the rewind button. See images speed up faster and faster as I whirled back through the last horrible thirty-two years ... Back through the exhumation, countless parole hearings, the awful court case.

I'd stop on the morning of 9 February 1988, press 'delete' and start again. I'd see myself hurrying down the stairs, tying my dressing gown, to catch Helen before she left for work. I'd tell her I loved her and that I'd pick her up from work that night. She'd go on her date, as planned. Shopping trips, holidays, parties, her wedding day, her babies, her thirtieth, fortieth, fiftieth birthdays would all unfold.

The life I should have had with her.

Simms had stolen all of that from me – and more. Not only had he taken my daughter's life, he had taken her body.

Hidden it. For more than thirty years he refused to say what he'd done with her.

And now. *Now*. Despite all of that they were letting him free.

My fingers trembled as I clumsily jabbed numbers for Michael, John and Fiona. I uttered three words: 'They're releasing him.'

Trembling like a leaf, I drove home. Within minutes, the story had broken online. My phone rang non-stop. James Thacker and his team were all in hearings but sent messages, urging calm.

We had two options. Following the John Worboys scandal, the Government had, just that summer, introduced a Parole Board Reconsideration Mechanism. It meant that for the first time, the Secretary of State for Justice (and the prisoner, of course, but not the victim or the victim's family) could ask for a decision to be reconsidered if they could show it was irrational or procedurally unfair.

A fresh judge would then examine the case and decide if a new parole hearing should be held.

I could also apply for a judicial review into the decision at the High Court – which is what victims of John Worboys successfully did in 2018.

We had three weeks to lodge an appeal for Robert Buckland to apply for a reconsideration – and three months to lodge a claim for a judicial review.

'Right, so we're not rushing into anything,' I agreed. Instead, we issued a simple statement reflecting my anger at the decision reached – for journalists and social media accounts.

'I am stunned, horrified, furious and absolutely devastated to find out that Simms could be released from prison before Christmas.

'Helen's Law is written and ready to go on the statute book. After my meeting with the Justice Secretary it was introduced to Parliament the very next day. It was also presented in the Queen's Speech but now, due to the election, it is on hold.

'After almost four years of fighting to get this law it is a disgrace that the Parole Board has chosen this time to release him.

'Six hundred thousand people signed this petition and hopefully the public will continue to support us in keeping killers like Simms in prison until they disclose where their victims' remains are.

'My greatest fear is that, once he has gained his freedom, he will never give us the information that we so dearly wish to have.'

For a few moments all was calm. Then a cacophony of ringing tones, notification beeps and email pings erupted.

'Sickened', 'horrified', 'disgusted', 'disgraceful' were just a few of the words that leapt out from screens. You could sense the anger, the disbelief, the horror, unfurling on my behalf.

The release summary left me shaking my head in disbelief. The panel had concluded: 'There is no prospect of Mr Simms ever disclosing the whereabouts of his victim even if he were kept in prison until he died'.

What, so we may as well let him go? I thought, incredulously.

They also acknowledged he had not completed any accredited offending behaviour programmes because of the denial. However, factors including 'the progress he had made' and 'the considerable change in his behaviour' meant he had 'met the test for release'.

An appalled Conor McGinn requested an urgent meeting with Robert Buckland. I also wrote directly to Mr Buckland, informing him that I was considering requesting a judicial review. However, with an election campaign underway, we were in purdah – a bizarre No Man's Land. Parliament had been dissolved, there was no Government in place – no one I could turn to.

Supporters like Professor Yardley, Claire Waxman from Voice4Victims and Dr Keri Nixon, the forensic psychologist who had supported our original campaign, all rallied.

Dr Nixon put me in touch with Harry Fletcher – a prominent victims' campaigner and Government adviser who took up our cause with gusto and ran with it. He was a whirlwind of action and a fount of legal knowledge.

We'd already considered launching a crowdfunding appeal to cover potential legal action; now it was time. Within two hours of our Justice for Helen McCourt appeal going live on GoFundMe, we'd raised £5,000. Within three days, we were at £20,000.

The comments had me reaching for tissues – former colleagues and commuters who remembered Helen well, a retired police officer who had worked on the case, and one message which simply said, 'Marie was there for me. I want to be there for her.'

Many said they were sorry they weren't able to donate more, which made me cry even more. So many expressed their anger and fury on my behalf. And others sent me strength and love and urged me never, ever to give up fighting for justice.

'Thank you for trying to keep other people safe,' one message said.

It worked. Their encouragement, their backing, their belief in me was fuel for my tank.

On 2 December, Robert Buckland replied. He said: 'I recognise the deep distress which the Board's decision has caused you, the more so as Simms continues to deny responsibility for murdering your beloved and much-missed daughter Helen and refuses to disclose what he did with her body.'

He understood my wish to apply for a judicial review but said he was considering asking for a reconsideration of the decision – which would save me embarking on legal action. He would let me know before the deadline on 12 December. However, he warned that if his application was rejected, the provisional decision to release would become final and legally binding: '[...] I must comply with the direction of the Board, and officials will finalise preparations for Simms' release.'

But it wouldn't come to that. Would it?

* * *

So, with Robert Buckland asking for a reconsideration, I needed to get my arguments to him. My legal team compiled written representations from myself (all the grounds for our belief that the decision was irrational and procedurally unfair).

Even to me, who had lived every moment of this nightmare, my submission made shocking reading. It included the threatening letter he had sent to me, evidence of his violence, both before and in prison, newspaper coverage of how he had threatened to kill and hide a body so well it would never be found, his macabre painting of Helen, his refusal to meet with police and co-operate in helping them find Helen's body, his continued denial of the offence and the appeal in which he argued that manslaughter should have been given to the jury as an option to murder (thereby admitting he had taken Helen's life).

Hopefully, Robert Buckland would agree. If he didn't call for a reconsideration of the decision, I'd have to launch a judicial review immediately – and argue for a stay of release (i.e. for Simms to stay in prison) until it had been heard. So, my legal advisers now focused all their attention on that – asking the Parole Board for the full decision summary and the dossier containing all the information on Simms over the years.

Journalists were still asking for interviews and now that I had a plan of action, I was happy to grant them.

'It cannot be right that a killer who shows no remorse and refuses to reveal where the body of his victim is, can be deemed fit for release,' I told them. 'I am begging the Minister for Justice, Robert Buckland, to intervene for my sake and the public's sake. Before my daughter's murder, Simms openly boasted of being able to kill and hide a body so well it would never be found. This may not have been his first murder – which makes him a dangerous person.

'I feel very vulnerable that this man who has threatened me and my family will be free to carry out his threats. And I do believe he will do so. He may wait a while until the authorities aren't watching him so carefully.

'I am putting my faith in the justice system that the Government will do the right thing and overturn this decision.'

Victims campaigner Harry Fletcher joined in furiously. 'Simms' refusal to say where the deceased can be found, violent behaviour in prison, refusal to show any remorse, which means he has not taken part in programmes of rehabilitation ... these are just some of the many reasons why he should not be granted freedom,' he said in a statement.

At lunchtime, on Tuesday, 10 December, two days before the General Election, we heard that Robert Buckland had asked for a reconsideration on the grounds that it was irrational.

I punched the air with delight. 'Thank God!' I cried. Simms would remain in prison until a decision either way. He wouldn't be released for Christmas.

The story got huge pick-up in the papers. 'Helen's Law Killer: Release Bid Halted ... Justice Chief Steps in to Demand Review,' said the *Mirror*'s headline.

On the eve of the General Election came more good news at the British Journalism Awards in London: Fiona Duffy and Louie Smith won Campaign of the Year for their work on Helen's Law. She sent me a photo of the two of them proudly holding the award aloft. I was so chuffed for them.

'Well done, you deserve it,' I told them.

In presenting the award, the judges said: 'This was campaigning journalism at its best. Fiona Duffy stuck with this story like a limpet over many years and has achieved a result.'

On election night, I heaved a sigh of relief as Conor McGinn was voted back in for St Helens North and Robert Buckland regained his seat in South Swindon. That was one less thing to worry about.

A week later, just six days before Christmas, I tuned in to the Queen's Speech in Parliament. Just two months after her last one this was lower-key with very little pomp and ceremony, but all that mattered to me was Helen's Law being re-included.

By now, I had come down with a sore throat, hacking cough and streaming cold. But I perked up with a jolt when I heard Her Majesty say, in her inimitable voice: 'My Government is committed to a fair justice system that keeps people safe [...] Legislation will be brought forward to support victims of crime and their families.'

Again, I logged into the briefing notes to check it was there, then emailed Robert Buckland and Home Secretary Priti Patel urging them to introduce Helen's Law as soon as possible when Parliament resumed.

Meanwhile, a vigorous game of ping pong was being played between my legal team – who wanted all the paperwork relating to Simms – and the Parole Board who didn't want to release it. Requests and rejections flew back and forth.

'The whole Parole system is biased towards the perpetrator and not the families of the victims,' stormed Harry Fletcher. 'It's a complete imbalance of power. They have all the reports and experts at their disposal, including defence reports. The families of murder victims have nothing.

'The Parole system has to change to make it fairer and more accessible to victims than it is at the moment.

'For the McCourt family to still be suffering this torment, almost thirty-two years after losing Helen, is appalling. It's a tragic situation to be in.'

I thanked God that I had such brilliant lawyers and supporters fighting my corner. There was no way I could have done this on my own.

Meanwhile, we had a big decision to make: we were just days away from our annual trip to India.

'Should we cancel?' I asked John for the umpteenth time.

It was the worst possible time to go away, but we were exhausted. Running on empty. Without recharging our drained batteries how could we possibly see this through? Plus, our widowed friend, Christine, was coming too – we couldn't let her down.

On 23 December, I was in the garden cutting some sprigs of holly to decorate Helen's marble seat when the phone rang.

Coughing, I dashed inside, clutching my secateurs. It was Robert Buckland, assuring me that Helen's Law would be reintroduced to Parliament as soon as MPs returned on 7 January 2020 and he would be pushing for it to be passed.

'Thank you, Robert. That's the best Christmas present, ever,' I said.

I was touched that he'd taken time out of his busy schedule to ring me and thanked him for his intervention in asking for reconsideration.

'There are other families just like me with killers due before the Parole Board. We need this on the statute books as soon as possible.

'For the Parole Board to accept that he had killed my daughter, was never going to tell me where he had hidden her, but was still fit for release is ludicrous.'

He listened as I explained all about the system in Australia, then urged me to enjoy Christmas and to go on holiday, as planned. 'Nothing will happen,' he assured me. Fiona, Michael and other family members agreed, insisting they'd look after everything.

So, on 30 December, we left the UK for Goa – it was a decision we would rue.

* * *

In India, my health plummeted. John spent his time nursing me, visiting countless chemists for remedies and spending a fortune in internet cafés printing off reams of legal documents for me to approve. Even though we were still waiting for a decision on the reconsideration, the paperwork for a judicial review needed to be in order so we could act quickly if we needed to.

I'd sit in the shade, shivering feverishly and coughing violently, urging my foggy brain to make sense of the words.

We were five and a half hours ahead so completely out of synch with what was going on, back home. At times, we'd find Wi-Fi and log on to find they were waiting for me to return something vital yesterday.

My phone refused to work, which was a blessing in one sense but a disaster in another – I felt like I'd lost a limb.

'We shouldn't have come away,' I sighed.

Poor Winnie Johnson was also playing on my mind. Tears welled behind my dark sunglasses whenever I thought of her and her tragic fate. The thought of following in her footsteps broke my heart.

On Monday, 6 January 2020, Michael rang.

'They're releasing their decision one day this week, Mum,' he said. 'I'll ring you as soon as I know.'

Simms would be informed first (no surprises there), then my victim liaison officer had thirty minutes to contact Michael before it was released to the press. (Again, the hurry to tell the world news that affected me so deeply, baffled me.)

I gathered that out of forty-seven reconsideration requests made, since the previous October, only three had resulted in a new hearing. Not great odds, granted, but we lived in hope.

I was like a stuck record asking John to check if his phone was charged, switched on, working ... On Wednesday afternoon, I'd just dozed off in the shade, after another sleepless night, when his mobile rang. Michael's name flashed up on the caller display – this was it.

John and Christine hovered anxiously as I answered; they saw my head drop and my shoulders slump. The Parole Board was standing by its decision. Afterwards, I ranted, 'Of course, they're going to back each other up, aren't they? What a ridiculous system!'

Again, the legal team urged caution and patience. The most important thing, now, was finding out a date for Simms' release.

We were also still hoping that there was a small chance that Robert Buckland would launch his own judicial review into the decision. After all, he'd believed it was irrational while asking for the reconsideration.

In the meantime, journalists were contacting Fiona and Michael for my reaction. We'd prepared two statements – one joyful, one miserable. Sadly, the miserable one was released.

> I am devastated, but more determined than ever to take this to the highest court in the land to get justice for families in this situation.
>
> I was assured that Helen's Law would be introduced to the statute book as soon as possible. For the killer of my daughter, the very person who has inspired this campaign, to be released before then would be such an insult.
>
> I have instructed my legal team to prepare for a judicial review at the Royal Courts of Justice in London, with immediate effect, and I look forward to challenging this appalling decision.

Ironically, the news came on the very day that Helen's Law was presented to Parliament for the third time.

Once again, messages of support flooded in. Conor McGinn tweeted: 'This is appalling and will devastate Marie McCourt and her family. It is hard to believe that the Parole Board could make such a flawed decision again. It is perverse and heartbreaking that this has happened on the very day that the Helen's Law Bill is presented in Parliament.'

The story was set to be the front-page lead in the *Daily Mirror*. We lost out to Prince Harry and Meghan Markle stepping back from royal life. But a picture of Helen still made it onto a front-page corner under the headline: 'Helen's Killer Free in Weeks' exclusive and a link to the story inside.

Fiona had been emailing Harry Fletcher for a couple of days now and was puzzled not to hear back. He normally responded to messages straight away. Sadly, the next morning, we heard the sad news: Harry had died of a heart attack.

We were left reeling. We'd only worked with him for a few short weeks, but with his knowledge and fighting spirit, he had quickly become an invaluable member of the team. We had never needed someone like him more on our side and now he was gone. I wept, not just for the loss of a great man, but at the enormity of what I was taking on.

Questions whirled around my head. If I launched legal action would they keep Simms in prison until then, or would he be released and recalled if I won?

And, dear God, how much would this cost me? I'd wake in the early hours in a cold sweat, thinking: *I could lose my home – the house that Helen loved … my grandchildren's money …* Then, in an instant, I'd be arguing with myself: *Some things are more important than bricks and mortar, we have to highlight this.*

By the time John woke, I'd be defiant and determined.

'To hell with the house, to hell with everything,' I'd say, 'this is more important.' He'd look a bit alarmed at the thought of losing the roof over our head, but he understood completely that this was our last chance when it came to getting the information we so desperately needed from Simms. We had to do this, even if it could cost us everything.

* * *

My legal team suggested we revamp my GoFundMe appeal to reflect that I was bringing this action in the public interest.

'Being able to bury a murdered loved one is a basic human right – and I am taking this stand in the interest of the public,' read the new wording. 'I truly believe that justice can only be served when families of missing murder victims are treated with respect and compassion and the public are protected from dangerous killers who refuse to show remorse for their actions. We need to acknowledge and prevent the significant anguish that innocent families of murder victims continue to experience. I am also calling for greater transparency and victim participation in parole proceedings.

'Money raised would go towards legal costs I might incur as a result of court action,' I explained. 'And any unused money would be placed into a fund to support future legal action by other families of missing murder victims.'

I finished with a poignant, 'This is my last chance to bring Helen home.'

More forms and statements were arriving daily for me to complete and email back. I was stunned to learn that my claim form for the judicial review, which asked for my address, telephone number and email address, would be shown to Simms. This man who had killed my daughter, hidden her body and threatened justice on his release would get full access to my personal details.

He already had my address from sending his letter, back in 1992. But what if I'd moved? What then? Advised by my legal team, I left the email and phone number blank.

I scanned the page and took in the words: There it was, for the first time, in black and white: 'The claimant challenges the decision of the Parole Board to release a prisoner, Ian Simms, on licence, and the subsequent refusal to reconsider that decision.

'I am seeking permission to proceed with my claim for judicial review ... seeking the following interim remedies.'

It then listed my short-term requests: an order staying Simms' release, an order for disclosure (of the information we'd been asking for) and a cost-capping order – to limit the costs I'd incur if I lost.

And my long-term requests: an order quashing the decision to release Simms and, if appropriate (i.e. if the decision went in my favour), declarations concerning a) victim participation in parole proceedings, and b) the principles which the board should apply when determining whether to release a prisoner who not only denies his or her guilt but refuses to reveal information as to the whereabouts of a victim's body.

This is why I am putting myself through this, I thought.

I had never been so sure of anything in my life.

I picked up a pen and with a sense of satisfaction, signed my name with a flourish. John scanned the forms and emailed them back – it was done.

Meanwhile, we were keeping a close eye on the Bill's progress. We already had great support in the Commons and hoped for similar in the Lords. Back at home, Fiona was busily arranging a date for me to visit Parliament in the spring to present my campaign to members.

* * *

On 29 January, the day of our flight home, we had just sat down to breakfast when John clicked on his emails. My cup of tea was halfway to my lips when I realised the colour had drained from his face.

'Oh, God! What?' I asked.

Unable to speak, he passed his phone silently to me: Robert Buckland would not be launching a judicial review. Simms was being prepared for released.

My cup clattered into its saucer; I was stunned. Urgently, I skimmed the rest of the message: 'It is my view that we have little option but to lodge an urgent judicial review today,' James Thacker had written.

I glanced up to see tears running down our friend Christine's face.

'Oh, love, don't – or you'll start me off,' I said.

'You're like that Emily Pankhurst,' she sniffed, wiping her eyes.

In spite of my tears, I found myself smiling weakly. *Wasn't it Emmeline?* 'No, I'm not,' I sighed. 'She was totally different, she was fighting for women's votes.'

Christine shook her head. 'Yes, but she wouldn't give up. You are doing exactly the same thing.'

She was right – I wouldn't give up. Not now. Not ever.

* * *

Hours later, Fiona picked us up from the airport (the first thing she noticed was my weight loss) and put us on the phone to the legal team.

With Simms set to be released in as little as five days' time, the Royal Courts of Justice had been put on notice that we would be lodging an urgent claim – both to apply for a judicial review of the decision and block Simms' release – and asking for a response within twenty-four hours.

James Thacker served the papers in person just before 1pm the following day: we were now in the system. If the court did grant a judicial review, our legal team asked that it be dealt with no later than 28 February – 'So at least we won't have to wait too long,' I said to John.

It was 30 January, the very day that the World Health Organization (WHO) declared a Public Health Emergency of International Concern regarding the outbreak of a certain coronavirus in Wuhan, China.

We had no idea what was about to hit us ...

In the meantime, the more I discovered about the parole process, the more furious I became. I learned that the date of Simms' parole hearing had been sent to the Secretary of State on 1 August 2019. So why hadn't I been notified in writing before 14 October – the day of the Queen's Speech – when the hearing was just three weeks away?

'It was the Secretary of State's responsibility, under the Victims' Code, to notify your client of the hearing,' said the Parole Board in one of its letters to my legal team.

More issues were bothering me. My representations to Robert Buckland hadn't featured at all in his application for reconsideration. There had also been a representative from his department present at the parole hearing. Why didn't this person argue the case at the time? Why wait until after the decision had been made to argue it was irrational?

My legal team had also asked me, on a number of occasions, if I'd ever been told that I could provide information regarding my concerns over Simms' risk.

'No,' I replied, frowning. 'I was simply told to write how the crime had affected me.'

I was furious to discover that, according to the Victims' Code, I could have done just that – making submissions either to my victim liaison officer or the probation service. However, it seems that there is no obligation for anyone to tell victims about this ... yet another area where victims and their families are forgotten.

We were hoping to keep our legal action quiet for a few days but by 8am the next morning, my phone started ringing off the hook. The story had already appeared on two news websites.

'It's best not to say too much,' the legal team advised, so I turned down interviews and simply issued a brief statement confirming we'd applied for a judicial review.

The court fired into action; a judge asked for responses from the other parties by 4pm that day.

My blood pressure rose when I read comments from Simms' representatives: 'Mr Simms submits that the Claimant is not a party to these proceedings, has no standing, and as such, the matter should be dismissed.'

Oh, does he now?

'The Reconsideration Process has been scrupulously followed in this case and found the Parole Board process, procedure and decision making to be lawful.

'Mr Simms urges the Court to respect Parliament's authority in setting legislation and to dismiss the claim as lacking standing.'

'How dare he!' I fumed. The only reason I was having to do this was because of his cruelty. And what was with the 'Mr Simms'? Surely, it's surname only when dealing with convicted killers?

At 7pm, that Friday evening, the court announced it would make a decision on the Monday – it was like having a plaster torn off excruciatingly slowly.

John and I spent the weekend poring over our finances. Because I was applying for a cost-capping order the courts wanted to know exactly how much I had – in addition to the crowdfunding account – right down to the last penny. We could lose the lot. Simms, on the other hand, would be granted legal aid.

On Monday, 3 February, the judge decided there would be an oral hearing with all parties before a Divisional Court the following day at 2pm.

Would this ever end?

On the Tuesday, I woke early to light candles and say my novena. Once again, we drafted two media statements and prayed we'd be using the 'I'm relieved' version.

Just before 3.40pm, my email inbox pinged: it was James Thacker. I held my breath as I clicked on it.

We'd lost.

Simms was being released. The court had relied on him having already been released on temporary licence and licence conditions being put in place. There was also a concession made that, should I win a judicial review, the court must recall him. But that was little consolation now.

Phone calls from reporters came thick and fast. I was too upset to speak, but released my miserable statement. The one glimmer of good news was that the court had ordered disclosure of all the information we wanted about Simms.

At 11am, on 5 February, I was loading the washing machine when the phone rang: it was my VLO. My knees buckled. There was only one reason why she'd be calling now.

'This is the phone call I've been dreading all these years, isn't it?' I said weakly.

There was a long pause. 'He's out, Marie,' she said simply.

My stomach twisted. 'What ... he's *being* released or he's *been* released?' I demanded.

'He's been released,' she repeated.

My grip on the phone weakened. Energy and strength leached from every pore. So, this was it: after thirty-two years, it had happened.

I imagined gates clanging shut behind him. The satisfying inhalation of fresh air as he stepped outside, blinking, clutching his possessions in a carrier bag.

It was probably just a regular door that clicked shut behind him. And, let's face it, he'd been sniffing fresh air for a while now on temporary release. But the principle of it crushed my insides.

He was free. Properly free. And Helen was still missing.

No sooner had I broken the news to Michael, John and

Fiona than the phones started ringing off the hook: 'Is it true?' journalists clamoured to know. 'Is he out?'

I'd planned not to speak to anyone, but the BBC begged to do an interview for the local news and I relented.

At one point, there was a TV crew in the conservatory, another in the living room, a reporter in the kitchen and another crew parked outside waiting to come in.

That evening, I watched the news bulletins numbly. 'I didn't think my heart could break twice,' I heard myself say. 'But today it did.'

I still have no idea where Simms is. He is under strict conditions not to come anywhere near the Northwest and is tagged to ensure he meets curfew and boundary regulations (with a fifty-mile exclusion zone around Billinge). Somewhere within that radius lies Helen's remains – and I don't want him coming anywhere near them.

When monitoring and tracking procedures are removed we will take security measures. However, we will not be frightened or intimidated – and refuse to spend the rest of our lives looking over our shoulders.

Simms could not hurt me any more than he has already done – he has done his worst.

Four days later, my heart still felt bruised as we took our seats in the House of Commons public gallery to hear the Prisoners (Disclosure of Information about Victims) Bill finally have its long-awaited second reading.

Conor McGinn spoke so beautifully on my behalf. Tears of emotion ran down my face as he mentioned Winnie Johnson and her plight – it was all getting so close to home now. Afterwards, he glanced up towards us. 'Thank you,' I mouthed.

I would never, ever be able to tell him how much this meant.

As the vote was announced, I scanned the chamber anxiously. My heart stopped beating. As it came to the 'ayes', there was a resounding response. And the 'no's? I strained my ears. The silence lasted for one second. Two.

'The ayes have it,' the Speaker announced. 'The ayes have it.'

I exhaled slowly and gratefully.

Outside, Conor introduced me to various MPs. 'Oh, Marie,' one said, shaking my hand. 'A constituent used to be babysat by Helen. She contacted me urging me to vote for this. I'm so pleased it's passed today's reading.'

I beamed proudly at the thought of grown-ups still remembering their lovely babysitter. Helen had adored those children and they'd never forgotten her.

On 3 March (another Tuesday) I tuned into Commons proceedings on our old laptop and was astonished when the Bill passed the next three crucial steps – the committee stage, report stage and third reading – one after the other.

Conor McGinn observed how bittersweet today was for me – coming after the release of my own daughter's killer: 'However, it is a testament to the character of Marie McCourt that her campaign continued so that other families would not have to suffer.

'I know that Members across the House send their sympathy and solidarity to Marie McCourt, on a day on which she can rightly take pride, although that, of course, does not return the remains of her beloved Helen.'

I wiped tears away as the Bill was officially passed by the Commons: it was on its way to the Lords. Then I glanced up at Helen's portrait: 'Did you hear that, love?' I asked. 'You were mentioned in Parliament.'

Then I cursed Brexit, general elections and every other delay that had prevented Helen's Law from being adopted into law before now. But I tried to stay positive. Any day now we hoped to hear about our application for a judicial review.

And on 11 March, we went to London to meet Professor Penney Lewis, the new criminal law commissioner at the Law

Commission – the body that makes laws. She gave me her undivided attention as I told her all about my campaign and explained that the burial laws in England and Wales were outdated and badly in need of reform.

'This has to be changed,' I implored. 'Everyone, whether you are religious or not, has the right to a funeral and their loved ones have the right to give them that last goodbye. It's part of the grieving ritual. Without a body, you can't believe they're gone.

'All I want is my daughter's remains. I want to give her, or whatever is left of her, a burial in our little churchyard.'

Professor Lewis explained how law reform projects were undertaken and advised me to request a review of these laws through the Government. Then she added: 'You should feel incredibly proud at the work you have done to get Helen's Law where it is. I am sure it will make it onto the statute books.

'You have already helped families immensely because of that legal change – even if you haven't been able to prevent Simms coming out. It is an immense accomplishment and an immense legacy for your daughter. Very few people manage to make that kind of difference. The fact that you have done it is tremendous.'

I nodded gratefully.

'But it doesn't help me give her a burial,' I said tearfully.

She nodded. 'I'm sure she would be really proud.'

I left feeling more positive than I had in weeks. Helen's Law was on its way to the Lords. We had a meeting lined up to meet members. We were campaigning for an overhaul of burial laws and any day now we'd hear about our judicial review.

But on that very day the World Health Organization declared a global pandemic. Coronavirus was spreading like wildfire. Soon afterwards, we entered national lockdown.

Chapter 20

To the High Court

All we needed now was a plague of locusts and we'd have completed the 'great hurdles of our time' challenge. Seriously, was there anything else that could be thrown at us?

As John and I were now both in our seventies (and therefore in the higher-risk category), we battened down the hatches. I didn't even leave the house for a daily walk. I'd made it this far – I was not going to let some deadly virus stop me having my day in court and seeing my campaign through.

Like every other part of society, legal cogs stopped turning. Clerical desks were abandoned. Judicial wigs packed away. Court doors slammed shut and locked. And I imagined dust settling, like the dewfall, on legal papers – including my application for a judicial review.

Weeks passed with no news – apart from the terrifying rise in the death toll. My heart went out to the thousands affected – and those grieving families denied final goodbyes before their loved ones slipped from this life. I knew only too well how tortuous this could be – I truly hope they have been helped through their pain.

Unsurprisingly, we had to cancel our trip to the Lords to meet members but I needn't have worried. They were all supportive when Helen's Law had its second reading in the Lords in late April 2020. It was largely virtual – various members zoomed in from their homes across the country (yes, another technical aspect I had to master).

The comments were supportive, positive and poignant. Members observed my 'formidable campaign' and the heart-breaking timing of this Bill – coming so soon after Simms' release. As one member said: 'It is not a "No Body No Parole" Bill, so it is not everything the campaigners wanted, but it sends a clear message to Parole Board panels that a refusal to give information that can ease a relative's pain, such as non-disclosure of remains, should be a significant factor in their decision-making.'

Members also recognised that much more needed to be done to support victims in the parole process. I've since spoken to many privately and this is something I would definitely like to see happen. If I can spare other families from this ordeal, something good will have come out of losing Helen.

Speech was muffled, connections lost and adjournments taken while technical hitches were sorted. But, finally, the reading was passed.

It was VE Day in May before I learned from my legal team via Zoom that, just before lockdown, the Court hadn't been able to make a decision from the paper application alone: it wanted an oral hearing by the end of July. By now, Tom Little QC – one of the top barristers in the country – had joined the team. We couldn't have been in safer hands and I will never, ever, be able to say thank you enough times to him for coming on board to help us.

While the rest of the country held socially distanced street parties, John, Michael and I had a huge decision to make. Did we opt for the 'rolled-up' hearing that the court had suggested – where they considered both the application itself, and the hearing, at the same time? Or did we go for the other option – asking for permission first and then a cost-capping order to cover a separate hearing?

There were huge pros and cons to both options. The first was quicker, but we would be going in without a capping on costs if I lost. Simms' team was currently estimating costs at a whopping £75,000. With my legal fund at a perilous £27,000, I would have to make up the shortfall.

The second option (applying for permission and cost-capping first and then a subsequent separate hearing) would take longer. There were already huge backlogs in the system. Who knew when the hearing might happen? And the longer Simms was out (and behaving himself because, let's face it, no one was leaving home), the less chance there was, realistically, of persuading a judge that the decision to release him had been wrong. Not to mention the toll all of this was taking on us. For more than thirty-two years, we'd lived this nightmare. But now, with our advancing years and the added stress of lockdown and terror of catching Covid-19, we were finding it so hard to think straight. To make decisions.

My legal team were absolutely brilliant in explaining everything but the final decision then lay with John and me. We had the weekend to think things over. It was one of the most miserable times we'd ever gone through together.

We went round and round, and over and over, the same grounds. Whichever decision we made could finish us off. We could risk everything – and win. Or we could save our home – the home that Helen loved, everything we'd worked so hard for – and lose.

By Monday afternoon, we'd aged ten years. The lowest point came when John took a deep breath and suggested withdrawing from the whole thing; cutting our losses and running.

What?

'But we've come so far, John. We can't pull out now, we'll always wonder "what if?" We have to see it through,' I said, gesturing to Helen's portrait. 'For Helen.'

Suddenly, he was crying. My brave, strong, stoic husband was sobbing like a child. 'I can't stand it,' he wept. 'I can't stand what this is doing to you. To us.'

I put my arms around him and we cried together. For three long decades we had lived under the darkest of rumbling, threatening clouds. Now, they were about to burst, leaving us engulfed and gasping for breath.

It took a week to make a final decision. We'd go for the first option and pull out all the stops to raise enough money through crowdfunding. To do that, we needed one final push.

'Helen's Law Mum Faces Losing Home in Court Battle' ... 'Simms Has Stolen My Daughter – Now He Could Take My Home,' screamed the dramatic headlines.

'This convicted killer was granted legal aid and I, the mother of a missing murder victim, am not entitled to a penny,' I told readers. 'Any help, even a single pound, would mean the world.'

It was a huge gamble. By then, businesses were folding, the economy was in crisis, jobs were being axed. But my wonderful, generous supporters – I could cry just thinking about how grateful I am – rallied. Money, love and strength poured in. Within a few days, we'd reached £40,000.

My brilliant, persuasive legal team successfully asked the other side to limit costs to those funds if we lost. Finally, we had a bit of breathing space.

We avidly watched Helen's Law pass its committee and report stages in the Lords. These were much lengthier hearings with one amendment made – requiring the Parole Board to create and maintain a database of the victim's family members so they could be kept fully updated on an offender's parole application. However, because a change had been made, this now had to be approved by the Commons. The result was a phase called 'ping pong' (seriously!), where the Bill would bounce back and forth between the two houses before an agreement was made. I prayed a huge match wouldn't entail. (On Tuesday, 6 October, the Bill returned to the Commons – only for the amendment to be rejected. MPs argued that, as a new pilot scheme had been undertaken to keep families updated on decisions, the amendment wasn't needed. Hopefully, at that point the Bill would then be approved by both houses and be presented to HM The Queen herself for royal assent. Finally, after five long years of campaigning, Helen's Law would enter the statute books).

So, we were on the home straight for seeing Helen's Law through, but when it came to getting Simms back behind bars, everything was hanging on this judicial review.

By sheer coincidence, the first day of the hearing was 29 July – Helen's birthday.

'That's a good sign, surely?' I said to John.

* * *

Like everything else these days, the hearing would be virtual, with everyone logging on. It involved mastering yet another platform: Skype Business. In desperation, John and I approached a local computer shop for help. We were so touched when the owners set everything up on a laptop and lent it to us for as long as we needed it – with no charge.

As the date drew nearer, I focused entirely on the hearing – and Helen's birthday. We issued a statement to journalists outlining my hopes and reasons for bringing the action – arguing that the Board's decision was wrong because it applied the wrong legal test (in respect of the appropriateness in releasing a convicted murderer who denies their offence and refuses to identify the location of their victim's body), was irrational and procedurally unfair.

Then we prayed.

As 29 July dawned, the story made all the papers and news bulletins – 'Mum Asks Judges to Quash Parole Decision' and 'Recall Killer to Prison' said the headlines.

Messages of support and good luck flooded in. Everyone was behind us.

No matter what the outcome, we were making legal history. This was believed to be the first time ever a decision to release a convicted murderer who refused to disclose information about the location of their victim's body had ever been challenged by the family.

Not surprisingly, Simms' team was disputing the claim in full.

But as the Parole Board was also questioning whether victims had a legal right to challenge its release decisions my claim would also cover the extent to which victims of crime could participate in parole proceedings. Like the successful judicial review challenge by victims into the release of convicted taxi rapist John Worboys in 2018, this could have huge ramifications.

'The success of that [judicial challenge] has given me the courage to launch this action,' I said in a statement. 'How can a killer who has consistently refused to disclose the whereabouts of his victim's body be deemed safe to return to society? Refusing to admit his guilt and face up to his crime means he has not taken part in any rehabilitation or reform programmes during his time in prison.

'I am making a stand for all families of missing murder victims and hope and pray that my claim succeeds.

'Ironically, the hearing is taking place on Helen's birthday. My daughter would have been fifty-five, yet the man who killed her has been released without saying where he hid her body.

'I want to see justice done.'

On the morning of the hearing, I placed fresh flowers in front of Helen's portrait. 'Happy birthday, love,' I said, as John switched on the laptop.

'Ready?' he asked.

I nodded.

Here goes, it was now or nothing.

He logged on. An ominous-looking message flashed onto the screen: 'No internet connection'.

We looked at each other, aghast.

Then we tried again. We restarted the laptop. Of all the times, of all the days for Virgin Media to crash, it had to happen now.

I clapped my hands to my mouth. 'What do we do? What do we do?' I shrieked.

We sped to my brother Tez's house – a full half-hour's drive away – notifying the legal team of our technical disaster. Finally, twenty minutes after the logging-in time – and with direct help from the High Court clerks – my name flashed up on the screen: I was in.

'And breathe,' I sighed.

For the next two mornings we listened avidly, mutely, as the legal teams thrashed out the case before Lady Justice Macur and Mr Justice Chamberlain – referring to countless other cases brought and decisions made.

Tom Little was superb – highlighting all the reasons why we believed the Parole Board had made the wrong decision – and a few extra faults along the way. In assessing whether Simms was safe to be released, he said the Parole Board should have pushed him to reveal where Helen's body was. He accused them of 'feather duster questioning'.

'There was no probing. Questions have to be asked, they have to be probed. Things that begged questions weren't followed up,' he argued.

I was shocked at the suggestion that Simms' painting of Helen had been presented to the board as a black-and-white photocopy rather than the colour original – losing its impact.

Tom rebuffed the argument that I had 'no standing' to

challenge this decision: 'There is no other person able to bring this challenge than the mother of the deceased,' he declared. 'In bringing this claim, Marie McCourt is acting in the public interest.'

And he dismissed the opposition's argument that granting this judicial review would open the floodgates for similar claims. (I longed to press the unmute button and say, 'Believe me, no one else would want to put themselves through this!')

Among many things, Simms' counsel argued that although the whereabouts of her daughter's body was 'a central issue for the claimant' the central issue for the Parole Board was whether Simms posed a risk to the public. There was a significant amount of evidence that Simms' risk had changed throughout his sentence, they insisted, adding, 'There is no suggestion that denial increased risk or that non-disclosure increased risk.'

Closing his argument, Tom referred to me as a champion for others suffering this ordeal: 'She has campaigned for a change in the law not just for herself but for other families who find themselves in this situation.

'It is a sad irony that the 29th of July is Helen McCourt's birthday and she would have been fifty-five today,' he concluded.

I scrutinised the judges' faces for a flicker of emotion, empathy, sympathy. There was nothing. Coolly and briskly, the hearing moved on.

And there, again, is my plea for kindness. I appreciate that judges have to be impartial but, somewhere, somehow along the road of evolution, we have lost our humanity. Our compassion. Surely, there must be a less brutal way of doing things.

In announcing she would reserve judgment, Lady Justice Macur acknowledged there were 'wide implications arising from this in terms not only for Mrs McCourt but for others in similar positions'.

This case really could make a difference.

And that was it: the hearing was adjourned. All we could do now was wait.

'I am pleased that I have had the opportunity to take my case to the High Court and raise the impact that this decision has had on us,' I said in a released statement. 'It has been particularly hard bringing this action on what would have been my daughter's fifty-fifth birthday, but I had to do it, not just for her but for all the other families who will find themselves in this situation. I have taken this stand in the public interest.

'I would like to thank my wonderful legal team for the amount of work and dedication they have put into this case in their own time because it is a cause they believe in. I would never have been able to do this without them.

'Again, I just hope and pray that justice will be done.'

* * *

We'd anticipated that a decision would come within two weeks but as we entered the third and fourth weeks of August, my hopes started to rise.

'It's a good sign,' John assured me. 'Don't forget they asked for more statistics from the Parole Board. There could have been a hold-up there or even more questions as a result of receiving them.'

I nodded.

'You can't rush justice,' I agreed. 'They can take all the time they need so long as they come back with the right verdict.'

All I could do was wait. Every Tuesday, I lit my candles and said my novena to St Martha.

On Bank Holiday Monday came news: the decision was being released the following morning – a Tuesday – at 10am. My legal team was allowed to give me the news half an hour before. We arranged a Zoom call for 9.30am. To comply with legal rules, I had to be alone when they delivered the news.

'I'm trying to prepare for the worst,' I told Fiona. 'I'd be devastated. I'm only human. You can't control your emotions, can you?

'But the judges have taken a full calendar month to consider this so I'm hopeful. Even if they don't put him back in prison, I am hoping that, at least, they agree that this has been very unfair.'

Next morning, Michael helped me log on. Then he went into the garden with his Cockapoo dog, Bob. John went into the living room and closed the door.

I was alone.

Nervously, I requested admission to the Zoom meeting. One by one, my wonderful, wonderful legal team appeared in boxes. My heart was thumping out of my chest as I scanned their faces for a clue to the verdict. They smiled as they wished me a good morning and asked how I was. Such lovely, pleasant young men, but I could see disappointment reflected in their eyes.

They didn't have to say a word – I'd lost.

I was being given the most awful news and I was completely alone. It wasn't my legal team's fault, they were just following rules. But, as John says, it's yet another cruelty for victims to contend with. In the great scheme of things would it really have mattered to have my son and husband holding my hands, comforting me? Surely, changes have to be made here, too?

On autopilot, I nodded and listened as they explained the ruling – that the decision by the Parole Board 'involved no arguable public law error'.

We had won one small victory: the High Court had ruled that I did have legal standing to bring this challenge, which meant other families would be able to take action in future.

'That's a huge achievement, Marie,' Tom Little said. 'And something to be proud of.'

But I still can't bury my daughter.

He told me afterwards that he could see the collage of Helen, designed by a local artist from newspaper cuttings and precious items, behind me as he delivered the heartbreaking news. My heart went out to the legal team – they had worked so hard on this and having to break such awful news couldn't have been easy.

I managed to hold it together while thanking them all, individually. 'I would never have come this far without you all,' I said, my voice breaking.

I'd had the best legal team in the country – and I'd still lost. What chance did anyone else have?

One by one, their faces disappeared until a black screen was all that was left.

I was alone again.

I called out for my husband and son. They took one look at my stricken face and, instinctively, came towards me with outstretched arms. We cried together. Then we broke the news to the rest of the team before releasing an emotional statement.

'Sadly, I have lost my bid for a judicial review into the decision by the Parole Board to release my daughter's killer.

'I am bitterly disappointed at the decision. This was my last chance to get my daughter's killer to admit where he hid her body.

'I did my best, and so did my legal team, but sadly, this hasn't produced the result we wanted in getting Simms back into prison. We are now discussing my next steps. However, I am celebrating one small victory – and that is the High Court's ruling that I did have legal standing to bring this challenge – something that Simms' legal team argued against.

'Although I have lost my own claim, I have successfully paved the way for any other family to now challenge a decision by the Parole Board. It is a small comfort but one that I hope will have implications for others – particularly in missing body murder cases.'

I thanked every single donor and every single supporter for helping me to get to this point. 'I could not have done it without you,' I added.

John and I had already decided we wouldn't be appealing if we lost. There was no guarantee another judge would think differently. And more legal action would cost our sanity as well as our life's savings.

I'd been through many disappointments and low points since losing Helen. But this defeat was something else.

For a few hours I functioned. I put the kettle on. I made tea. But, suddenly, without warning, I crashed. And burned. A bubbling sensation in my chest took my breath away. My voice constricted. I cried silently, noiselessly, and couldn't stop. I was inconsolable. It was over, I'd lost. He'd won. And I couldn't bear it.

In the past, I had always, always answered the phone to journalists. For the first time in thirty-two years, I let it ring. And ring. And ring. I couldn't speak with them. The despair, the pain, was all-consuming.

* * *

I could see the concern on Michael's face. He spoke to John, who agreed. It was like the awful 'no' years all over again.

'Marie, I think we should go away,' he suggested.

I shrugged.

Whatever …

With quarantine corridors opening and closing by the day, our options were limited, but three days later, we landed in a quiet resort in Turkey. And there, with my wonderful, adoring husband at my side – my rock, my soulmate – I turned my face to the sun and began to heal.

We hadn't had a proper holiday in years – we had always, always been campaigning, researching, answering our support group's helpline. But this was different.

John switched off our phones. Disabled our emails.

Initially, I was oblivious to our surroundings. But, over time, I was able to take in the glorious sunrises and dramatic sunsets, sparkling seas and endless stretches of sands. And, slowly, I came to terms with my loss.

I had done my best for my daughter, that was all I could ever do.

And now ...

As you turn to this page, I would love nothing more than to bring you a happy ending.

To be able to finish this book by telling you that, by some fluke, I managed to appeal the decision and get Simms back into prison. Or, better still, that he had finally faced up to his crime and told me where we could find my daughter's remains.

That we had brought Helen home and seen her laid to rest in consecrated ground. That I was visiting her grave every day to lay flowers. That I had found some peace.

Sadly, that hasn't happened. This isn't a fairy tale or fiction, this is real life. And, as we all know, there isn't always a happy ending.

However, I do have some good news to report. The Bill was passed by the Lords and on Wednesday 4 November 2020 Helen's Law was given royal assent. The Ministry of Justice announced that, at midday, Her Majesty the Queen had signed the Bill.

When Conor rang to give me the news, that Helen's Law was now enshrined in law, I felt so proud. Then I looked at Helen's portrait. 'Well, love, you've done it. You've finally done it.

Everyone will remember you, Helen. Your name will go down in history and you will never, ever be forgotten.'

I'd dreamed of posting triumphant photos taken outside Parliament but because of Covid that was out of the question, of course. Instead, John and I celebrated with a rare meal out, and raised a glass to our Helen, hours before England entered a second lockdown at midnight.

My update on social media, saying how the news had made me the proudest mum in the world, unleashed an avalanche of congratulations. Bouquets of flowers and 'Well done' cards arrived while hundreds of messages flooded my Facebook and Twitter accounts. '"Helens Law"; what a legacy to have accomplished in such tragic circumstances. Your tireless days and nights will help many in the future,' wrote one woman. Others thanked me for not giving up – and for making the world a safer place, and told me, over and over, how proud Helen would be. I read the comments through a cloud of tears.

At the time of writing – December 2020 – Helen's Law is due to be officially added to the statute book in early 2021. I like to think this law, in my daughter's name, will strengthen over time and make a real difference. My judicial review claim, although not successful, has also paved the way for others to follow. The McCourt judgment from September 2020 is now enshrined in case law – establishing that families in this situation do have legal standing to challenge Parole Board decisions.

Simms is still a free man. He could still end this torture at any time. I pray he does – it is not too late for him to do the right thing.

Peter Faulding of Specialist Group International will continue his work in trying to locate Helen's remains. By the time you read this, we will have already embarked on new searches. And Merseyside Police assure me the case will remain open until Helen is found.

Until my dying breath, I will continue to look for my daughter and fight passionately for victims of homicide and their families. For far too long the scales of justice have been tipped in favour of the criminals, the killers – and to hell with the rest of us. It has been hugely, grossly unjust and inflicted immeasurable pain.

Before I go, please allow me to make one thing clear: I am not a vindictive woman. My aim was never to see killers locked up and the keys thrown away. It was only ever about highlighting a cruel injustice and ending this cruel torture that has been inflicted on families for far too long.

Had Simms confessed and made attempts to put things right – by revealing where my daughter was and saying sorry for taking her life – I could have learned to accept what happened, forgiven even. I wish no harm to anyone – least of all my daughter's murderer. I, more than most people, have seen the awful, tragic results of violence and anger. However, in a civilised society, this double-edged cruelty in not only taking a life but hiding the body – continuing to inflict the most awful pain on the victim's loved ones – cannot be allowed to happen.

Human rights laws, when used correctly and in principle, are commendable. But let's not forget the most basic human right of all: the right to life. And the right to lay our loved ones to rest.

Our ancestors understood the importance of this. Sadly, somewhere along the line, these priorities, this respect for the dead, has been forgotten – pushed aside. We have put men on the moon, created a World Wide Web, invented driver-less cars yet laws respecting our deceased have been allowed to wither and stagnate.

We need to revive and reform our ancient burial laws if we wish to live in a modern, considerate, kind world. This is something I will continue to campaign for. Helen's Law is just the start of a whole raft of changes in favour of missing homicide victims and their families that I would like to see enshrined in law. I am already lobbying MPs, Lords and Ministers to ask the Law Commission for a much needed review of outdated laws relating to the treatment of dead bodies. Conservative MP Dr Kieran Mullan raised the issue in the House of Commons in December and, as a result, Alex Chalk, the Parliamentary Under-Secretary of State for Justice, said he would be 'delighted' to meet with us to discuss further steps.

And that's not all. Just before this book went to press I had a lovely letter from the Victims Commissioner for England and Wales Dame Vera Baird to say that, as a result of my letter, she has taken up the matter with the Lord Chancellor.

In the meantime, I have requested a meeting with the Director of Public Prosecutions to establish exactly why Simms was never charged with these outstanding offences and why these ancient laws of preventing a burial and obstructing a coroner aren't being applied more often. Admittedly, they're outdated and in need of reform but, until that happens, they're all we've got. Let's use them. As a result of my request the victim liaison manager for the CPS contacted me to say Helen's case file is being retrieved from storage. I look forward to hearing from them and will be sure to post regular updates on my Helen's Law Facebook page.

My ultimate dream (after finding Helen, of course) is to establish an official charity devoted to the families of missing murder victims, offering emotional support, practical help with searches and an official, extensive database of missing homicide victims. (The Home Office only started officially recording homicide convictions without a body since 2007/2008.) Just days before this book went to press we received a response to our Freedom of Information Request to the Home Office regarding figures for homicide convictions where the body of the victim was not recovered. The figure (from 2007/8 when records first began to March 2019) now stands at fifty-four.

Back in the eighties, it was rare for a killer to be convicted without a body. These days, it's commonplace. The thought of fifty-four more families joining me in this ordeal, over just the last ten years, is heartbreaking. And, without further changes in legislation I can guarantee there will be more.

And it is for this reason that I will continue to fight for justice – both for the missing victims and their eternally-grieving families – until my dying breath.

I feel honoured and humbled that my campaign for Helen's Law is now having an impact in other countries. A campaign for similar legislation, called Suzanne's Law, was launched in Scotland by the families of missing murder victims Suzanne Pilley and Arlene Fraser. As a result the Scottish Government is amending Parole Board (Scotland) rules, ensuring that 'failure to disclose a victim's body' will be taken into account when determining release. The amendments will be introduced by late 2021/early 2022.

A similar campaign is also underway in Northern Ireland, spearheaded by the families of missing murder victims Charlotte Murray and Lisa Dorrian. (Tragically, in Lisa's case, there hasn't even been a conviction – but her family want to ensure that, once caught, her killer will reveal her location). We've had lots of encouraging chats and were thrilled when a motion to 'introduce legislation equivalent to Helen's Law' was passed by Members of the Legislative Assembly at Stormont in September.

As a result, the Justice Minister Naomi Long is now consulting with the campaigning families, plus other organisations, including the Parole Commissioners for Northern Ireland, the Probation Board and the Prison Service.

Parole rules are also being amended to ensure families have more access to information surrounding decisions and are able to challenge those decisions if they believe they are unreasonable, unfair or unlawful. And Paul Givan, Democratic Unionist Party MLA and chair of the Justice Committee, said he would like to see further changes including longer sentences for non-disclosure.

I felt beyond proud for Helen when Joanne Dorrian, sister of Lisa, told me: 'All the work you have done has really paved the way for other countries to follow. People here are constantly referring to Helen's Law. Her life and death have really made a difference, Marie. You're changing the world!'

Astonishingly, Joanne has now been approached a family in the Republic of Ireland keen to campaign for a change in legislation there too. We are now in contact with the family of mum of one, Fiona Sinnott, nineteen, who went missing, believed to have been murdered, in County Wexford in 1998, and I'll help them all I can. Ironically, Fiona went missing on 9 February – ten years to the day that Helen was murdered. My heart goes out to them.

Even further afield, we have reached across the Atlantic to support Canadian MP Dane Lloyd, in Alberta, who is pushing for similar legislation in the form of McCanns Law (after elderly husband and wife Lyle and Marie McCann who were killed in 2010).

I will do whatever I can to help them – and any others fighting for legal changes. Now that we've got the ball rolling, we need to keep it moving. I would love to see a version of Helen's Law on every statute book in the world.

Every Tuesday, I still light a candle and say my novena to St Martha. I always will. My faith has been sorely tested, but remains strong.

I hope my story triggers reaction and response – particularly among those who are just starting out in their careers as lawyers, police officers, journalists, probation officers. Please remember, victims and their families would never, ever choose to be in this situation. Believe me, this is definitely not the path I would have carved for myself, but once Helen had been taken from us, I had no choice: this is something I had to do.

I am proud that I have taken it – and I hope Helen would be proud of me too.

She really was a dream daughter (I so wish you'd got to meet her, you'd have loved her) and I like to think that, together, we have made a difference by illuminating a murky, dark area of cruelty and injustice and establishing a springboard for change.

So many people I have met on this journey had no idea that such horrors were possible, that killers really could be released while continuing to twist the knife so cruelly – plunging families of the victims into a continual, worsening hell. Together, however, we can insist on change.

It can be done. The louder the shout, the more chance we have of being heard. And I truly believe that good will always, always prevail.

I am seventy-eight on my next birthday (July 2021) – the same age Winnie Johnson was when she slipped, heartbroken, from this life. Winnie's dream, like mine, was to be reunited with her child in this world as well as the next. Sadly, it didn't happen for her. And, lately, I have started to accept that it may well not happen for me, either. Slowly, I am coming to terms with that.

I live in hope that Helen will be found – even if, sadly, I am not here to see it.

If that's the case, please can I ask that my daughter is brought home with love and dignity. Give her a requiem mass. Sprinkle her coffin with holy water and, perhaps yellow rose petals, then lay her to rest beside me, in our family plot in St Mary's churchyard, where she belongs.

Mediums have told me over the years that Helen was there, waiting, with outstretched arms when my mum died.

I pray she'll be there for me, too, when my time comes.

My breath will catch in my throat as I catch that first glimpse of my long-lost daughter and run towards her, calling out her name:

Helen! It's me.

Clasping her tightly to me, letting the tears run down my face, I will ask her, 'Where have you been? I've been looking everywhere for you.'

I'll stand back, then, to take in her pretty face, her sparkling eyes and sweet smile. I'll tell her how much I love her. How much I've missed her and how hard I tried to find her and bring her home. 'But it's OK, now, love,' I'll say. 'Mum's here, now.'

I've found you at last!

I'll gather her to me once more.

And, this time, I will never, ever, let her go.

Acknowledgements

I could fill an entire book thanking each and every lovely person who has helped me since the loss of my daughter. I apologise in advance if I have missed anyone. Please know that you have made a difference and will always be here, in my heart.

With love and heartfelt thanks to:

My wonderful children Helen and Michael. Helen – you were a dream daughter and I was blessed to have you in my life for twenty-two years. I only wish we could have had longer…

Michael – you are the best son a parent could ask for. You have made me so proud over the years. You, your wife and my special grandchildren have made life worth living. I love you all very, very much.

John – my soulmate, my rock, my strength, my husband. Words will never be enough to say just how much you mean to me.

My lovely Mum and wonderful family – particularly my sisters and brothers for picking me up and carrying me through those awful early years. You are my best friends as well as my siblings.

All the officers at Merseyside Police, Greater Manchester

Police and Cheshire Police, and forensic scientists, for their brilliant detective work in catching Helen's killer and securing a conviction – and for continuing to support me over the years. Particular thanks to Paul Acres, Eddie Alldred, Kevin Conroy, Mike McDermott and John Ross. I feel honoured to count you as friends.

All the family and victim liaison officers who have supported us over the years – particularly our current victim liaison officer.

The members of the jury and every witness who had the courage to come forward. You will never know the difference you made.

Every single journalist, producer and photographer who has helped keep Helen's story alive for more than three decades – in particular, Louie Smith and the *Daily Mirror*, Carole Richardson at *Yours* magazine and the Press Association.

Helen's friends and colleagues who have kept in touch over the years and assured me she will never be forgotten.

Everyone involved with SAMM Merseyside; this charity has saved me on countless occasions and I am so proud to have been a part of it for all these years; with particular thanks to our patrons Lady Kirsty Pilkington and the late Sir Ken Dodd and Lady Anne Dodd.

All those families affected by homicide or the disappearance of a loved one. This is a group that no one wants to join. But I feel humbled to have met such wonderful people – including Ann West, Winnie Johnson, Joan Lawrence (mum of Claudia), Pat Green, John Suffield and Margaret Dodd in Australia.

All families of the missing murdered who have fought so valiantly alongside me. There aren't enough pages to name you all individually but you know who you are. This fight has been for every single one of you – past, present and, sadly, future. Hopefully, together, we can continue to make a difference and prevent more from joining us.

Acknowledgements

My many dear friends, including Kath Moodie and Helen Hill for their unwavering support and love over the years and all the members of my Pilates class who have kept me going through rain and shine.

Our brilliant academics including Professor Liz Yardley, Dr Keri Nixon, Dr Graham McBain and Dr Imogen Jones, for their tireless support and research.

All the politicians and lawmakers who have helped in my quest for Helen's Law; including Conor McGinn (St Helens North) and his predecessors Dave Watts and John Evans), Stephen Metcalfe (South Basildon and East Thurrock), Dr Kieran Mullan (Crewe and Nantwich), Lord Tim Clement-Jones, Baroness Liz Barker and Justice Ministers David Gauke and Robert Buckland. The Bill had cross party support and I am so grateful to each and every member who voted in favour.

The teams at change.org and GoFundMe; each and every one of the 750,000 people who signed my petition on change.org and all those who contributed so generously to my fundraising campaign on GoFundMe – providing me with the opportunity to challenge the Parole Board's decision.

All those who have supported me on social media – your love and encouragement have lifted me on dark days and kept me going.

James Thacker, Tom Rainsbury and Tom Little at 9 Gough Chambers and Craig Hunn at Thomson's Solicitors; thank you for stepping forward when I needed you most – and representing me so diligently on a pro bono basis. Plus Robin Makin for his legal support in the 1990s. I am so, so grateful.

Pope John Paul II, Aunt Bibby, my late local priest Father Ashton, and every member of the clergy. You have restored and strengthened my faith.

Peter Simkins, Peter Faulding, Brian Houlton, Professor John Hunter and every single person who has given up their valuable time, over the years, to assist in the physical search for my daughter's remains.

Joe McDonough, Helen Hill (again!), Mackenzie France, Michelle Francis and all those who have patiently helped me to master technology and social media accounts.

Judge Rob Rinder and all the TV documentary makers who have highlighted Helen's murder over the years.

Students who have helped raise the profile of my campaign; particular thanks to Charlie Bell, James Saville and the late Adam Painter, who created a brilliant documentary on Helen's Law, and Jessica Perrin who (encouraged by her senior policing lecturer Brian McNeill – a former DCS at Merseyside police who was very involved in Helen's case) wrote her Master's thesis on No Body Homicide and is now assisting with further research.

To Adam Houghton at Loft Print in Wigan for so kindly offering to support our campaign with eye-catching Helen's Law T-shirts and tote bags.

My agent Robert Smith and editors Ciara Lloyd and Justine Taylor, at Bonnier, for their faith, patience and encouragement in bringing this book to life.

Fiona Duffy – who has co-written this book with me. She first came into my life, as a journalist, more than twenty years ago. Over time we have become very close friends. She has always been there to help and support me and without her investigative work I would not be where I am today. She has worked tirelessly and encouraged me along the way. Fiona, you will always be an important part of my life. Thank you!

And finally, thank you for reading my story and ensuring my daughter will never be forgotten.

God Bless you all.
Marie
x

Contact Marie McCourt

Thank you for reading my story.

If you have any information regarding the location of my daughter's remains, would like to contact me after reading my book, or would like to assist in my future work in securing justice for missing murder victims and their families please email me at: justiceforhelenmccourt@gmail.com

You can also reach me via social media:

Facebook: Helen's Law

Twitter: @helens_law_

Instagram: helens_law_campaign

Support and useful organisations

Find Our Lost Loved Ones (FOLLO): follo.org.uk
This is a website Fiona and I have founded, to unite families of missing homicide victims. It is still in the early stages but we hope to develop it further. If you would like to be involved, please contact us at justiceforhelenmccourt@gmail.com

Support After Murder and Manslaughter (SAMM), Merseyside. Despite the geographical location, the organisation offers nationwide support.
https://samm-merseyside.org.uk/contact-us/
24-hour helpline: 0151 207 6767

Victim Support National Homicide Service
www.victimsupport.org.uk
0300 303 1984
Supportline: 08 08 16 89 111

Support and useful organisations

Roadpeace
www.roadpeace.org
Helpline 0845 4500 355

Murdered Abroad
http://www.murdered-abroad.org.uk/
Helpline 0845 123 23 84

NOVENA TO
ST MARTHA

Many people have asked me about the Tuesday novena that I
have said every week since losing Helen. This prayer, said while
kneeling in front of a lit candle, has brought me immeasurable
comfort and kept my faith strong over three decades. There are
different versions but this is the one I always say.

> O St Martha, I resort to thy protection
> And, as proof of my affection and faith, I offer thee
> the light which I will burn every Tuesday.
> Comfort me in my difficulties and, through the
> great favour thou didst enjoy when our
> Saviour lodged in thy house, intercede for my family
> that we may be provided for in all our wants.
> I beseech thee to have pity on me with regards to
> the favour I ask of thee (State your request…)

Say one Our Father, three Hail Marys and light a candle each
Tuesday for nine in succession.